PLAUTUS: THE COMEDIES

Complete Roman Drama in Translation

David R. Slavitt and Palmer Bovie, Series Editors

PLAUTUS:
THE COMEDIES
Volume II

EDITED BY

DAVID R. SLAVITT

AND PALMER BOVIE

THE JOHNS HOPKINS UNIVERSITY PRESS
Baltimore and London

© 1995 The Johns Hopkins University Press
All rights reserved. Published 1995
Printed in the United States of America on acid-free paper
04 03 02 01 00 99 98 97 96 95   5 4 3 2 1

The Johns Hopkins University Press
2715 North Charles Street
Baltimore, Maryland 21218-4319
The Johns Hopkins Press Ltd., London

Library of Congress Cataloging-in-Publication Data

Plautus, Titus Maccius.
   [Works. English. 1995]
   Plautus : the comedies / edited by David R. Slavitt and Palmer Bovie.
      p.   cm — (Complete Roman drama in translation)
   Includes bibliographical references.
   Contents: v. 1. Amphitryon / translated by Constance Carrier — Miles gloriosus /
translated by Erich Segal — Captivi / translated by Richard Moore — Casina /
translated by Richard Beacham — Curculio / translated by Henry Taylor . . . [etc.]
   ISBN 0-8018-5070-3 (v. 1 : alk. paper). — ISBN 0-8018-5071-1 (v. 1 : pbk. :
alk. paper)
   1. Plautus, Titus Maccius—Translations into English.   2. Latin drama
(Comedy)—Translations into English.   3. Greece—Drama.   I. Slavitt, David
R., 1935–   .   II. Bovie, Smith Palmer.   III. Title.   IV. Series.
PA6569.S55   1995
872'.01—dc20   94-45317

ISBN 0-8018-5056-8 (v. 2 : alk. paper). — ISBN 0-8018-5057-6 (v. 2 : pbk. : alk. paper)
ISBN 0-8018-5067-3 (v. 3 : alk. paper). — ISBN 0-8018-5068-1 (v. 3 : pbk. : alk. paper)
ISBN 0-8018-5072-X (v. 4 : alk. paper). — ISBN 0-8018-5073-8 (v. 4 : pbk. : alk. paper)

A catalog record for this book is available from the British Library.

Acknowledgments of prior publication appear at the end of this book.

CONTENTS

PREFACE

Plautus's characters are descended from the conventional types portrayed in Greek New Comedy (Menander's, for instance), but they have a new individuality. In the *Rudens*, Daemones, the disillusioned but respectable exile, is trying to live a moral and decent life, and he delivers pious lectures to Gripus, his young slave. The slave answers that he has only heard such talk from *actors on the comic stage*, but then, as he explains, the spectators all return home and conduct their lives in the same old way:

> Spectavi ego pridem comicos ad istunc modum
> sapienter dicta dicere atque eis plaudier,
> cum illos sapientis mores monstrabant poplo;
> sed cum inde suam quisque ibant divorsi domum,
> nullus erat illos pacto ut illi iusserant.

> [At times I've seen actors acting in this fashion, repeat sayings in a wise manner and being applauded for them, when they pointed out prudent conduct to the public. But when each one went back to his own home, none of them behaved in the manner recommended.]

> Rudens, ll. 1249–53

Gripus falls back on cynicism, but the disgruntled Daemones we met at the beginning of this unusual comedy of character is no longer just a "character." He begins as the conventional grouch, but by the end, with his daughter restored to him, he is a happy father who rejoices and invites all present to share in his good fortune.

Euclio, in the *Aulularia*, is another conventional grouch who must deal with a most unconventional problem when the household god bestows a pot of gold on him. The pot (*aula*) is intended as a reward for Euclio's daughter Phaedria (*illa*), and in a climactic scene

vii

the two words are confused. Throughout the play Plautus allows for a considerable amount of language at cross-purposes. The poor rich man is driven to distraction by his own greed, or perhaps by his fear that he will lose what is most precious to him.

Unlike Daemones, Euclio is a figure of fun, someone to jeer at. Molière's Harpagon, the manic hero of *L'Avare*, takes his name from Plautus's use of the Greek *harpago* (for "hook" or "rapacious person") in several passages where Euclio expresses his distrust of everyone in town and his fear that they may bilk him.

In *The Rope* the dignified Daemones well deserves his good fortune after the lonely years spent longing for his daughter. In *The Pot of Gold*, Euclio is a nervous wreck but finally comes to his senses, recognizing the value of his true treasure, his peerless daughter. In the *Bacchides* the fathers succeed in making perfect fools of themselves. In *The Entrepreneur* the father (a *mercator*) outnegotiates his son (also a *mercator*) for possession of the son's mistress. But his profit nearly results in the loss of his son, about to leave home for permanent exile—until the father is made to see the foolishness of his double dealing.

So, Plautus seems to be studying the various affections and passions of fathers and children. These are not naive examples of filial piety or absolute parental authority. Strong emotional currents bind and challenge the older and the younger generations.

In the *Truculentus* a resourceful woman takes over the scene. The heroine, Phronesium, is, as her name suggests, intelligence personified. Smart, ruthless, and inordinately attractive, she knows how to get what she can out of the life of a courtesan, playing her suitors off against each other while remaining interesting and seductive to them all. The question is whether her skills are enough to allow her to manage the young country slave, Truculentus, "savage," who is characterized as he appears as *violentissimus*. But she conquers him, and the glorious captain, too. The play is not so much one of action and plot as it is of comic downfall. Lovers never learn: as James Tatum has said, Plautus's method here is "a relentless exposition of the jaded and the gullible." The work is a pageant of susceptibility. Tatum calls it "the sharpest delineation in Roman comedy of specifically male folly."

At the end of the play, Phronesium stands alone, facing the

audience and explaining: "I've handled my affairs well—perhaps I could do the same for you? Do applaud, for Venus's sake: she is in charge of this play. And so, spectators, a fond farewell. Give us a good round of applause as you leave."

Spectatores, bene valete, plaudite atque exsurgite.

Palmer Bovie

THE ROPE

(*RUDENS*)

Translated by Constance Carrier

INTRODUCTION

On a lonely seashore near Cyrene in North Africa there stands, at one side of the stage, the cottage of Daemones and, at the other, the forecourt of a small temple of Venus. The middle distance looks out toward the seacoast. It is the day after a heavy storm, which has done considerable damage to Daemones' cottage, and, as the action begins, Daemones and his servant Sceparnio are at work repairing the damage. But before the play begins Arcturus, the Prologue, addresses the audience to introduce this unusual situation, an unfamiliar setting for Roman comedy. He tells us that the gods are watching over the characters in this play. Their emissaries, the stars, survey the scene of humanity during the day and return to report to Jupiter at night. And since Jupiter will not let men get away with wickedness, Arcturus assures us, their misdeeds are entered in his records, and punishments are assigned for wrongdoing. Arcturus, the stormy weather sign, brewed up a tempest during the night to overwhelm the ship and the nefarious plans of the procurer Labrax and his Sicilian crony Charmides, who had sailed off with two attractive young women in their possession. They intended to sell the women in Agrigentum, where such luxuries command a higher price than in North Africa. The planned escape was compounded by fraud: Labrax had already tricked the young man Plesidippus into paying half the purchase price for the young woman, Palaestra, and was to hand over the girl to her suitor at a meeting at the chapel of Venus on this very site on this very morning after the storm.

The storm mounted by Arcturus swamped and capsized Labrax's ship, and the passengers were washed overboard. The young women, Palaestra and her companion Ampelisca, were able to jump into a skiff and make their way to shore. Labrax and Charmides clung to some rocks; they eventually waded ashore after the women had clambered safely onto land near Daemones' cottage.

Plesidippus and some of his friends now arrive at the scene of the supposed rendezvous with Labrax. They question Daemones and Sceparnio about the slave dealer when, all at once, Sceparnio sees Labrax and Charmides in the distance making their way ashore. Plesidippus sets off to accost them. And no sooner has this sighting come about, than Sceparnio discerns "two girls sitting alone in a boat" and describes how they have clambered ashore safely from the rocks onto the lonely sand. At this point Daemones summons Sceparnio indoors to work on the cottage roof. The stage is thus left empty for the young women's appearance—first Palaestra alone and forlorn. She has lost everything because her traveling case, which contained the tokens identifying her parents and herself as an Athenian citizen, has been, she believes, irretrievably lost in the shipwreck. Ampelisca hears her friend's voice, and they are reunited. Seeing the chapel of Venus, they seek refuge there and the priestess offers them her protection, slight as it is.

By gaining refuge in these precincts Palaestra and Ampelisca become "daughters of Venus," their sheltering goddess who rose from the sea. When they are threatened by Labrax later, Plesidippus's slave Trachalio, who has taken a fancy to Ampelisca, offers a prayer to Venus in pointed language, using the vulgar word *concha* for these "daughters of Venus":

> tu ex concha natam esse autumant, cave tu harum conchas
>   spernas
> [they say that you were born of a shell: take care that you do
>   not despise these she-sells!]

(l. 704)

Earlier, the gifts and the refusals of the sea had been chanted of in detail by a chorus of fishermen going to pay their respects at the shrine of Venus before their day's work of casting for "sea-urchins, rock-mussels, limpets, shell-fish, fluted scallops." If they can't scrape a haul from the rocks, the fishermen fish with rod and hook. But today, because of the previous night's storm, they believe that there won't be anything to catch; so, they are asking Venus to help them. This modest choral interlude is unique in Roman comedy—as *The Rope* is unique in its setting among Plautus's other plays. The theme of the poor fisherman's chancy lot is more like a page of music torn out of Benjamin Britten's *Peter Grimes* than an episode in Roman comedy.

In a brilliant analysis of the imagery and diction of Plautus's *Rudens*, Eleanor Winsor Leach describes the sea as "the center of the landscape, as the goddess herself becomes the central figure in the mythical pattern of the story."[1] The innocent victims will be saved from a forlorn fate as victims of their own *conchae* (in the erotic sense) by a goddess herself born of a seashell (*concha*).

Plautus's tempest proves to be a lucky blow. As the play continues, another slave of Daemones, the young Gripus, having cast his net after the storm, hauls in a traveling trunk instead of the fish he had been counting on. But seeing this considerable catch, Gripus can afford to indulge in some colorful, wishful thinking about becoming rich and buying his freedom. But there is a catch to his catch: as he hauls the traveling trunk across the stage in his net, a rope dangles from one end of the net. Trachalio appears at just this moment, only to recognize the trunk as Labrax's lost gear. Trachalio grabs the rope and gets into a tug of war with Gripus for possession of the trunk over the lawful possession of the contents. The Latin word for "rope" is *rudens*, and the conventional manuscript title for Plautus's play derives from it. But by coincidence the adjective, *rudens, rudentis*, means "roaring" (as of an animal roar or other loud noise), so it sounds as if the roaring tempest that started the action is turning into a prize possession with a rope attached. Labrax's traveling trunk contains Palaestra's jewel case with her birth tokens. They will disclose her identity as the long lost daughter of Daemones.

Everyone involved somehow profits from the disaster. The hard-pressed, grumpy Daemones changes into a happy father and a congenial host who invites the company to dinner, including the two procurers. As the players stroll off the stage, Daemones says to the audience that he would like to invite them as well. But he isn't really giving a dinner party; besides it would be slim pickings, and he knows that they are already going out to dinner elsewhere. But he will invite them all some time in the future—shall we say, sixteen

[1]"Plautus' *Rudens:* Venus Born from a Shell," *Texas Studies in Literature and Language* 15 (1974): 915–31.

years from now?—if they liked the play, and are prepared to give it a
good clear round of applause!

> spectatores, vos quoque ad cenam vocem,
> ni daturus nihil sim neque sit quicquam pollucti domi,
> nive adeo vocatos credam vos esse ad cenam foras.
> verum si voletis plausum fabulae huic clarum dare,
> comissatum omnes venitote ad me annos sedecim.

Palmer Bovie

THE ROPE

CHARACTERS

ARCTURUS, as the Prologue
DAEMONES, an old Athenian gentleman, now living at Cyrene
SCEPARNIO, a servant of Daemones
PLESIDIPPUS, a young Athenian gentleman, now living at Cyrene
TRACHALIO, a servant of Plesidippus
PALAESTRA, a young Athenian woman, now owned by the slave
    dealer Labrax
AMPELISCA, Palaestra's companion, also owned by Labrax
LABRAX, a slave dealer and procurer
CHARMIDES, a Sicilian and a companion of Labrax
PISCATORES, fishermen of Cyrene
PTOLEMOCRATIA, a priestess of Venus
TURBALIO, a house slave of Daemones
SPARAX, a house slave of Daemones
GRIPUS, a fisherman and servant of Daemones

SCENE: *In the vicinity of Cyrene, in North Africa, near the coast.
The cottage of* DAEMONES *is in the foreground. In the background,
across the stage, can be seen a small temple of Venus, with a forecourt, surrounded by a wall.*

7

PROLOGUE

I am Arcturus, citizen of the heavens,
Like him who governs sea and lands and skies.
Behold me, on whose forehead shines a star
That here and in those heavens will arise,
Unfailing in its season. Jupiter
Assigns to each of us our stated place,
That we may know mankind, its deeds, its thoughts,
And he rewards or punishes through his grace.
The scoundrel who repudiates his debts,
Who lies, who bears false witness in the court—   10
It is his immorality we mark,
For Jupiter; his name that we report.
For Jove would know men who are evildoers,
Who break their oath before a magistrate.
Those who use perjury to win a case
Must learn that Jove himself will arbitrate,
And that his fines are greater than their gains.
He keeps a listing of good men, I'm told,
And those who try to gain a place upon it
By bribes are wasting time and strength and gold.   20
He'll touch no tribute from a guilty hand,
And although a good man's prayers will move his heart,
A knave's are wasted. Let me beg you, friends,
Who live by his rule, oh, do not depart
From the straight way you've chosen,
And you'll be glad, after the fact.
                                    Let me now
Explain why I stand here addressing you.
Diphilus chose to call this town Cyrene.
Here lives Daemones, an Athenian who,
Exiled from Athens through no fault of his,   30
Settled in that small cottage by the coast.
His bad luck came from efforts to help others;
It is his goodness that has cost him most.
And, worse than loss of wealth, his little daughter

Kidnapped and carried here, or so they say,
By the worst of pimps. A young Athenian
Has fallen in love with her, seeing her one day
On her way home after her music lesson.
He offered the pimp a good sum, paid him half,
Promised the rest. But to the pimp the oath   40
Was air, the youth a mere moon-calf.
He had a guest from Sicily, prepared
To sell his soul for money, and his peer
In evil. This man praised the young girl's looks,
Saying, *A beauty, like the others here*
In this house, and he urged the pimp at once
To take himself and them to Sicily—
Oh, what a crowd of our hot-blooded men
They'll draw! And you—how rich you're going to be!
Who could resist? A ship was hired in secret   50
And filled with everything the pimp possessed.
To the young fellow who had made the contract
He says, *A vow to Venus would be best*
To seal the bond—her shrine is over there.
We'll meet for lunch after the sacrifice.
Then, before noon, he and his pal set sail
And the young man is left to pay the price
Of gullibility, and to discover
That fate can make a fool out of a lover.

I saw the innocent girl thus carried off,   60
And in one swoop saved her and ruined her master
By stirring up a storm and savage seas—
For I, Arcturus, can incite disaster,
In rage arising, setting still in rage.
The two men, pimp and friend, cling to a rock,
Their ship gone down. The girl and another slave,
Jumping from ship to boat, huddle in shock,
But even now the waves carry them on
Straight toward the beach and old Daemones' hut—
The roof stripped of its tiles by furious winds.   70
Look—the door opens that those winds blew shut.

Here comes his slave; here comes the young man, too.
So farewell—grief to your enemies, luck to you.

ACT I

Scene 1

SCEPARNIO: Ye gods, that was a downpour Neptune sent
  Last night! The wind ripped all our roof clean off—
  Wind, did I say? that was hurricane *Alcmena*,
  Out of Euripides; not one tile left.
  All I can say is, now we have more light
  With all the holes there are to let it in.

Scene 2

PLESIDIPPUS: I do apologize—I've kept you all
  From your affairs, and had no luck myself   80
  In what I'd hoped for. He slipped through our fingers,
  That pimp, that pander, on this very deck.
  I can't give up, despite discouragement;
  That's why I've kept you here so long, my friends.
  Let's take a look now at the shrine of Venus—
  That's where he said he'd make his sacrifice.

SCEPARNIO: If I had sense, I'd start to dig this clay.

PLESIDIPPUS: Who's talking there? I heard—

DAEMONES: Sceparnio!

SCEPARNIO: Who's calling me?

DAEMONES: The one who paid hard cash   90
  For you.

SCEPARNIO: Aah, call me slave, why not?

DAEMONES: Go back to digging. We'll need lots of clay;
  The whole roof's got to be replaced, I tell you.
  It's like a sieve—look up and there's the sky.

PLESIDIPPUS: Good morning, Father—to you both.

DAEMONES: And you.

SCEPARNIO: What are you, man or woman, calling him father?

PLESIDIPPUS: A man, of course.

SCEPARNIO: Look for your father farther on.

DAEMONES: I fathered one young daughter, but I lost her
  And never had a boy.

PLESIDIPPUS: God send you one.   100

SCEPARNIO: And send bad luck to you, whoever you are,
  Keeping us from our work with all your jabber.

PLESIDIPPUS: You live here?

SCEPARNIO: Hmph. Why do you want to know?
  Staking it out? Planning to rob the place?

PLESIDIPPUS: It takes a valuable and trusted slave
  To put words in his master's mouth as you do
  And to address a gentleman so roughly.

SCEPARNIO: And it's a funny kind of gentleman
Who comes into a man's house uninvited,
Pestering people who don't owe him anything.   110

DAEMONES: Quiet, Sceparnio. What do you want, young man?

PLESIDIPPUS: To see that fellow whipped for impudence.
Even with you right here, he thinks he's master.
Sorry to trouble you, but I've some questions.

DAEMONES: I'll try to answer, although I'm rather busy.

SCEPARNIO: Go on down to the swamp, why don't you? Reeds
Are what we want. Go cut some while it's clear.

DAEMONES: Be still, I said. How can I help you, sir?

PLESIDIPPUS: Well, have you seen a stranger, curly-haired,
Not young, full of smooth talk, a good-for-nothing?   120

DAEMONES: By the dozen! Men like him have ruined me.

PLESIDIPPUS: Here at the temple, I mean. With two young girls?
Ready to sacrifice? Today or yesterday?

DAEMONES: No, sorry. No one's come to sacrifice
For several days—I see the ones who do.
They're always asking me for fire or water,
Or borrowing knives or pots or spits or dishes.
It's Venus owns my kitchen more than I do.
But no one's come a-begging now for days.

PLESIDIPPUS: And with those words you've spoken my death
     sentence.   130

DAEMONES: What do you mean? You're safe enough with me.

SCEPARNIO: Hanging around in hopes of a free meal
    Here at the shrine? Go home and fill your belly.

DAEMONES: You mean that you were asked to have lunch here
    And now can't find your host?

PLESIDIPPUS: That's it exactly.

SCEPARNIO: Oh, go home hungry—we're not interested.
    Go say your prayers to Ceres, not to Venus—
    Venus takes care of lovers; Ceres feeds 'em.

PLESIDIPPUS: I'm taking no more insults from this lout—

DAEMONES: Good Lord, Sceparnio, what's that over there?   140
    Two men at the water's edge?

SCEPARNIO: If you ask me
    They're headed for a banquet.

DAEMONES: What do you mean?

SCEPARNIO: I mean they've had a bath since breakfast time.

DAEMONES: They must have been shipwrecked.

SCEPARNIO: What else?
    Right here
    We've got our own wreck, with the roof all gone.

DAEMONES: How small they look—half-drowned, and swimming
    still—

PLESIDIPPUS: Where? I can't make them out.

DAEMONES: There, to the right.
    See? Coming toward the shore.

PLESIDIPPUS: Come on now, friends.
Please God this is the wretch I'm looking for.   150
Take care!

SCEPARNIO: Thanks for the warning, know-it-all.
Holy Palaemon, now what's this I see?

DAEMONES: What? What?

SCEPARNIO: Two girls—two young girls—in a skiff.
The waves are battering it. Oh, but what luck!
They've missed the rock and headed for the shore!
No pilot could have done a better job
In surf like this. I never saw it worse.
Wait, though—those breakers! Can they get through them?
It's now or never. One girl's overboard—
But look—it's not too deep to wade ashore.   160
Hooray! She's safe! She's made it! But the other—
She's jumped out—now she's trying to make shore—
Oh, Lord, she fell—too scared to keep her balance.
Ah! Now she's made it. There she is on land.
Damn it, she's turned away, off toward the right.
Poor kid, she's got a good long hike ahead.

DAEMONES: What's that to you?

SCEPARNIO: She's headed toward the cliff.
That's the last hiking that she'll ever do.

DAEMONES: If you were going to dine with them tonight,
I'd say that your alarm was justified,   170
But if I'm going to feed you, earn your keep.

SCEPARNIO: Yes sir; you're right.

DAEMONES: Then come along.

SCEPARNIO: I'm following.

Scene 3

PALAESTRA: Tales of the horrors men have suffered through
　　Can never equal what the sufferer knows.
　　Does it please God to throw me, terrified
　　And helpless, on this inhospitable shore?
　　Was it for such misfortune I was born,
　　For this I led a modest, virtuous life?
　　It would be punishment that I deserved
　　If I had wronged the gods or shamed my parents—   180
　　But if I've done my best to honor you,
　　Then surely, gods, this penalty's unjust.
　　What stigma will you give the guilty now,
　　If this is the reward of innocence?
　　How have we sinned, my family or I?
　　If I knew that, I could accept your wrath.
　　It is my master's sin I suffer for.
　　And now he's lost his ship and all his wealth—
　　Nothing of value left; even the girl
　　Who shared the boat is lost. There's none but me.   190
　　If somehow she is still alive, my grief
　　And terror would be almost bearable.
　　Without her, I can find no spark of hope.
　　Rocks all around, an ever-sounding sea,
　　No other living being anywhere!
　　Nothing to call my own but these wet clothes,
　　Nowhere to beg for shelter or for food.
　　Since there's no hope, why should I care to live?
　　Here in a place I've never seen or heard of,   200
　　Oh, is there no one who will rescue me,
　　Show me a path to lead me back to life?
　　Should I go right or left? How can I tell?
　　There's not a field around that's known a plow.
　　All I can feel is chill and doubt and fear.

Thank heaven my parents cannot see me now!
I was freeborn, but what is that to me?
No slave is more the slave of fate than I am,
And what reward am I to those who reared me?

Scene 4

AMPELISCA: What's left? What good is life? I'll end it, here and
  now,
Rather than drag it out in dreadful, shivering fear.   210
I've come so close to death there's no hope left to stay me.
Search high and low—and search I have—no sign of her,
The other slave, although I call her through the shadows
I'll never find her—no, however I may seek,
And I see no one else who might tell me about her.
I swear there never was a desert more deserted—
But while I live I'll hope still for a miracle.

PALAESTRA: Whose voice is that? Hark now, it's growing louder.

AMPELISCA: Somebody's there. O heavens, how I'm shaking.

PALAESTRA: Faith of the terrified, be with me now—   220
Pity me, save me from more grief, I pray.

AMPELISCA: Surely that was a woman's voice that spoke?

PALAESTRA: Could it have been a woman that I heard?
Could it be Ampelisca?

AMPELISCA: O Palaestra!

PALAESTRA: I'll call her name aloud, so she can hear:
Dear Ampelisca!

AMPELISCA: Who's that?

PALAESTRA: It's Palaestra.

AMPELISCA: But where are you?

PALAESTRA: Here, in the midst of trouble.

AMPELISCA: And I no less, my friend, I swear it to you.
  But oh, I need to see you—

PALAESTRA: And I you.

AMPELISCA: Let's let our voices guide us. Where are you?

PALAESTRA.   Here!   230
  Come this way; here I am!

AMPELISCA: I'll do my best.

PALAESTRA: Stretch out your hand.

AMPELISCA: Here!

PALAESTRA: Truly, you're alive?

AMPELISCA: It's you who make me want to go on living
  So I can reach you. Oh, I can't believe it,
  That I'm alive to take you in my arms.
  Hold me and give me hope. My cares are gone.

PALAESTRA: Oh Ampelisca, what more can I say?
  We can't stay here, though—

AMPELISCA: But where can we go?   240

PALAESTRA: Along the beach?

AMPELISCA: You lead, darling; I'll follow.
   Should we go on, though, in these soaking clothes?

PALAESTRA: We have no choice. But what's that?

AMPELISCA: What?

PALAESTRA: My dear,
   Can't you make out a shrine?

AMPELISCA: Where?

PALAESTRA: To the right.

AMPELISCA: A place for some god and his worshipers—

PALAESTRA: Some of those worshipers may be around,
   With such a splendid shrine. I pray the god
   Himself, whoever he may be, to bring
   Help to us undeserving, shipwrecked women.   250

Scene 5

PTOLEMOCRATIA: Who comes to seek my patroness's favor?
   Their voices raised in prayer brought me out here.
   Lucky they are! The goddess they beg aid from
   Is kind and generous, never harsh or grudging.

PALAESTRA: Good morning, Mother.

PTOLEMOCRATIA: And to you. But where
   Is it you've come from, wet through to the skin?

PALAESTRA: Just now from somewhere near here—before that
   They brought us from a place a world away.

PTOLEMOCRATIA: In a light-footed ship through sun-blue seas?

PALAESTRA: Well, sort of.

PTOLEMOCRATIA: But you should have come in white, 260
 Your arms outstretched with offerings. No one
 Comes to this fane in such a state as yours.

PALAESTRA: But where could we have found fit offerings,
 Two shipwrecked girls, alone and lost? Tell me—
 We kneel before you, praying for your help.
 Where are we? Lost and losing hope—
 Oh, take us in, we beg, take pity on us!
 Homeless and hopeless, what have we to live for?

PTOLEMOCRATIA: Give me your hands, my poor dears, and
  stand up.   270
 You could not find a friend more sympathetic.
 I must confess I haven't much to offer—
 Living's hard here; I give my all to Venus.

AMPELISCA: This is a shrine of Venus?

PTOLEMOCRATIA: Yes, my dear;
 My title is the priestess of her shrine.
 Though I can't give you any lavish welcome,
 I'll do my best. Come with me, both of you.

PALAESTRA: O Mother, bless you for those kindly words.

PTOLEMOCRATIA: They are what you deserve, I'm sure of that.

ACT II

Scene 1

PISCATORES: If you're poor, we can tell you, your life will be
    tougher.
No trade, no profession? Get ready to suffer.   280
Make do with the little we've got, that's our setup;
No one takes us for bankers, no—not in this getup.
Hook, line, and sinker, that's our wealth, more's the pity.
We cover the waterfront, out from the city.
Instead of a ring and a ref and gloved wallops,
Our fights are with oysters and shellfish and scallops
And limpets and snails and sea-urchins and mussels—
And never believe that they don't offer tussles.
Or maybe we fish from a rock with our rods
And eat what we catch, with a bow to the gods,   290
And if they refuse us so much as a bite,
We go home, cleaned and salted, and starve through the night.
Today is no good—the sea's running too rough,
Although a small haul of shellfish would earn us enough.
So let's go worship Venus before she forgets
To smile on our efforts and fill up our nets.

Scene 2

TRACHALIO: I've looked in all directions, but no sign.
He said that he was headed for the harbor
When he went out—I was to meet him here.
There are some men there—maybe they have seen him.   300
Hey there, hello, you heroes of the fishline,
You hook-and-shellers, brothers of starvation—
How are you doing? How are you dying? Tell me.

PISCATORES: As do all fishermen: by thirst and hunger.

TRACHALIO: Did any of you see a young man passing?—
    Businesslike, husky, red-skinned? And three
    Others besides him, cloaked and carrying swords?

PISCATORES: No one we've seen would answer that description.

TRACHALIO: Maybe a Bacchus-type? Old, with a belly
    And bushy eyebrows and a mean expression,   310
    Hateful to gods and men, vicious and evil,
    And having two young girls for company?

PISCATORES: A character like that, with all those virtues,
    Ought to be on his way to meet the hangman,
    Not sucking up to Venus.

TRACHALIO: Have you seen him?

PISCATORES: No one like that has come our way. So long.

(*They exit*)

TRACHALIO: Goodbye. Well, I was right, as I suspected.
    The rat's run off, now that he's tricked my master—
    Shipped out, kidnapped the girl. A fine sleuth I am!
    And all that talk of how he'd treat my master   320
    To lunch! Well, all I can do now is wait
    Until he comes. The priestess may know something.
    If I see her, I'll ask; she'll tell me, surely.

Scene 3

AMPELISCA: (*Calling back inside*)
    I am to go to the house next to the temple
    And ask for water. Is that it?

TRACHALIO: Whose voice
  Is carried on the wind?

AMPELISCA: Who spoke? Who's there?

TRACHALIO: Is it Ampelisca coming from the temple?

AMPELISCA: Is it Plesidippus's serving-man, Trachalio?

TRACHALIO: It is.   330

AMPELISCA: It is! Trachalio, hello!

TRACHALIO: Why, Ampelisca, what are you doing here?

AMPELISCA: Wasting the best years of my life, I think.

TRACHALIO: May God forbid.

AMPELISCA: People should tell the truth,
  And listen to it. Tell me, where's Plesidippus?

TRACHALIO: Don't be an idiot. In the shrine, of course.

AMPELISCA: He's no such thing, and hasn't been all day.

TRACHALIO: Not here?

AMPELISCA: You've hit it on the head, my friend.

TRACHALIO: There had to be a first time. Is lunch ready?

AMPELISCA: Lunch? What lunch?

TRACHALIO: Well, you're sacrificing,
  aren't you?   340

AMPELISCA: Wake up!

TRACHALIO: Your master, Labrax—he invited
  Mine to have lunch with him today, right here.

AMPELISCA: That's no surprise to me. Cheat men, cheat gods:
  He'll do the second as he does the first.

TRACHALIO: Then none of you are here to sacrifice?

AMPELISCA: You've guessed it.

TRACHALIO: Then why are *you* here?

AMPELISCA: Well, we were almost dead with what we'd gone
      through,
  No help in sight, and danger all around us,
  When the priestess gave us shelter in the temple,
  Palaestra and myself.

TRACHALIO: My master's girl?   350
  She's here as well?

AMPELISCA: Indeed she is, praise heaven.

TRACHALIO: O Ampelisca, that's the best news yet!
  But what about your sufferings? Tell me more.

AMPELISCA: Last night, Trachalio, our ship went down.

TRACHALIO: Your ship? What kind of a story is that?

AMPELISCA: You mean you haven't heard? The pimp was set
  On taking us to Sicily, with none the wiser;
  He sailed with everything he owned on board, and then
  Suddenly all was lost.

TRACHALIO: Praise be to Neptune!
Nobody's better with the dice, but *this*—   360
This was a master stroke: a liar lost.
And now where's Labrax?

AMPELISCA: Dead of drink, no doubt,
The great god Neptune having quenched his thirst.

TRACHALIO: No dregs left in his glass, I'll guarantee.
Oh Ampelisca, how I love you, girl—
You and your words are sweet as honey. Tell me,
How were you saved, the two of you?

AMPELISCA: You'll see.
We were so scared we jumped into the skiff—
The ship was going to crash. I loosed the rope;
Nobody else dared move. And then the storm   370
Carried us off away from them. All night
Gales blew us about, waves washed around us—
How we lived through it, who can tell? At daybreak,
We were cast up on shore, more dead than living.

TRACHALIO: That's Neptune for you—always the businesslike
Inspector: what's no good goes overboard.

AMPELISCA: You and your wit.

TRACHALIO: And yours, my Ampelisca!
I had a hunch that he was plotting something,
That pimp of ours. I wonder: should I grow
A beard and set up as a prophet?

AMPELISCA: Tell me: 380
Couldn't you two have stopped him in his scheming?

TRACHALIO: How?

AMPELISCA: You ask *me* how? Plesidippus loves her:
He should have shielded her, protected her,
Been always at her side. Plesidippus!
If he had loved her, he'd have been on guard.

TRACHALIO: Why do you say that?

AMPELISCA: Why? Because it's true.

TRACHALIO: When a man goes into the public baths,
He'll keep a sharp eye on his clothes, and yet
They disappear, as like as not—and where?
The thief can spot the owner, sure enough,   390
But who spots *him?* Well, take me where she is.

AMPELISCA: Go in the temple and you'll find her there,
Crying her heart out.

TRACHALIO: What's to cry about?

AMPELISCA: She's really broken up because the pimp
Made off with a little box she kept some things in—
Things that might help her find her family.
She thinks it's lost.

TRACHALIO: Where was it?

AMPELISCA: In Labrax's trunk, where nobody could get it.

TRACHALIO: The dirty devil, claiming she's his slave,
A freeborn girl!

AMPELISCA: It's down in Neptune's locker   400
Along with all his gold and silver now.

TRACHALIO: Somebody could dive down and bring it up.

AMPELISCA: Maybe, but now it's gone; that's why she's weeping.

TRACHALIO: So much more reason why I should go in—
Give her a little comfort, smooth her down.
Hope springs eternal, as the saying goes.

AMPELISCA: Hope is a crutch that can't support much weight.

TRACHALIO: Keeping your head—it may be that's the answer.
Can I do anything for you? Then I'll go in.

(TRACHALIO *exits to the temple*)

AMPELISCA: Yes, do, And I'll obey the priestess's orders   410
And ask for water at the house next door.
Mention my name, she said, and they'll oblige you.
I couldn't hope to meet a sweeter person
Than that old lady; she deserves the best
That heaven and earth can offer, bless her heart.
The welcome that she gave us, warm and gracious—
And we all drenched and half-alive and fainting!
She couldn't have done more were we her daughters—
Tucking her skirts up, heating our bathwater.
Mercy, I'm dawdling! This is the house now.   420
Is anybody here? Please come! Hello!

                              Scene 4

SCEPARNIO: Who's making all that racket at the door?

AMPELISCA: I am.

SCEPARNIO: Oho, and here's a bit of luck—
A woman, and a pretty one at that!

AMPELISCA: Good morning.

SCEPARNIO: And the same to you, my dear.

AMPELISCA: I've come—

SCEPARNIO: I'd show you a good time if it was evening.
   Why not come back then? Mornings aren't for parties.
   How about it, doll? Hmm?

AMPELISCA: Take your hands away.

SCEPARNIO: By all the gods, she could stand in for Venus.
   Why she's a muddy—I mean, bloody—marvel!   430
   Look at those breasts, and that mouth made for kissing!

AMPELISCA: I'm not a feast for peasants. Let me go!

SCEPARNIO: You won't so much as let a fellow squeeze you?

AMPELISCA: A little later on we'll have our fun.
   Now I'll explain what I was sent here for.

SCEPARNIO: What?

AMPELISCA: Nobody could mistake it: for some water.

SCEPARNIO: Nobody could mistake what's on *my* mind.

AMPELISCA: It was the priestess at the shrine who sent me.

SCEPARNIO: I'm lord and master here, girl; my word's final.
   Not one drop do you get unless you beg me.   440
   We dug that well and used our tools to make it.
   You'll have to butter me up if you want water.

AMPELISCA: Even a little? A stranger wouldn't grudge it.

SCEPARNIO: Even a little love? No friend would grudge it.

AMPELISCA: (*Aside*) Oh, but I never said that I'd refuse you.

SCEPARNIO: (*To* AMPELISCA) Aha, that's better! Now she's coming
    'round.
  You'll have your water, just so you can't say
  Love brought you nothing. Let me have the pitcher.

AMPELISCA: Here, then, but hurry with it, there's a dear.

SCEPARNIO: I'll be right back. Don't go away, sweetheart.   450

(*He exits*)

AMPELISCA: What reason can I give for being so long?
  —Oh—even a glimpse of sea can make me shudder!—
  But who's that standing far off on the beach?
  Good heavens! It's the pimp and his Sicilian—
  And I was certain both of them had drowned.
  That's double trouble now in store for us—
  Palaestra there and me. I'll run and tell her,
  And we'll take refuge at the holy altar
  Before they've had a chance to catch us here.
  We'll hide together, if there's only time.   460

(*She exits*)

Scene 5

SCEPARNIO: I've never had a good word until now
  For water. Even drawing this was easy—
  I'd swear the well was deeper yesterday.
  I didn't need to use a muscle this time.
  I'm quite a guy, I am, with my new baby—
  Well, here you are, doll; carry it this way,
  The way a lady does, and then I'll love you.
  Where are you, kid? I've got the water for you,

Wherever you are. By Jove, she's fallen for me:
This playing hide-and-seek is proof of it.   470
Where are you? Aren't you going to take your pitcher?
Look, no more fun and games. Come on, where are you?
Where in the world—and don't you want the water?
No sign of her. She'd make a fool of me,
Would she? I'll put this pitcher down right now,
Here in the middle of the road—but wait:
Suppose somebody stole it? After all,
It's Venus's, and I'd be in a jam.
Hey, wait a minute. What if it's a trap
To get me caught with Venus's pitcher on me?   480
Never a judge who wouldn't take my head off
If anybody saw me carrying this.
And—oh, the devil! Look, there's an inscription—
The goddess's own name, to prove it's hers.
I'd damn well better get it back right now.
I'll call the priestess. Ptolemocratia!
Come out and take your blasted holy pitcher.
Some girl—I don't know who—got me to fill it.
Nobody there? It's my job to deliver it?
What do they think I am, their water boy?   490

Scene 6

LABRAX: You want the worst that land and sea can offer?
Then trust yourself to Neptune—he's the greatest.
You can be fair in all your dealings with him,
But you'll be lucky to get home alive.
Wasn't it Liberty who wouldn't board
A ship if Hercules was there? Smart girl!
But where's the guest who caused the whole disaster?
Ah, there he is!

CHARMIDES: O Labrax, what's the rush?
Breaking track records, are you? Come on, slow down.   500

LABRAX: I wish I'd seen you hanged in Sicily—
It's all because of you I'm in this fix.

CHARMIDES: And me: I wish I'd stayed in bed in jail
And never seen the inside of your house.
The worst that I can wish you is a flock
Of guests, and every one of them like you.

LABRAX: Bad Luck came through my door the day you entered.
Good god, why did I listen to you, leave,
And board a ship that lost me all my fortune?
All that I owned is gone, and more besides.   510

CHARMIDES: I doubt a ship could ever stay afloat
With you, you misbegotten crook, aboard it.

LABRAX: You and your lies! A fool I was to listen.

CHARMIDES: Tereus and Thyestes—what they dined on
Was no more appetizing than the food you served.

LABRAX: I think I'm going to vomit. Hold my head.

CHARMIDES: Okay, throw up your guts. That I'll enjoy.

LABRAX: Palaestra, Ampelisca—Oh, where are you?

CHARMIDES: Food for the fish, no doubt.

LABRAX: Well, you're to blame
For that, and leaving me bankrupt.   520

CHARMIDES: You should be grateful, man. You used to be
Dry as a bone. Now you're the salty type.

LABRAX: Oh, go to hell! Get out!

CHARMIDES: My idea too.

LABRAX: Nobody in the world's worse off than I am.

CHARMIDES: Except for me, although you won't believe it.

LABRAX: Why?

CHARMIDES: I don't deserve bad luck the way you do.

LABRAX: I envy those bulrushes: they stay dry.

CHARMIDES: I think I'm training for the infantry—
    My teeth are chattering so I swear they rattle.

LABRAX: An icy bath it is Neptune's in charge of.   530
    Even here I'm freezing, and with all my clothes on.

CHARMIDES: No hot drinks, either—just ice water, salted.

LABRAX: Now blacksmiths—they're the fellows that I envy—
    A good hot fire to warm them while they work.

CHARMIDES: Even a duck is luckier than we are—
    It spends all day in water and stays dry.

LABRAX: Maybe I'll hire out as Jaws BigMouth,
    Chewing on nothing at a country fair.

CHARMIDES: Why that?

LABRAX: Because my teeth are chattering so.

CHARMIDES: I had it coming, losing all I owned—   540

LABRAX: How so?

CHARMIDES: Taking you on as shipmate. It was you,
   I'll bet it was, who conjured up that tempest.

LABRAX: Where I went wrong was listening to your come-ons.
   That's where the money was—in girls, you said,
   And all I'd have to do was stuff my pockets.

CHARMIDES: And you were set to swallow Sicily whole,
   You shameless hog.

LABRAX: So far as swallowing goes,
   That's what some whale's done with my trunk and all
   The gold and silver in it, I expect.

CHARMIDES: My wallet too—that was his appetizer.   550
   There was some silver tucked away inside.

LABRAX: All I've got left to cover me is this—
   One filthy tunic and one worn-out cloak.
   I'm ruined.

CHARMIDES: Me too. Well, there's an equal basis;
   Why not set up as partners?

LABRAX: If they're safe—
   The girls, I mean—though if Plesidippus—
   The one who paid part payment for Palaestra
   If he should see me here, he'd have my hide.

CHARMIDES: Oh, stop your blubbering. Whatever happens,
   That tongue of yours can get you out of it.   560

Scene 7

SCEPARNIO: What the hell's happening? Two girls in the temple
   Carrying on and hanging onto the altar,

Scared witless of I don't know who or what—
Claim they were shipwrecked in the storm last night
And thrown up on the beach.

LABRAX: What's that? Where are they?

SCEPARNIO: At the shrine.

LABRAX: How many?

SCEPARNIO: Two, like you and me.

LABRAX: They're mine; they must be.

SCEPARNIO: How would I know that?

LABRAX: What do they look like?

SCEPARNIO: Well, I'd go for either—
If I were drunk enough, that is.

LABRAX: They're young?   570

SCEPARNIO: Look for yourself—what you are is a pest.

LABRAX: Charmides, they're my girls—they've got to be.

CHARMIDES: You think I give a damn one way or the other?

LABRAX: I'm heading in there, shrine or not, this minute.

CHARMIDES: I wish it was the gate of hell and Pluto.
And you, my man—I need a place to sleep.

SCEPARNIO: Well, then, lie down; nobody's stopping you—
It's a public place.

CHARMIDES: But look: I'm sopping wet.
Take me home with you; lend me some dry clothes.
I'd do as much for you in the same fix.   580

SCEPARNIO: This blanket is the only thing I've got.
Take it. Sometimes I use it as a raincoat.
Give me your things—I'll see that they get dried.

CHARMIDES: Hey, wait: those rags are all that I've got left.
Do I get further stripped now that I'm on shore?

SCEPARNIO: Stripped, cleaned out—give it any name you want.
If you need trust, you give security.
Sweat to death, freeze to death—get sick, get well;
No foreigners come in this house. That's final.

CHARMIDES: Now wait a minute! You're one real slave driver,   590
No heart at all. Well, why stand here and drip?
Why not drop in on Venus and sleep it off?
I got a whole lot drunker than I meant to—
And not so much on wine as on seawater.
Neptune the druggist, with his dose of salts!
If he'd gone on, we'd be asleep out there
Instead of barely living and back home.
Let's see now how my drunken pal is doing.

ACT III

Scene 1

DAEMONES: The dreams the gods think up to plague us mortals!
Not even night and sleep can bring us peace.   600
Take me, for instance: never slept a wink
Last night—too busy having nightmares.

I saw a monkey climbing up a tree,
Trying to snatch some swallows from their nest.
No luck. The monkey asked me for a ladder,
But I protested—swallows are descendants
Of Philomela and of Procne, Greeks
Like me. The monkey grew more insolent, her threats
More sharp; she swore we'd go to court.
Before I knew it, I had lost my temper,   610
Seized her and chained her so she couldn't move.
If there's a sensible interpretation
Of all this nonsense, I don't have a clue.
But tell me—what's that racket at the shrine?

Scene 2

TRACHALIO: Citizens! Citizens! I implore your aid!
Farmers who till the furrows of these fields,
Comfort the comfortless, cheer those afraid,
And show the world our spirit never yields!
Prevent the power of the impious
From overwhelming all poor innocents   620
Who otherwise are known only to us
As victims of malicious malcontents.
Now let the shameless reap what they deserve,
And give the good their hard-achieved reward.
Let men be safe within the law they serve
Nor tremble underneath a threatening sword.
Come here, come here, gather at Venus's shrine.
I beg your aid, all you who hear my plea:
Help those who, hoping for the goddess's sign
Of favor, seek her in her sanctity   630
And beg protection from her priestess here.
Choke the iniquity that's drawing near—

DAEMONES: What's this about?

TRACHALIO: O kind sir, on my knees
  I beg you, sir, whoever you may be—

DAEMONES: Come, come now, let me go, and make it plain
  What's on your mind.

TRACHALIO: O sir, this: if you want
  A healthy crop of asafoedita,
  Enough to export to the Capuans
  And to keep your eyes free of bleariness—   640
  O sir, I do implore you to consider
  Granting the favor that I beg of you.

DAEMONES: For God's sake, I beseech you by your hide—
  Unless you want a healthy crop of scars
  From birch rods and their earnest application—
  Come to the point. What are you trying to say?

TRACHALIO: O sir, I only mean to wish you well.
  You're not fair.

DAEMONES: Yes, I am. I'm wishing you
  What you deserve—no more, no less.

TRACHALIO: O sir,
  Do let me tell you.

DAEMONES: Out with it!

TRACHALIO: Well, sir,   650
  Inside here are two women, innocent, helpless.
  They've come to grief through no fault of their own
  And right before the altar. Even the priestess
  Has been insulted. It's outrageous, sir.

DAEMONES: Who in the world would dare profane a shrine,
  Manhandle women—ah, but who are they,
  These women? How are they being hurt?

TRACHALIO: I'll tell you:
  They're clinging to the statue of the goddess—
  The man, who'll stop at nothing, trying to seize them.
  He has no right—

DAEMONES: Who is this brute? Be quick.   660

TRACHALIO: There's not a good word to be said for him,
  No crime he's not committed, no god he fears—
  In other words, a pimp. Is that enough?

DAEMONES: God help us, hanging's far too good for him.

TRACHALIO: He tried to choke the priestess—

DAEMONES: He will pay,
  I swear it. Sparax! Turbalio! Where are you?
  Come here!

TRACHALIO: O sir, it's up to you to save them.

DAEMONES: Come here, you louts; this time is the last time
  I'll call you. Here! Come over here, I say!

TRACHALIO: Tell them to pound him until his eyes pop out,   670
  The way cooks do with fish.

DAEMONES: Drag him out bodily
  Like a stuck pig.

TRACHALIO: Ah, listen to them! Great!
  They'll blacken his eyes, I hope, and break his jaw.
  But here come the two women, pale as death.

Scene 3

PALAESTRA: Nothing is left us, not a shred of hope,
No place of safety, no protecting arm.
Security's a long lost dream; we turn
Frantic in our uncertainty. In there
My master showed himself the brute he is—
Knocking the priestess down, dragging us off   680
The altar statue we were clinging to.
Bruised as we are, and broken, what is death
Except a welcome ending? For all like us
The boon we pray for.

TRACHALIO: That's no kind of talk.
I'll cheer them up. Palaestra!

PALAESTRA: Who is there?

TRACHALIO: Ampelisca?

AMPELISCA: Who's that?

PALAESTRA: . Who calls me by my name?

TRACHALIO: Look here and you'll find out.

PALAESTRA: My rescuer!

TRACHALIO: Don't worry. Just stay calm; I'll manage things.

PALAESTRA: It's violence I fear—the fear of it
Will drive me to do violence to myself.   690

TRACHALIO: There's no more danger, girl. Be sensible.

PALAESTRA: Don't think there's any comfort left in words.
You've got to do something, Trachalio.

AMPELISCA: I'll die before I let that pimp near me
Although I'm a woman and afraid of death.
Oh, I could curse the day that I was born!

TRACHALIO: Courage!

PALAESTRA: And where do I find courage? Tell me that.

TRACHALIO: Don't be afraid, I tell you. Stay by the shrine.

AMPELISCA: No more protection there than by the statue
Inside the temple, where the brute attacked. 700

TRACHALIO: Okay. Sit down here and I'll keep you safe—
This is your camp, I'll be your general,
And with the help of Venus I'll protect you.

PALAESTRA: Whatever you say. O Venus, we implore you,
Here on our knees before your holy altar,
Take us beneath your wing; watch over us;
Avenge us on these scoundrels who profane
Your holy place, which is our refuge now.
We've been ill-used by Neptune all night long— 710
We would not lose your favor—oh, be kind!
Forgive us if, unwitting, we offend you.

TRACHALIO: Venus, be just. Here's one plea you must grant.
Forgive them; they've been nearly mad with fear.
Born of a shell, you might shell out some pity
For these conch-ientious objectors, casting their perils
Before such swains as take your name in vain.

Scene 4

DAEMONES: Come on, you blot on all humanity!
Girls, sit down at the shrine. But where are they?

TRACHALIO: Right over there, sir!

DAEMONES: Good! Just as I'd have it.
Let him go near them! Does he think we'll watch   720
While he insults the gods? Give him a good one!

LABRAX: You'll pay for these insults.

DAEMONES: You're threatening me,
You scum?

LABRAX: I've got my rights! These girls
Are mine, you thief!

DAEMONES: We'll leave that to the judgment
Of any senator, any reputable man:
Let him decide whether these girls are yours
Or freeborn; whether you should be jailed
And kept there until the prison walls fall down.

LABRAX: I've better things to do than spend my time
With any hangdog fool—and that means you.   730

DAEMONES: He is the one that knows you. Have it out
With him.

LABRAX: It's you that I'm concerned with.

TRACHALIO: Concern yourself with me. These are your slave
girls?

LABRAX: You bet they are!

TRACHALIO: Just put a finger on them—

LABRAX: And what?

TRACHALIO: I'll make a punching bag of you,
Smash every bone you've got, you lousy liar!

LABRAX: I can't take my own slaves out from the temple?

TRACHALIO: That's it exactly, man. We have a law—

LABRAX: You think I give a damn about your laws?
I'm taking both these girls with me—and if   740
You've got your eye on them, you'll pay me plenty.
Or else let Venus keep them, at any price.

DAEMONES: You're dunning Venus? Listen—and take this in—
If you so much as lift a hand to them,
Even pretend to—why, I'll send you home
So beat up that your mother wouldn't know you.
(*To servants*)
Come over here. Unless you knock his eyes out
When I give you the sign, I'll lash you both
Until the whips tie you like a bunch of stalks.

LABRAX: You're threatening me!

TRACHALIO: You talk of threats, you
bastard?   750

LABRAX: You keep your mouth shut. I know you, you jailbird.

TRACHALIO: Well, even if I am and you're a gentleman,
Does that mean that these girls shouldn't go free?

LABRAX: Free? Them? Ho!

TRACHALIO: They're your betters, from free Greece,
And this one comes of good Athenian stock.

DAEMONES: What's that? What do you mean?

TRACHALIO: That she's freeborn
And an Athenian.

DAEMONES: So she's my compatriot.

TRACHALIO: Oh no, sir. You're Cyrenian, aren't you, sir?

DAEMONES: Not by a long shot. I was born in Athens,
And reared there too.

TRACHALIO: More reason to protect her.   760

DAEMONES: The girl brings back my grief of long ago
When I lost my three-year-old. By now she'd be
About this girl's age, if she were alive.

LABRAX: I paid their owner hard cash for the two.
What do I care where they were born? I say
They're slaves, and, what's more, slaves of mine.

TRACHALIO: You loud mouth, so it's you who steal our girls
As youngsters—snatch them from their families
And wear them out, still young, as whores. You rat!
As for this one, wherever she was born,   770
She deserves better than you ever will.

LABRAX: You sound as though you owned them.

TRACHALIO: Let's compare
Our backs—which one's more scarred with marks of beatings?
You've got more welts than any ship has nails,
I'll bet, or I'm a liar. I'll count yours first,
Then you can have your turn. If mine's not smooth
Enough to make a first-rate leather cover
For any flask (some glassmaker can judge),
Then tell me why I shouldn't take a whip
And flog you until I'm sick of it. And stop   780

That winking at the girls. Look, knock it off
Or I'll knock you—

LABRAX: Just wait and see: I'll take them
Along with me because you say I can't.

DAEMONES: And how do you propose—

LABRAX: With help from Vulcan.
Venus he hates, and has since she betrayed him.

TRACHALIO: Watch out there—where's he headed?

LABRAX: Who's inside?

DAEMONES: You touch that door, man, and I'll slice your face
As if I had a hayfork for a fist.

SLAVE: No coals in here. All that we eat is figs.

DAEMONES: I'll give you coals to burn, but on your head.   790

LABRAX: I'll find them somewhere else, by God.

DAEMONES: And then?

LABRAX: I'll send this temple up in flames.

DAEMONES: To rid
Yourself of spleen?

LABRAX: No. Rid of these two wenches.
Burn them alive before the shrine, I will.

DAEMONES: Splendid. And then I'll take you by the beard
And toss you in the fire as well, and when
The flames have half devoured you, pull you out
And feed you to the vultures.

(*Aside*)

                               It may be
This character is the monkey in my dream—
Trying to get those swallows from the nest   800
Against my will.

TRACHALIO: I think what we should do,
Sir, is—you keep the girls from danger
And I'll go fetch my master.

DAEMONES: Good. Go find him.

TRACHALIO: But watch this good-for-nothing.

DAEMONES: Don't you worry.
I'll beat him up if he tries anything.

TRACHALIO: You swear?

DAEMONES: I do. Now off with you. Be quick.

TRACHALIO: And watch in case he tries to get away.
If he escaped, we'd owe the hangman cash.

DAEMONES: Off. On your way—I'll manage.

TRACHALIO: I'll be back.

                            Scene 5

DAEMONES: It takes a beating, then, to shut you up?   810
Or can you do it by yourself? You choose.

LABRAX: Say what you want to. I don't give a damn.
I own those girls; I'm going to drag them off
Out of this shrine with me right now. To hell
With you and all your gods.

DAEMONES: Go ahead. Touch them.

LABRAX: Who's going to stop me?

DAEMONES: Go on. There they are.

LABRAX: Well, tell those oafs, *Move off.*

DAEMONES: The only way
They'll move is toward you.

LABRAX: They wouldn't, would they?

DAEMONES: They move, and what do you do?

LABRAX: I back up.
But let me tell you this, old man—if ever   820
I catch you in the city, I swear you'll get
What you deserve, or I'm no pimp.

DAEMONES: Meanwhile,
You touch these girls, I'll mash you to a pulp.

LABRAX: Oh? So you're going to pummel me? How hard?

DAEMONES: Hard as a pimp deserves.

LABRAX: Oh, shut your mouth.
I'm sick of all your threats. I want my girls.

DAEMONES: Touch them. Go on.

LABRAX: I will, by God.

DAEMONES: Go on
  And find out what you get. Turbalio!
  Run home and bring me back a club or two.

(*The servant exits*)

LABRAX: Clubs?

DAEMONES: Mind you, good solid ones. Go on now! Move!   830
  You'll get the kind of welcome you deserve.

LABRAX: Wouldn't you know I'd lose my helmet too,
  Last night, just when I'd find it handiest?
  I'll have a word with the girls, at least—

DAEMONES: No way.
  Ah, splendid! here's my clubman back, well-armed.

LABRAX: Just looking at those clubs makes my head spin.

DAEMONES: Come on now, Sparax, you take one of them
  And stand this side of him. You, over there.
  That's right. Now hold it. Listen: if he tries
  To get at either girl against her will,   840
  You use these clubs on him until he can't tell
  Which end is up, or else you'll get the same.
  And if he tries to speak to them, you answer,
  Or if he tries to get away, why, clip him
  Across the shins.

LABRAX: You mean you're holding me
  As prisoner?

DAEMONES: You're right. And when that slave
  Gets back here with his master, hurry home.
  See that you do exactly what I've told you.

LABRAX: I'd always thought this was a shrine of Venus.
　　All of a sudden Hercules takes over   850
　　And sets up these two statues at the gate,
　　Complete with clubs. Where do I head for now?
　　Everything's turned against me, sea and land.
　　Palaestra!

SPARAX:　　What do you want?

LABRAX:　　　　　　　　　That's not her voice.
　　Hey, Ampelisca!

TRACHALIO:　　　Labrax, you watch out.

LABRAX: Oh, shut up. Still, it's pretty good advice,
　　Coming from statues. Look, you guys, what harm
　　In moving a little nearer to the girls?

SPARAX and TURBALIO: (*In unison*) No harm at all, for us.

LABRAX:　　　　　　　　　　　　　　　For me?

SPARAX and TURBALIO: Watch out.

LABRAX:　　　　　　　　　For what?

SPARAX and TURBALIO: For these. You might get hurt, you
　　know.   860

LABRAX: For heaven's sake, let me get out of here.

SPARAX and TURBALIO: Sure. Go away.

LABRAX:　　　　　　　　　　Great! Thank you—
　　oh, I see.
　　Oh well, I'll stick around.

SPARAX and TURBALIO:　　Not one step farther.

LABRAX: Nobody has this kind of luck but me.
Okay. If I don't budge I'll wear them down.

Scene 6

PLESIDIPPUS: You mean the pimp had the effrontery
To try to drag my girl out of the shrine?

TRACHALIO: You're right, sir.

PLESIDIPPUS: You should have killed him then
and there.

TRACHALIO: I didn't have a sword, sir.

PLESIDIPPUS: Well, a club?
A stone?

TRACHALIO: I couldn't treat him like a dog,   870
Could I? No matter if he *is* a dog—

LABRAX: Oh God,
Plesidippus! I'm in hot water now.
He'll make an end of me, and no trace left.

PLESIDIPPUS: The girls were by the altar when you came
To look for me?

TRACHALIO: And there they are, sir, still.

PLESIDIPPUS: But who is with them now to keep them safe?

TRACHALIO: Venus's next-door neighbor, some old man
Who's been a lot of help. He and his slaves
Will watch them; he's quite clear about his duty.

PLESIDIPPUS: Take me to Labrax, double-quick. Where is he?   880

LABRAX: Good day, sir.

PLESIDIPPUS: Don't go wishing me good day.
    Make up your mind. Which would you rather be:
    Dragged off or collared with a noose? Come on,
    Take your choice.

LABRAX: Neither.

PLESIDIPPUS: So? Trachalio,
    Quick—run down to the beach and tell my friends
    To meet me at the harbor. We'll join forces
    And turn this fellow over to the hangman.
    When you've done that, come back to stand guard here.
    I'll take the criminal to court right now.
    Come on. The judge is waiting.

LABRAX: What have I done?   890

PLESIDIPPUS: Forgotten everything? You stole my cash—
    Part payment for this girl—and took her off.

LABRAX: You lie. I never took her off.

PLESIDIPPUS: Who's lying now?

LABRAX: I carried her on board, that's all I did.
    I swore I'd meet you at the temple here,
    And here I am. You can't deny it.

PLESIDIPPUS: Oh,
    Save all that stuff for court. Now come along.

LABRAX: Charmides, help! Rescue me! Can't you see
    He's got me with a noose around my neck?

CHARMIDES: Who called my name?

LABRAX: You're blind? You see the way   900
  He's hauling me along?

CHARMIDES: A splendid sight!

LABRAX: For God's sake, help me!

CHARMIDES: Who's that with the rope?

LABRAX: Plesidippus!

CHARMIDES: My, he's the very one
  That you were after. Better go along—
  Most people pray for what you've got.

LABRAX: What's that?

CHARMIDES: What suits them.

LABRAX: Charmides, be my good friend.
  Come with me.

CHARMIDES: There's an invitation, now—
  I'm off to prison. You come too. Still fighting?

LABRAX: This is the end.

PLESIDIPPUS: I hope you're right. Palaestra,
  You and your friend stay there until I come back.   910

SLAVE: Maybe they would be safer in our house, sir,
  Till you get back.

PLESIDIPPUS: I think you're right.

LABRAX: You robbers!

SLAVE: Who're you calling robbers? Get a move on!

LABRAX: Palaestra, save me!

PLESIDIPPUS: Oh, come on, you rascal!

LABRAX: Friend—

CHARMIDES: You're no friend of mine. What makes you
    think
  I want your friendship?

LABRAX: There's no pity in you?

CHARMIDES: Nope. Just one drink with you was plenty.

LABRAX: God send you straight to hell.

CHARMIDES: You'll be there first.
  Sometimes I think that men get changed to beasts—
  Labrax, now: he's a bird, a lousy jailbird.   920
  They'll wring his neck and keep him in a coop.
  Maybe I ought to go and see him through
  And get the judge to let him go—to jail.

ACT IV

Scene I

DAEMONES: I got my good deed done today, all right—
  Helping those nice young girls. And my reward?
  Two new friends, charming as you'd hope to see.
  If it weren't for my wife—it's her hawk-eye
  That's on me day and night: no winks, no passes.
  What's Gripus up to? Fishing trips at midnight?
  I'd like a slave of mine to have more sense.   930
  He'd be far better off at home in bed—

Twenty-four hours now this gale's been blowing;
He's wasting both his nets and his own time.
And his catch? I could fry it with my fingers.
There's the old lady calling me to lunch,
And every dish will have a sauce of gossip.

(*He exits*)

Scene 2

GRIPUS: Now bless you, Neptune, just as you've blessed me.
Patron of sailors, god of fishermen,
Look how you've sent me home, my boat weighed down
With such a catch as no man's made before,   940
My rowboat just as sound as when I launched it.
I praise the sea god, though the fish I caught
Fit in a basket and don't weigh it down.
At midnight I got up
Ready to try my luck.
In spite of all the storm
I hoped I'd made a buck
For old Daemones—and
For me as well, of course.
I'm not the kind of slave   950
A master has to force
Before he'll do his job.
I have no use for such.
You have to stay awake
Or you won't profit much.
If Master has to shake you
Before you're up and out,
You're only asking trouble
To offer you a clout.
Why, look at me! Up early—   960
And look at the reward:
Freedom and all the pleasures

That money can afford.
This is the trunk—too heavy
Almost for me to hold!
What's in it? Well, my guess
Is that it's full of gold.
And no one in the world
But me knows it's been found.
Gripus, you're as good as free: 970
Fortune has turned you around,

Now here is what I've got in mind to do:
Go to Daemones, offer him spot cash
(And up the offer, if it's necessary)
For freedom. Then I'll build a little house
And buy some land and slaves to till it for me
And then a fleet of ships—before you know it,
I'll be the richest man in Greece—one men
Bow down to. And I'll have my private yacht
And sail around like old Stratonicus.   980
And when my name's a household word—why then
I'll found a city—let's see: Gripusville?
With walls two feet thick, ten feet high—and that
Will be the center of my empire. Lord,
Lord, it's enough to take your breath away.
But now I think I'd better find a place
To hide this trunk. Meanwhile my majesty
Will have to make do with a salty lunch.

Scene 3

TRACHALIO: Hey, wait a minute!

GRIPUS: What's the matter?

TRACHALIO: Look:
(*Starts to coil up rope at bottom of the net*)
This rope is going to trip somebody up.   990

GRIPUS: Take your hands off that!

TRACHALIO: All I want to do
Is help. My good deed for the day, you know.

GRIPUS: That was some storm last night. I've got no fish,
Young man; don't get up any hopes. That net
Is all I'm bringing back, and no fish in it.

TRACHALIO: What makes you think I want your fish? I want
A little conversation.

GRIPUS: Well, I don't.
I'm sick of listening to you.

TRACHALIO: Don't go 'way.
Wait.

GRIPUS: Now what's this about? Take care
Or you'll get hurt. Let go; I'm in a hurry.

TRACHALIO: Listen to me.

GRIPUS: Shut up.

TRACHALIO: You'll listen later.   1000

GRIPUS: Oh well, what have I got to lose?

TRACHALIO: Now pay attention, or you'll wish you had.

GRIPUS: What is it, for God's sake?

TRACHALIO: Can anyone hear us?

GRIPUS: What has that got to do with it?

TRACHALIO: A lot.
But tell me: can you keep your mouth shut?

GRIPUS: Lord,
What is this all about?

TRACHALIO: You've got to promise
That you'll be fair. Promise and then I'll tell you.

GRIPUS: Whoever you are, I promise.

TRACHALIO: All right, then.
I was a witness to a robbery—
And since I knew the man who was the victim,   1010
I made a proposition to the thief:
You split with me and I won't split on you,
Although I know the man you robbed. He didn't answer.
What should have been my share? Half, would you say?

GRIPUS: No less, in my opinion; maybe more.
And if he won't pay up, why, tell the owner.
That's my advice.

TRACHALIO: I'll take it. Keep on listening—
This has to do with you. You want to miss it?

GRIPUS: What in the world?

TRACHALIO: I recognize that trunk.
I know who owns it.

GRIPUS: *What?*

TRACHALIO: And how it came
  To disappear.

GRIPUS: Well, what I know   1020
  Is how it came in sight again, and who
  Saved it, and who it is that owns it now.
  Nobody in the world, including you,
  Has any chance of making off with it.

TRACHALIO: The owner, even, if he came along?

GRIPUS: What do you mean, the owner? *I'm* the owner.
  I caught it, fishing.

TRACHALIO: Fishing? You don't say.

GRIPUS: Look, I don't claim fish while they're in the ocean,
  But if I catch them, they belong to me.
  They're mine. Nobody else can claim them, see?   1030
  I sell them at fair prices. Look: the sea's
  An open market; we take our chances there.

TRACHALIO: Well, if it's free to all, what's to prevent me
  From claiming what it gives us, even trunks?

GRIPUS: Of all the nerve! Where would we fishermen be
  If the law went that way? We'd take our fish
  To market, but the villagers would yell
  That it was theirs by right as much as ours,
  And never pay a cent.

TRACHALIO: You lowlife sneak,
  Trying to make a trunk the same as fish!   1040
  You think they are the same?

GRIPUS: It's not my doing.
  I drop my net and take whatever's in it—
  And that *whatever* you can bet is mine.

TRACHALIO: Not if it's something useful, like a jug.

GRIPUS: What do you think you are? A lawyer, maybe?

TRACHALIO: Look, you low scum, whoever saw a trunk-fish
  Caught in this bay or sold in the market stall?
  What do you think you are? Do you make trunks
  Or do you fish? Maybe you're good at both,
  Or want me to think so. Show me your trunk-fish—   1050
  For if you don't, I'll see you don't make off
  With something that no ocean ever spawned.

GRIPUS: You never heard of trunk-fish? Ignorant lout!

TRACHALIO: You bet I never have. There's no such thing.

GRIPUS: Of course there is. What do you know about it?
  It takes a fisherman to know. They're scarce, of course,
  One in a thousand at the very most.

TRACHALIO: Think you can fool me by *handing out words,* you
  jerk?

GRIPUS: They're different colors, too: the little satchels
  Like this—and great big ones, dark red or black.   1060

TRACHALIO: You'll turn into a trunk yourself one day—
  First red, then black.

GRIPUS: What's happened to my luck?

TRACHALIO: Come on, make up your mind. We'll find
  somebody—
  You name him—who can settle this for us.

GRIPUS: Settle it for us? Leave it to the trunk.

TRACHALIO: You fool!

GRIPUS: Well, wise guy?

TRACHALIO: You're not leaving here
  Until you find someone to act as judge.

GRIPUS: Are you in your right mind?

TRACHALIO: I must be crazy—

GRIPUS: Me too—but this trunk stays with me,
  No matter what.

TRACHALIO: Another word, you dope,   1070
  And I . . . will . . . break . . . your . . . neck. Let go of it,
  Or else I'll strangle you with my bare hands.

GRIPUS: I'll squeeze the blood out of you like the ink
  Out of an octopus. You want to fight?

TRACHALIO: Oh, what's this all about? Let's split the deal.

GRIPUS: You can have half the grief, if there is any.
  I'm off now.

TRACHALIO: Ha! No way. Come on around.
  I'm at the helm; you're not the skipper now.

GRIPUS: The hell you say. I'm still the captain.
  Watch that rope!

TRACHALIO: I'll drop it if you'll drop the trunk.   1080

GRIPUS: Pull till your arms drop off. The trunk stays here.

TRACHALIO: It's share and share alike or call a judge.

GRIPUS: What do you mean? I caught that trunk myself—

TRACHALIO: Didn't I watch from here?

GRIPUS: —with my own net
     All by myself, with nobody to help me.

TRACHALIO: Suppose the owner comes—since I looked on
     While you were fishing—would he charge me too?

GRIPUS: You bet he would!

TRACHALIO: He couldn't, idiot,
     Unless I took my share.

GRIPUS: Oh. That's the law?   1090
     That's not for men like me. The trunk is mine.

TRACHALIO: But I maintain that it belongs to me.

GRIPUS: Hey, wait! You needn't be a thief *or* share.

TRACHALIO: How's that?

GRIPUS: You go your way and I go mine,
     And neither of us tells another soul.
     You don't take anything and I don't give.
     The slate's wiped clean.

TRACHALIO: So there's no deal at all?

GRIPUS: I offered you one—drop the rope and scram.

TRACHALIO: I've got a better thought.

GRIPUS: Think about leaving, man.

TRACHALIO: Who lives around here? Do you know them?

GRIPUS: Sure.   1100
   They're neighbors.

TRACHALIO: Where do you live?

GRIPUS: Over there,
   Yonder.

TRACHALIO: Any reason not to let the man
   Who lives in this house be the referee?

GRIPUS: Loosen the rope and let me think it over.

TRACHALIO: Okay.

GRIPUS: Boy, my luck's back! The trunk stays with me—
   Imagine, my own master to be judge!
   He wouldn't let his slave be gypped, he wouldn't.
   This chap is playing right into my hands.

TRACHALIO: Well, what do you say?

GRIPUS: Although by rights it's
   mine,
   Rather than fight with you, I'll let him say.   1110

TRACHALIO: I knew you had some sense. Who this man is
   I've no idea—if he's fair-minded, then
   Although we'd never met I'd want to know him;
   If he's unjust I'd never recognize him.
   Afterward, even if we were acquainted.

Scene 4

DAEMONES: If I could help you girls, I would, but then
   That wife of mine would get the wrong idea—
   That I was showing off my mistresses

In front of her. I'd rather it was you
Than me who begged for help from Venus.

PALAESTRA and AMPELISCA: Will no one save us?

DAEMONES: Now I give
    my word   1120
You're in no danger. Guards, you're both excused
From further duty. Go inside again.

(*They exit*)

GRIPUS: Good morning, Master.

DAEMONES: Gripus, hello! How are you?

TRACHALIO: This is your servant, sir?

GRIPUS: And proud to be.

TRACHALIO: I want no words with you.

GRIPUS: Well, then, get out.

TRACHALIO: I must know, sir. This is your slave?

DAEMONES: Yes, mine.

TRACHALIO: My luck's improved. I'm glad to know you, sir.

DAEMONES: Thank you. But you're the one, I think, who left
    A little while ago to call your master.

TRACHALIO: That's me, sir.

DAEMONES: What's up now?

TRACHALIO: Is this your slave?   1130

DAEMONES: It is.

TRACHALIO: Great!

DAEMONES: But what difference does that make?

TRACHALIO: A liar and a sneak, that's what he is.

DAEMONES: What harm has he done you?

TRACHALIO: I'd like to see
   Somebody break his neck.

DAEMONES: What *is* all this?
   What's all this squabbling?

TRACHALIO: Sir, let me explain.

GRIPUS: Shut up, you. I'll take care of the explaining.

TRACHALIO: I'm ready to present my case—

GRIPUS: Better be ready
   To show your heels if you've got any conscience.

DAEMONES: Gripus, enough, enough. Just let me hear him.   1140

GRIPUS: Before I've had a chance to tell my story?

DAEMONES: Quiet. You, now, say what you have to say.

GRIPUS: You'd rather hear a stranger than your slave?

TRACHALIO: What does it take to shut him up? Now, sir,
   You know that pimp you chased away from here?
   That's his trunk that this guy's somehow come up with.

GRIPUS: I have not!

TRACHALIO: Lunatic! It's right before our eyes!

GRIPUS: Oh, shut them and shut up! What's it to you
   Whether I have the trunk or not?

TRACHALIO: The point
   is whether you have any right to it.   1150

GRIPUS: If I didn't find it in my net, so help me
   You've every right to hang me. But if I did,
   Why should I let you claim it?

TRACHALIO: A lot of bluff!
   I'm giving you the facts.

GRIPUS: You are, are you?

TRACHALIO: I'm speaking first, I am. Make him shut up,
   Sir, if he's yours.

GRIPUS: You want me to be handled
   The way your master handles you? Daemones
   Gives better treatment.

DAEMONES: Gripus, that's your round.
   Now, man, what do you want?

TRACHALIO: You can be sure
   I'm claiming nothing of what's in that chest—   1160
   I never said that it was mine. But in it
   There's a small case—I told you all about it;
   How its real owner is a freeborn girl.

DAEMONES: The girl you said came from the same place I did?

TRACHALIO: That's it, sir. In the smaller case are toys
    She played with as a child—who would want those?
    But someday they might help the girl prove
    Who her parents were.

DAEMONES: I'll see she gets them. Quiet!

GRIPUS: There's not one damned thing I'll give up, by God!

TRACHALIO: Only the small chest and the toys, that's all.   1170

GRIPUS: They could be solid gold.

TRACHALIO: Well, you'd be paid
    Gold if they're gold, silver if they are silver.
    Nobody's out to gyp you.

GRIPUS: Show your gold
    And maybe you can see the chest.

DAEMONES: Enough!
    What were you saying?

TRACHALIO: Do me this one favor:
    If the trunk is the pimp's—that I'm sure of—
    Protect the girl. It all may come to nothing—

GRIPUS: See? He admits it. And you'd trust a liar?

TRACHALIO: Keep still until I finish. If the pimp
    Is the real owner, the girls will know the trunk.   1180
    Have him show it to them.

GRIPUS: Show it? You're crazy.

DAEMONES: Gripus, for heaven's sake, why?

GRIPUS: It isn't fair.

DAEMONES: Why not?

GRIPUS: You let them see it—right away
   They'll swear it's his; of course they will.

TRACHALIO: You think
   Because you've got no morals, no one has?

GRIPUS: You and your pious talk! My master knows me.
   He's on my side.

TRACHALIO: He'll listen to the other.

DAEMONES: Now Gripus, pay attention. Come to the point.

TRACHALIO: I thought I had, sir, but I'll try again.
   These girls should both be free. This is the one   1190
   (*Points to Palaestra*)
   Stolen from Athens when she was a child.

GRIPUS: It's trunks we're talking of, not kidnapped children.

TRACHALIO: You want to waste our time repeating facts?

DAEMONES: Enough, enough! Just answer what I asked you.

TRACHALIO: Once more: inside the trunk's a chest of reeds,
   And in the chest mementos of her parents,
   Things she had with her when the kidnapper
   Stole her from Athens years ago.

GRIPUS: Oh, dry up!
   What's with the girls? They're dumb? Should I suppose
   They haven't got the words to tell their troubles?   1200

TRACHALIO: They're silent because a woman who keeps still
   Is a good woman, more than the chatterbox.

GRIPUS: Then you're not man or woman.

TRACHALIO: What do you mean?

GRIPUS: Your speech is just as worthless as your silence.
   When do I get a chance to tell my side?

DAEMONES: One more word out of you and you'll regret it.

TRACHALIO: You will see, sir, that he returns the chest?
   Even give him a reward—and anything
   Else in the trunk, of course, he's free to keep.

GRIPUS: So you admit it now: it's mine by right.   1210
   Not long ago you were for getting half.

TRACHALIO: And I am still.

GRIPUS: A hawk can chase its prey
   And not get anything.

DAEMONES: Will you keep still,
   Or must I beat you?

GRIPUS: Just let him keep still
   And I will too. He talks and so do I.

DAEMONES: Give the trunk to me, Gripus.

GRIPUS: Well, all right—
   But give it back if there's no cash inside.

DAEMONES: I will.

GRIPUS: So. There it is.

DAEMONES: Palaestra, you
  And Ampelisca both, hear what I say.
  Is this the trunk that held your chest?   1220

PALAESTRA: Oh yes!

GRIPUS: Well, damn it, that's the end. She never
  Looked at it, even—that's how sure she was.

PALAESTRA: If you should doubt me, sir, I'll give you proof.
  Inside the trunk you'll find a small reed box,
  And I can tell you everything it holds—
  Blindfold me, I could do it. If I'm wrong,
  Wrong even once, why then I lose my claim
  And you can keep the contents for yourself.

DAEMONES: Yes. I agree to everything you say.   1230

GRIPUS: Well I don't. What if she's got second sight
  and names the things by magic? That's not fair.

DAEMONES: Magic won't help her. If she makes mistakes,
  She doesn't get a thing. Open the trunk,
  And let's get on with this.

GRIPUS: Enough of her.
  The straps are loose.

DAEMONES: Come, open it. A box!
  Is this the one you meant?

PALAESTRA: Oh yes, Oh yes!
  All I have left of family is here—
  The only way I have of knowing them.

GRIPUS: The gods are going to have it in for you,   1240
   Keeping your parents prisoned up in this!

DAEMONES: Gripus, come here. What happens now involves you.
   Palaestra, over there. Now turn your back
   And name each thing inside the chest. Describe it
   As clearly as you can. Don't skip a thing.
   Be right the first time 'round. Correcting later
   Will do no good.

GRIPUS: That's straight enough.

TRACHALIO: She's not
   The crooked one. You are.

DAEMONES: Speak up, Palaestra.

PALAESTRA: A rattle, with some little toys.

DAEMONES: That's right.

GRIPUS: Damn it, I'm losing. Hey, don't let her see it.   1250

DAEMONES: Describe the toys.

PALAESTRA: Well, one's a little sword,
   Golden, and something's written on it.

DAEMONES: What?

PALAESTRA: My father's name. Then there's a tiny axe,
   Two-headed, and my mother's name on it.

DAEMONES: Wait! Tell me, what's your father's name?

PALAESTRA: Daemones.

DAEMONES: I don't believe—I can't—

GRIPUS: I wish I couldn't.

TRACHALIO: Go on, Palaestra.

GRIPUS: There's no need to rush her.

DAEMONES: And on the ax? your mother's name?

PALAESTRA: Daedalis.

DAEMONES: This comes to me from heaven.

GRIPUS: To me from hell.

DAEMONES: This is my daughter, Gripus!

GRIPUS: What do I care?   1260
  Damn you, Trachalio, for what you've done
  Today—Lord, what a fool I was
  To net that haul and not see who was watching!

PALAESTRA: And there's a sickle, silver, and a pair
  Of clasped hands, and a windlass—

GRIPUS: Would you were!

PALAESTRA: And a gold heart, my father's birthday gift.

DAEMONES: It is my daughter, it must be my girl.
  Oh, let me take her in my arms—my dear,
  My dear, I am your father, I am Daemones,
  And there's your mother, Daedalis, in the house.   1270

PALAESTRA: Father! Oh, I had never dared to hope—

DAEMONES: The joy of having you here in my arms!

TRACHALIO: It does me good to see such happiness.

DAEMONES: Trachalio, will you take this box inside?

TRACHALIO: Poor Gripus—watch him suffer! Hey there, Gripus!
Accept my heartiest congratulations.

DAEMONES: Come to your mother, child. She will remember
More of your childhood. You can talk together.

TRACHALIO: Let's all three of us go and share the joy.

PALAESTRA: And Ampelisca, come—

AMPELISCA: God bless this day!   1280

GRIPUS: Lord, what a fool I was to show that trunk!
I should have hidden it in a safe place.
Proud of myself, I was, hauling it in
On such a night—and think of all the treasure
There is inside it that I'll never see!
Well, what's to do? Go hang myself, I guess—
Until tomorrow. Then I may feel better.

Scene 5

DAEMONES: No happier man than I
Has ever lived, who's found
A daughter so long lost.   1290
I'll make a joyful sound
To praise the gods who've helped
A man who sought their grace
Humbly and without hope.
I look upon a face
So many years unseen—
Join me while I rejoice!
And I've a husband for her—
She will approve my choice:

Athenian, he is, 1300
And rich, and a relation.
I want him here. I should
Have sent an invitation—
I told his slave to go
And bring him right away.
He should be here by now . . .
(*Looking into the cottage*)
Well, look at this, I say:
My daughter and my wife,
Their arms around each other,
Kissing and crying—that's 1310
Enough of all that, Mother.
We have a sacrifice
To make at our own shrine,
Now that she's home again,
This girl of yours and mine.
Get the beasts ready now—
Lambs, pigs—but send him out,
Send out Trachalio.
Find him! What's he about?

Scene 6

TRACHALIO: I'll find him for you, sir, and bring him back 1320
No matter what—Plesidippus, I mean.

DAEMONES: Tell him Palaestra's here—my daughter's home.
Don't let him waste a minute getting here.

TRACHALIO: Okay.

DAEMONES: And tell him he can marry her.

TRACHALIO: Okay.

DAEMONES: His father is my relative and friend.

TRACHALIO: Okay.

DAEMONES: Now quick, be off with you! Right now!

TRACHALIO: Okay.

DAEMONES: See that he hurries. We'll be at dinner.

TRACHALIO: Okay.

DAEMONES: Everything seems all right?

TRACHALIO: Okay.
    It looks as though you need reminding, sir—
    This is the day you promised I'd go free.   1330

DAEMONES: Okay.

TRACHALIO: And you remind Plesidippus
    To set me free.

DAEMONES: Okay.

TRACHALIO: Your daughter might
    Put in a word and get him to agree.

DAEMONES: Okay.

TRACHALIO: And then I marry Ampelisca.

DAEMONES: Okay.

TRACHALIO: You owe me quite a little, sir,
    For all I've done.

DAEMONES: Okay.

TRACHALIO: Are we agreed okay's the word
  For everything?

DAEMONES: Okay indeed. You'll get all you deserve.
  Now hurry to the city and back again.

TRACHALIO: Okay. I'll be here pronto. While I'm gone,
  You check that everything gets done.

DAEMONES: Okay,   1340
  Okay, okay—I'm sick of those two sounds;
  I think that word's his whole vocabulary.

                              Scene 7

GRIPUS: I'd like a word with you, if that's okay.

DAEMONES: What is it now?

GRIPUS: About that trunk. A man
  With any brain would use it, wouldn't he,
  And keep the things luck sends him?

DAEMONES: So to you
  It's quite all right to claim what's someone else's?

GRIPUS: I was the one who saved it.

DAEMONES: Just by luck—
  Luck for the owner. Luck doesn't make it yours.

GRIPUS: No wonder that you're broke, you're so damned
    holy.   1350

DAEMONES: O Gripus, Gripus, life is full of traps—
   No man can manage to avoid a fall.
   The bait is something few men can resist,
   And if our greed would have us gulp it all,
   Why, there we are, only ourselves to blame.
   It takes a lot of honesty and will
   To make a man stay on the straight and narrow,
   Keeping his self-respect and honor still.
   Touch dirty money and your hands are soiled.
   If I should hide the trunk, I'd share the guilt.   1360
   None of that for Daemones; he won't work
   With you to make the scales of justice tilt.

GRIPUS: A great performance, sir; you'd have been cheered
   Like any actor with that same routine.
   The trouble is that once the crowd is gone
   There's never one who took the words to heart.

DAEMONES: Oh, go inside; you're nothing but a pest.
   And hold your tongue—you'll get what's coming to you
   From me, and that will be not one damned thing.

GRIPUS: I hope whatever may be in that trunk,   1370
   Whether it's gold or silver, turns to ashes.

DAEMONES: No wonder all our slaves are scamps and rascals—
   If he'd got in with someone like himself,
   He'd be in jail, charged with grand larceny.
   He had his eye on loot, the law would have
   Its eye on him. Well, I should go inside
   And offer up that sacrifice, and then
   Order that dinner be prepared at once.

Scene 8

PLESIDIPPUS: Tell me all over again, don't skip a word—
   Trachalio, you treasure, you free man—   1380
   I'll owe my family itself to you! My girl
   Has found her mother and her father then?

TRACHALIO: That's right.

PLESIDIPPUS: And she's from Athens?

TRACHALIO: So they say.

PLESIDIPPUS: She'll marry me?

TRACHALIO: I wouldn't be surprised.

PLESIDIPPUS: Her father gives consent today?

TRACHALIO: No doubt.

PLESIDIPPUS: Should I congratulate him, now she's found?

TRACHALIO: Yes, I guess so.

PLESIDIPPUS: Her mother?

TRACHALIO: So I'd judge.

PLESIDIPPUS: What *is* your judgment?

TRACHALIO: Well, in my opinion—

PLESIDIPPUS: Hand it down, now; I'm listening, I'm all ears.

TRACHALIO: I'll buy that.

PLESIDIPPUS: Should I run?

TRACHALIO: Yes, yes; why not?

PLESIDIPPUS: Or should I walk quite slowly?

TRACHALIO: Yes, why not?   1390

PLESIDIPPUS: Should I speak to her when I get there?

TRACHALIO: Yes, why not?

PLESIDIPPUS: Her father, too?

TRACHALIO: Why not?

PLESIDIPPUS: And then her mother?

TRACHALIO: Why not?

PLESIDIPPUS: And then? Should I embrace her father?

TRACHALIO: I'd say not.

PLESIDIPPUS: Or her mother?

TRACHALIO: I'd say not.

PLESIDIPPUS: Palaestra?

TRACHALIO: I'd say not.

PLESIDIPPUS: Oh, damn it, damn it,
    He votes me down, and walks out on the meeting.

TRACHALIO: Out of your mind, you are.

PLESIDIPPUS: Lead on, my patron!

ACT V

Scene 1

LABRAX: Nobody has such rotten luck as I do.
   Plesidippus—the law's all on his side;   1400
   He even gets Palaestra, and I'm ruined.
   We pimps—what are we? Sons of Joy? We give
   Other men pleasure mocking us, that's sure.
   I've got one girl left, though; I'd better check—
   Get her to a safe place, out of that temple.
   She's my whole fortune now.

Scene 2

GRIPUS: I swear nobody
   Sees me alive tomorrow without my trunk.

LABRAX: Oh, that word *trunk*—each time I hear it said
   I'd swear a sword goes through me.

GRIPUS: Him that's guilty
   The gods let off—and me who fished that trunk up   1410
   With my own net—they hit me when I'm down.

LABRAX: Let me get close; I mustn't miss a word.

GRIPUS: God is my witness—I'll go put up posters
   Half a yard high that nobody can miss—
   IF ANYONE HAS LOST A TRUNK OF CASH,
   They'll say, APPLY TO GRIPUS. That should do it.
   You won't get one red cent, just wait and see.

LABRAX: Well, glory be to God, I think he knows
   Who's got my trunk. I'll ask him—heaven help me.

GRIPUS: Who wants me in there? Why? I want to stay here   1420
   And polish this spit up; there's more rust to it
   Than iron. If I rub the thing much more
   It's going to fade away into thin air
   Between my hands.

LABRAX: Good day to you, young man.

GRIPUS: And you. You looking for a barber, maybe?

LABRAX: How are things going?

GRIPUS: Spit and polish does it.

LABRAX: How are you feeling?

GRIPUS: You an M.D., buster?

LABRAX: Off by one letter. Busted's what I am.

GRIPUS: You look it, that's for sure. Whatever happened?

LABRAX: Sea washed me out last night—ship lost   1430
   And everything I owned.

GRIPUS: Like what, for instance?

LABRAX: A trunk of money.

GRIPUS: Tell me what was in it.

LABRAX: Oh, what the hell—it's gone. let's change the subject.

GRIPUS: Maybe I know who found it. You got proof
   It's yours?

LABRAX: There were two sacks of gold,
    One with a hundred pieces, one with eight hundred,
    The hundred in a wallet by itself.

GRIPUS: My luck is in. What a reward I'll get!
    Before he leaves here, I'll have cleaned him out.
    It's his trunk, sure enough. What else was in it?   1440

LABRAX: A lot of silver, separate, in a purse,
    And silverware besides—a bowl, a jug,
    A pitcher, and a ladle, and a bucket.

GRIPUS: Lord, you had
    A lot to travel with.

LABRAX: *Had*—that's the trouble.

GRIPUS: Supposing I told you—for a price, of course—
    That I could get it back. What would you give?

LABRAX: A thousand dollars.

GRIPUS: Skinflint!

LABRAX: Well, twelve hundred.

GRIPUS: Cheapskate!

LABRAX: Fifteen.

GRIPUS: That's chicken feed.

LABRAX: Two thousand,
    And that's my limit.

GRIPUS: Then get out of here.

LABRAX: Look, if I go I go. Twenty-five hundred?   1450

GRIPUS: Can't even hear you.

LABRAX: Oh well, what's your price?

GRIPUS: Five thousand flat. Add on some, if you like.
   Don't think you'll get away with less. Agreed?

LABRAX: You've got me over a barrel.

GRIPUS: This way, then.
   Venus will be our witness.

LABRAX: Oh, okay.

GRIPUS: Put your hand on the altar. Give your oath.

LABRAX: What am I swearing?

GRIPUS: What I tell you to.

LABRAX: Name it; I'll swear. I'm an old hand at this.

GRIPUS: Hand on the altar.

LABRAX: Sure.

GRIPUS: You give your word
   I'll get the cash the day you get the trunk.   1460

LABRAX: Amen.

GRIPUS: Repeat: *by Venus of Cyrene*
   I swear that if my lost trunk's found intact
   And is returned to me, I'll give this Gripus—
   Say what I've said, and touch me.

LABRAX: I'll give this Gripus
   (you hear me, Venus) five thousand dollars cash.

GRIPUS: And furthermore, say, *If I pull a trick*
  May Venus curse me all my life. In fact,
  Whether or not you pay, may the curse hold.

LABRAX: If I should break my word, goddess of love,
  May all pimps find their luck has run out, too.   1470

GRIPUS: Whatever you do, that's bound to come about.
  Wait here. I'll call the old man. Speak up then;
  Tell him you want your property returned.

LABRAX: Return the trunk or not, he'll get no money.
  It's up to me to say what oaths to keep.
  Here he is back again, with the old man.

Scene 3

GRIPUS: Over here, sir.

DAEMONES: Where is he?

GRIPUS: Labrax! Hey!
  This is the man that has the trunk. Here, sir.

DAEMONES: I do, and if it's yours, why, you shall have it.   1480
  You'll get it back, with all it holds untouched.
  Take it, if it belongs to you.

LABRAX: It does.
  Immortal gods, it's mine, my trunk!

DAEMONES: You're sure?

LABRAX: How can you ask? If Jove himself had owned it,
  He doesn't now. No doubt about it, sir.

DAEMONES: Everything's safe inside except one thing:
A little chest of toys. Because of that
I found my long lost daughter.

LABRAX: Who is she?

DAEMONES: That same Palaestra whom you called your
slave.   1490

LABRAX: Oh, fine! It's quite a day you've had. That's great!

DAEMONES: I doubt it makes you happy.

LABRAX: Oh, it does!
To prove it, I won't ask a penny for her.

DAEMONES: Generous of you.

LABRAX: Nothing at all.

GRIPUS: The trunk—
You've got it now.

LABRAX: I have.

GRIPUS: Well then, come on.

LABRAX: Come on?

GRIPUS: Pay up.

LABRAX: I don't owe. I don't pay.

GRIPUS: What do you mean, *don't owe?*

LABRAX: Right on the nose.

GRIPUS: You gave your word.

LABRAX: That's where my giving stops.
Giving your word saves giving anything else.

GRIPUS: Hand me the cash, you lying good-for-nothing. 1500

DAEMONES: What is all this about?

GRIPUS: He swore to pay me!

LABRAX: This is a court of law? What harm's in swearing?

DAEMONES: What is the money for?

GRIPUS: He swore he'd pay me
Once he had got the trunk back.

LABRAX: Oh, go on
And find an advocate. Then we can see
What the judge rules—whether I'm not a minor
And whether you made a fraudulent agreement.

GRIPUS: Let him decide.

LABRAX: No, I want someone else.

DAEMONES: You promised that you'd pay him?

LABRAX: Sure I did.

DAEMONES: What's promised to my slave would come
to me, 1510
And I'm not having any of your bribes.

GRIPUS: You thought you'd found somebody you could gyp,
Is that it? Well, we'll talk hard money now—
All for my master, so he'll set me free.

DAEMONES: Now let's consider what I've done for you—

GRIPUS: What have *you* done? *I* did it! Tell the truth!

DAEMONES: Keep out of this. You should play fair with me
And be as decent as I've been to you.

LABRAX: You realize I have my rights?

DAEMONES: But not
To use against a man who's helping you.   1520

GRIPUS: He's weakening! I've got the edge!

DAEMONES: My slave
Gripus it was who found the trunk. Agreed?
I was the one who gave it back untouched.

LABRAX: Well yes, you did. The cash I promised him—
No reason why it shouldn't go to you.

GRIPUS: Money you promised me you pay to me.

DAEMONES: One more word and I'll beat you.

GRIPUS: You pretend
To help me, when it's you you're working for!
I want my money and I want it now..

DAEMONES: You want that whipping?

GRIPUS: Thrash me until I
    bleed   1530
But I'll yell till you stuff my throat with cash.

LABRAX: Shut up. He's on your side.

DAEMONES: Labrax, come here.

GRIPUS: No tricks now—open and aboveboard, see?

DAEMONES: What did you pay for Ampelisca, tell me?

LABRAX: Twenty-five hundred dollars.

DAEMONES: Want an offer?

LABRAX: Try me.

DAEMONES: Split the five grand.

LABRAX: Why not?

DAEMONES: Half for the girl, the rest for me.

LABRAX: Okay.

DAEMONES: My half sets Gripus free, because through him
     You found the trunk that gave me back Palaestra.

LABRAX: All settled, then, and fair enough, I'd say.   1540

GRIPUS: And when do I get mine?

DAEMONES: Don't worry, Gripus.
     I've got it.

GRIPUS: But I want it for myself.

DAEMONES: You haven't got a chance. Skip it. Oh wait—
     We're not to hold him to his oath, you hear?

GRIPUS: That's the last straw, by God. I'll hang myself—
     Nobody's going to cheat me ever again.

DAEMONES: Stay on for dinner, Labrax.

LABRAX: Thanks, I will.

DAEMONES: Come on in, then.
   (*To audience*)
                    Patrons, I'd ask you, too,
  Except there'll be no dinner with no food
  Worth serving, and you're all tied up as well.   1550
  But if you'd care to shower us with praise
  You all must come and make a night of it—
  Say, sixteen years from now. Come on, you two.

LABRAX: That will be fine.

DAEMONES: Farewell then, and applause.

THE POT OF GOLD

(*AULULARIA*)

Translated by Palmer Bovie

/

INTRODUCTION

Plautus's *fabula aulularia* is the story of the pot, *aula* or *aulula* (also spelled *olla* or *ollula*), containing a treasure of gold coins found by Euclio, a poor citizen of Athens. Euclio's grandfather originally discovered the treasure, but hid it to keep his son from finding it. But the Lar Familiaris, the tutelary god of this household, let Euclio find the pot in gratitude for the reverent worship accorded him by Euclio's daughter and in deference to her excellence of character. No one knows that Euclio has had this windfall, and he is anxiously determined to keep anyone from finding out about it or stumbling onto the pot, hidden behind his hearth near the niche reserved for the Lar's statue.

When his friendly neighbor Megadorus asks for his daughter's hand in marriage, without a dowry, Euclio at first suspects that Megadorus has somehow learned about his treasure. But after Megadorus explains his preference for a woman of good character over a rich wife and delivers a harangue against imperious, propertied wives, Euclio is convinced of his neighbor's sincerity and consents to his request.

Megadorus sends extra servants to help in Euclio's house with the preparations for the wedding feast. Euclio becomes worried about the possibility that they will find his pot, so he drives them out of the kitchen and smuggles out the pot hidden under his cloak. He first tries to hide it in the shrine of *Fides* (Trust, or Credit), but as he leaves the shrine to return to his house he is overheard talking to himself about the new safe place by a slave who happens to be standing nearby. And on his way home Euclio hears a raven cawing ominously, so he rushes back to the shrine and finds the slave snooping around inside. After he hauls the slave out for questioning and inspection and sees that the pot is still safe, Euclio decides to find a

89

better hiding place for it and heads for the grove of Silvanus. But again he is overheard by the slave as he talks to himself about the new plan. The slave runs ahead of Euclio and climbs a tree to see where he is going to bury the pot. When Euclio has buried it and left, the slave digs it up and steals it, intending to report his good luck to his master, Lyconides, and win his freedom.

Meanwhile, Lyconides, who had ravished Euclio's daughter at the festival of Ceres in the darkness nine months earlier, now wants to marry her and has explained himself to his mother Eunomia, the sister of Megadorus. She assures Lyconides that Megadorus will agree that his nephew is the more suitable husband for Euclio's daughter. And she is prompted to intercede immediately when from within Euclio's house the cries of the daughter's labor pains are heard. Lyconides hails this offstage sound as final evidence of the situation he has been explaining, and goes in search of Euclio.

Euclio returns to the scene, having discovered the theft of his gold, and frantically implores the help of all his fellow citizens, including the audience, in apprehending the thief. When Lyconides encounters Euclio howling with rage, he assumes that the miser has found out about his daughter's condition. But Euclio is, of course, lamenting the loss of his pot of gold, the possession of which everyone has been as unaware of as Euclio has been of his daughter's pregnancy. Ironically mistaken in what they are referring to, Lyconides and Euclio talk heatedly at cross-purposes until the truth of their real concerns emerges. Lyconides admits his guilt in taking something belonging to Euclio and says that impulsive love made him do it. Euclio berates Lyconides for taking "it" (*illa*, which could also be assumed to refer to the pot, *aula*); Lyconides apologizes but maintains that there is even more reason now for his continuing in possession. But when Euclio accuses Lyconides outright of stealing his pot of gold, Lyconides not only denies it convincingly but promises to help Euclio catch the thief. He can then tell Euclio about his daughter's predicament, accept the responsibility, offer himself as the prospective husband, and congratulate Euclio on having become a grandfather.

Lyconides' slave proudly informs Lyconides that he has stolen Euclio's gold, and Lyconides sends the slave to fetch it. The manuscript of Plautus's play breaks off at this point, but from the few

fragmentary lines remaining we can infer that Lyconides returns the
pot of gold to Euclio, who then confers it on the young couple as a
dowry. Among the lines are: "I used to dig ten ditches a day"; "I
couldn't sleep day or night, but now I will sleep." These words, taken
with the play's acrostic argument, imply that Euclio has decided to
unburden himself of his worrisome weight and resume his familiar,
frugal existence.

The action of Plautus's farce bounces almost haphazardly off the
impulsive movements of the persons of the drama until it coincides
with the double discovery of the treasure and the plight of Euclio's
daughter. The pot of gold is a magnetic force, luring Euclio in one
direction after another and making him even more miserable than
usual. As a classical skinflint, like his father and grandfather, he is an
object of ridicule—a man who ties a bag under his chin at night so
that his breath will not be lost; someone who takes home the parings
when his toenails are clipped by the chiropodist; one who files a
complaint with the praetor against a hawk that swooped down and
carried off his breakfast. His habitual fear of losing anything has been
magnified by the possession of a secret hoard. It threatens his well-
known reputation for poverty.

Euclio's daughter, invisible in the action, is an even more shad-
owy character than the pot of gold, but an equally strong influence.
Her virtue and her reverence for the household god have led the Lar
to reveal the treasure to Euclio, against the grandfather's express
wishes. Like the treasure, she is a blessing in disguise, attractive to
two suitors—the older Megadorus, a sworn bachelor, and the ardent
young Lyconides. The secret hidden in the swollen contours of her
body helps free Euclio from his mind-rattling compulsions.

When the housemaid Staphyla chides Euclio for being afraid
someone might steal something from a house "full of emptiness and
cobwebs," Euclio tells her to make sure that the cobwebs are not
disturbed. And if anyone comes to borrow something, he continues,
say that burglars have broken in and stolen everything. Euclio goes
off to collect his two drachmas, but the supervisor is not there to pay
the wages. His precious pot is stolen. It is this absurd *reductio ad
nihil* that governs Euclio's antics and turns him into a comic figure.
He blocks the extravagant behavior of the other players, who mean
him no harm but whom he suspects of trying to take advantage of

him. He is determined to prevent others from doing anything for, to, or with him; and, while he yields to the request to marry off his daughter without a dowry, he will thereby lose one more possession. The marriage transaction seems to disappear from view when Euclio suffers the catastrophic blow of losing his treasure, and the whole drama almost falls apart, out of its senses like Euclio. But the confrontation scene between Lyconides and Euclio, beginning in total confusion and ending in new understanding and unexpected reconciliation, brings Euclio back to himself and enables him to shed the anxiety he had inherited with the treasure.

The psychology of character classically associated with avarice can be traced back to Theophrastus and to Menander's comedy *The Grouch*, but there is no extant model for Plautus's play. Here, Euclio is as much the rugged individualist as he is the begrudging miser, a needy citizen bound by his own frugality, whose attitude has become distorted and inflated by the sudden acquisition of money. The poor citizen is treated by the affable Megadorus, for instance, with respect and sympathy. The money had alienated him even further from the world of his fellow men, and when the truth became known, he could revert to character as a poor but respectable, penny-pinching, hard-working, stonefaced clown.

Molière's *L'Avare*, first produced in Paris at the Théâtre du Palais Royal in 1668, with Molière in the part of Harpagon, makes use of several elements in Plautus's *Aulularia*. The name of Molière's miser derives from Plautus's use of the noun *harpago, -onis*, (grappling hook; rapacious person) in several plays and his verbalizing of this noun, as in Euclio's suspicion, expressed in an aside at lines 200–201: "Ei misero mihi / aurum mi intus harpagatum est" ["Too bad for me / My gold has been snatched from inside the house"]. Like Euclio, Harpagon consistently suspects everyone of wanting his gold hoard. Harpagon has buried his cash box containing ten thousand écus in his garden, but his son's servant finds it and steals it. When Harpagon accuses his prospective son-in-law of having designs on and of stealing his "treasure," Valère assumes he is referring to his daughter; the same ironic misunderstanding dominates the dialogue until Valère eventually gets Harpagon to realize that the "crime" he has confessed to is that of becoming secretly engaged to Harpagon's daughter. Her first suitor, who has arranged with

Harpagon to marry his daughter without asking for a dowry, is the older man Anselme, much like Megadorus in his generous and affable character; he withdraws in favor of Valère, who turns out to be his long lost son. Harpagon's cook, chauffeur, and factotum, Jacques, blunders about cheerfully interfering in matters and comes in for his share of beatings, like the kitchen crew in the *Aulularia*.

Harpagon is mocked mercilessly for his absurd penny-pinching and candle-snuffing habits; obsessed by the fear that he may be taken advantage of, like Euclio, he seldom goes for long on the stage without becoming an object of ridicule. But here his resemblance to Euclio ends, for Molière's miser is an unscrupulous, crafty shark, whose sole interest is money. When the cash box is restored to him after the miraculous recognitions in the last act, Harpagon has the final word: "Et moi, voir ma chère cassette" ["And I'll go and gaze on my beloved gold"]. Despite his intentions to marry the young girl (who has turned out to be Anselme's long lost daughter) and his clever way of inveigling his son into admitting that he, the son, was secretly his rival, Harpagon has lost virtually all contact with human reality and can only concentrate happily on the cash in his cash box. In Molière's sparkling prose drama, with its perfectly constructed story and engagingly precise counterpoint of characters, Harpagon remains alone, ironically defeated by all the others over whom, he continues to believe, he has the advantage. Molière has capitalized on the theme of rapt devotion to one thing to the exclusion of all else. Harpagon indeed has his money. But that is all he has. Plautus's version, more loosely assembled and more naturally farcical, is not as fascinating a study in behavior as Molière's dramatic exposition of the consequences of money-grabbing as a primary craft, but his Euclio is someone we are willing to meet and even to nod to pleasantly. Harpagon is better left alone.

Palmer Bovie

THE POT OF GOLD

CHARACTERS

LAR FAMILIARIS, the household god
EUCLIO, an old man of Athens
STAPHYLA, an old woman and Euclio's housekeeper
EUNOMIA, an Athenian matron
MEGADORUS, an Athenian gentleman and the brother of Eunomia
STROBILUS, a slave and the major-domo of Megadorus
EEL, a cook
CHARCOAL, a cook
LYCONIDES, the son of Eunomia and a young gentleman of Athens
SOBERSIDES, the slave of Lyconides
PHAEDRIA, the daughter of Euclio
PHRYGIA, a flute-girl
ELEUSIUM, a flute-girl
SCENE: *Athens, before the houses of* EUCLIO *and* MEGADORUS *and the shrine of Trust* (Fides).

AULULARIA

Acrostic Argument

A pot of gold, which is discovered by Euclio.
Upsets him and makes him anxious to keep it hidden.
Lyconides has ravished Euclio's daughter, but,
Unaware of that, Megadorus wishes to marry her, and
Lavishes money on the wedding feast, and wants no dowry.
Anxious, Euclio suspects some plot and hides his gold outside,
Running into the slave of Lyconides, who watches him while
    hiding
In a tree. The slave then steals the gold, but Lyconides takes it
And returns it to Euclio. Lyconides gains the gold, a wife,
    a son.

PROLOGUE

(*Enter* LAR FAMILIARIS, *from* EUCLIO's *house*)

LAR FAMILIARIS: Hello. Don't be surprised. My name is Lar
    Familiaris. I'm the Guardian Spirit of that house
    I just came out of. I've lived there many years,
    Looking after the grandfather and the father
    Of the man who lives there now. You know: Euclio.
    The grandfather secretly trusted me with a hoard
    Of gold, and buried it under my niche by the hearth;
    An embarrassment of niches, because he prayed to me
    To keep it safe for him. He was so greedy
    That he didn't even tell his son about the treasure   10
    But preferred letting his poor son live in need
    To telling him about the treasure; and all he left him

Was a small plot of ground that it takes a lot of work
To carve out a bare existence from. So when he died—
The man who had left the gold in my safekeeping—
I began to watch his son to see if he would pay
Me more respect than his father had; but he took less,
Much less, care of me and neglected my worship.
So I neglected his. And then he died, and left
The son who lives here now and acts just like   20
His father and his grandfather. But this man, Euclio—
You know—has an only daughter, and every day she
Prays to me with incense, wine, or something,
And makes me garlands. So, it's for her sake
That I've let Euclio discover the treasure.
Now he can see her married if he wants to.
In fact, a young nobleman has ravished her
And knows who it is that he has ravished.
But she does not know him; and her father here
Does not know she has been ravished. So today   30
I'll have the old gentleman next door here
Ask for her hand in marriage, and I'll do that
To make it easier for the man who's ravished her
To marry her. Because: the man next door
Is the uncle of the man who ravished her
In the dark of night at the festival of Ceres.

But there goes Euclio, shouting around the house
As usual, pushing his housekeeper outdoors
So she can't see what he's doing. I suppose he wants
To peek at his gold, to see if it's been stolen.   40

ACT I

Scene 1

(*Enter Euclio driving out Staphyla*)

EUCLIO: Out, I tell you, out! You have to be outside,
　　You prying snoop, with eyes popping out of your head.

STAPHYLA: Why beat me? I'm bad enough off.

EUCLIO: To keep you well off,
　　And let a bad thing get the worst it deserves.

STAPHYLA: But why did you shove me out of the house just now?

EUCLIO: You want reasons from me, you bundle of bruises?
　　Move over there, away from the door. Just look
　　At her creep. Would you like to know what you're in for?
　　Let me lay my hands on a club or a slat, and I'll raise
　　The beat of that tortoise pace.

STAPHYLA: I wish the gods
　　Would drive me to hang myself, and not make me slave   50
　　In your house on these terms.

EUCLIO: Just listen to that
　　Old windbag grumbling and mumbling. And those eyes,
　　You witch. I'll gouge them out, so you don't keep on
　　Watching everything I do. Now, get over there,
　　More, over there, farther. All right, hold it:
　　And don't budge. If you make a move from that spot
　　As much as a finger's width, no, a fingernail's,
　　Or look back toward the house until I tell you
　　I'll send you off to the gallows for further study.
　　(*Aside*)

I never saw a shiftier creature than that old witch.   60
I'm scared to death she'll play some trick on me
When I'm off guard, and get a whiff of the place
Where the gold is hidden. She has eyes in the back of her
head,
The pain in the neck! I'll just step inside and see
If the gold is where I hid it. It has me worried
And gets me down in so many ways.

(He exits)

STAPHYLA: I can't imagine
What's gotten into my master, what insane idea
Makes him drive me out of the house like this,
Ten times a day, poor me! Some wild obsession
Has hold of him. He stays awake all night   70
Then sits around the house day after day,
Like a crippled cobbler. I can't imagine, either,
How I'm going to hide his daughter's pregnancy
From him, now that she is so near her time.
I guess there's nothing better for me to do
Than string myself up with a rope around my neck
And dangle out into one big capital I.*

Scene 2

(Euclio reenters from house)

EUCLIO: At last my mind's at ease: I can leave the house
Since I've seen that everything is safe inside.

---

*This striking image is expressed by Plautus in lines 77–78 as follows:

ut unam faciam litteram
longam, meum laqueo collum quando obstrinxeram
[Tie a rope around my neck and dangle myself out into
one long capital I]

(*To* STAPHYLA)
Back inside now, and look after things.

STAPHYLA: Look after   80
What things in there? Or are you afraid someone
Will walk off with the house? There's nothing else
Of value in our place for thieves. Everything there
Is full of emptiness, and draped with cobwebs.

EUCLIO: It's a wonder Jove doesn't turn me into a Philip
Or a Darius loaded with ducats, just for your sake,
You triple-witch. And as for those cobwebs,
I want them taken care of; they bring me good luck.
I'm poor, I admit it. And I put up with it.
I take what the gods give me. So, back inside,   90
And lock the door. I'll be back soon. Make sure
You don't let any stranger into the house.
Should anyone come around looking for coals,
I want you to put the fire out; and then no one
Will have any reason to ask you for a light.
If that fire keeps burning, I'll put you out.
If anyone asks for water, say it's run out;
Or an ax, or mortar and pestle, or some cooking pots,
Things the neighbors are always wanting to borrow:
Tell them that thieves got in and stole the lot.   100
I don't want a single person let in my house
While I'm away, I tell you. And I also tell you:
If Good Fortune herself comes along, don't admit her.

STAPHYLA: Heavens, I'll bet she sees that she's not let in.
She never comes to our house, though she lives nearby.

EUCLIO: Shut up, and get inside.

STAPHYLA: I'm shutting up and going in.

EUCLIO: Make sure you close the door with both bolts. I'll be
Right back. It's torture to have to leave the house.

I dislike the whole idea. But still, I know
What I'm doing. The supervisor of our ward   110
Told us to pick up our bonus of two drachs a man;
If I don't go and try to collect it, they'll all think,
I'm sure, that I've got some gold at home. It's not
In keeping with the character of a poor man
To think so little of even a little cash
As not to go and ask for his two drachs. And now,
While I'm trying as hard as I can to keep everyone
From finding out, they all seem to know. All of them
Greet me in a friendlier way than they used to;
They walk up, stop to talk, put out their hands,   120
And ask me how I am and what I'm up to,
And how things are. Well, now, I'd better be off
Where I started to go, and then I can turn around
And get back home as fast as I can make it.

ACT II

Scene 1

EUNOMIA: Brother, I hope you'll take these words as proof
    Of a loyal sister's interest in your welfare,
    Which a sister is entitled to express.
    I know of course that men find women hopeless:
    We talk too much—and there's some truth in that.
    They say no day or age has ever seen   130
    A woman who was mute. But Brother, all the same,
    Remember this one thing: that I am closest
    To you, and you to me. And so we ought
    To think of what is best for both of us,
    To give each other counsel and advice,
    Not hide our thoughts and be afraid to speak
    Right out, but share them: I with you, and you

With me. That's why I've asked you out here now,
Where we could talk about some private matters
That have to do with you.

MEGADORUS: Give me your hand,   140
Best woman.

EUNOMIA: Where is she? Who is that best?

MEGADORUS: You are.

EUNOMIA: And you say that?

MEGADORUS: If you say no,
Then I say no.

EUNOMIA: But you ought to say what's true.
No woman can be picked out as the best;
It's just that one is worse in one way, Brother,
Another in another.

MEGADORUS: I have to agree;
I'm sure I won't argue that point with you.

EUNOMIA: Then kindly give me your attention.

MEGADORUS: It's yours:
Use me; ask me to do whatever you want.

EUNOMIA: I'm here to counsel you about something   150
That is, I think, very much to your advantage.

MEGADORUS: That's quite in keeping with your character, Sister.

EUNOMIA: I hope it is.

MEGADORUS: And what is it?

EUNOMIA: Something
Of everlasting good for you. What you ought to have
Is children—may the gods grant you this increase—
And I want you to take a wife.

MEGADORUS: That's the death of me.

EUNOMIA: How so?

MEGADORUS: The discussion gives me a concussion, Sister,
You are speaking stones.

EUNOMIA: Come, do what your sister says.

MEGADORUS: I would, if I liked it.

EUNOMIA: It's to your own advantage.

MEGADORUS: Indeed, if I die before I marry. But I will,   160
On these conditions, marry anyone you want:
She arrives tomorrow, and the day after tomorrow
She is carried out of the house feet first.
Do you wish to give her to me on these terms?
Bring on the festivities!

EUNOMIA: I have someone
For you with a huge dowry, Brother: an older person,
A woman of middle age. If you tell me to ask for her,
Brother, for you, I'll ask.

MEGADORUS: May I ask you something?

EUNOMIA: Of course, ask anything you want.

MEGADORUS: Well, suppose a man
Well along in years at last brings home a wife   170
Well along in years, and the old fellow happens to get
The old girl pregnant. Can you doubt that the name

In store for the son is Postumus? So let me now
Spare you that task, Sister, lighten your work.
Thanks to the gods and our parents, I'm rich
Enough, and have no use for good connections,
The pride of place they bring with juicy dowries,
Their shouting, their ordering you about,
Their carriages inlaid with ivory panels,
Their linen robes and crimson cloaks, the things   180
Whose cost reduces men to slavery.

EUNOMIA: Then tell me, please, who is it you would take
For a wife?

MEGADORUS: I'll tell you. You know Euclio,
Our neighbor here, that rather poor old man?

EUNOMIA: I know him: not a bad sort, by my stars.

MEGADORUS: His daughter is the maiden I would pledge
My heart to. Now, don't be upset, Sister.
I know what you'll say: she's penniless.
But this penniless prospect pleases me.

EUNOMIA: May the gods favor your choice!

MEGADORUS: I hope so, too.   190

EUNOMIA: Is there something I can do?

MEGADORUS: No, just fare well.

EUNOMIA: You too, Brother.

MEGADORUS: I'll go see Euclio
If he's at home. Oh here, I see him now,
The very man, heading back home from somewhere.

Scene 2

EUCLIO: I just knew, when I left home, there'd be no point
  In going out there. That's why I didn't want to leave.
  None of the men from the district came, or the master
  Who should have paid out the money. So now I'm hiking
  Along in a hurry to get home where my heart is.

MEGADORUS: Greetings, Euclio. I hope everything is fine.   200

EUCLIO: God bless you, Megadorus.

MEGADORUS: And how about you?
  Things all right? Feeling as well as you wish?

EUCLIO: (*Aside*) When a rich man speaks so nicely to a poor man,
  It's not unintentional. That fellow knows
  I've got the gold: that's why he's greeting me
  So kindly.

MEGADORUS: You say you're feeling fine?

EUCLIO: Heavens, no!
  I'm far from well off.

MEGADORUS: But, heavens, if your mind
  Is at rest, you can live quite well enough.

EUCLIO: (*Aside*) By Hercules, the old woman has tipped
    him off
  About the gold; clearly, the secret's out.   210
  I'll cut off her tongue and dig out her eyes
  When I get in the house.

MEGADORUS: What's that you're saying to yourself?

EUCLIO: Oh, I was grousing about my poverty.
And I have a grown-up girl without a cent
For her dowry, who cannot be married off,
And I can't find a husband for her.

MEGADORUS: Cheer up,
Euclio: don't take it so hard. She will be married,
And you will be helped by me. Speak up and say
What it is you need.

EUCLIO: (Aside)   He wants something, so he promises
Something. His mouth is wide open, waiting to eat   220
Up my gold. He's carrying a stone in one hand
And showing bread in the other. I don't trust any
Rich man who speaks so very pleasantly
To a poor man. He gives you a cordial handshake
And at the same time does you some damage.
I know those octopuses: they take hold of something
And hang on.

MEGADORUS: I wonder if you have a moment, Euclio.
I wanted to talk to you about something
Of interest to both of us.

EUCLIO: (Aside)   Too bad for me.
My gold has been snatched* from inside the house: 230
I see. He wants to talk to me about it
And make some deal with me. I better go in
And have a look in the house.

MEGADORUS: Where are you going?

EUCLIO: I'll be back with you in a moment. There's something
I have to see to now in the house.

(Runs inside)

*Plautus writes: "aurum mi intus harpagatum est" ["my gold's been hooked"]. *Harpago,
-are* means "hook," that is, rob or plunder. The name of the chief character in Molière's
comedy *L'Avare*, "Harpagon," derives from this verb and its cognate noun, *harpago, -onis*.

MEGADORUS: Oh Lord,
I suppose when I bring up the subject of his daughter
And ask him for her hand, he's bound to think
I'm making fun of him. There's not a poor man around
More begrudging than he is.

EUCLIO: (*Reenters*)   The gods are with me.
    (*Aside*)
The stuff is safe—safe, unless some is missing.   240
I was really worried. Before I got in the house,
I nearly died.
    (*Aloud*)
                    I'm back with you, Megadorus,
If there's something you want.

MEGADORUS: I thank you. Yes,
I have some questions to put to you, if you
Don't mind being asked.

EUCLIO: I don't mind, unless
They're questions that I wouldn't want to answer.

MEGADORUS: Tell me, what do you think of my family
    connections?

EUCLIO: They're good.

MEGADORUS: And my reputation?

EUCLIO: Oh, it's good, too.

MEGADORUS: And my conduct in general?

EUCLIO: Not bad at all,
Above reproach.

MEGADORUS: You know how old I am?   250

EUCLIO: I know you're right up there, and so is your money.

MEGADORUS: I've always thought of you, by heaven, I have,
As a citizen free of every trace of guile,
And I still do.

EUCLIO: (*Aside*) He smells my gold.
(*Aloud*)
                           So now,
What do you want of me?

MEGADORUS: Since you know me,
And I know you, for what we are—and may this
Turn out well for your daughter and for you
And me—I ask for your daughter as my wife.
Do tell me this can be.

EUCLIO: Really, Megadorus!
That's not in keeping with your usual conduct,   260
To laugh at me, a poor man who has never harmed
Your family or you. I've never said
Or done a thing to earn this kind of treatment.

MEGADORUS: Heavens, I'm not out here to laugh at you,
I'm not laughing at you, and I don't think
You deserve such treatment.

EUCLIO: Then why do you
Ask for my daughter's hand?

MEGADORUS: To make life better
For you because of me, and for me because of you
And yours.

EUCLIO: Here's what comes to my mind, Megadorus:
You are wealthy and a man of influence,   270
But I am poor, the poorest of the poor.
If I married my daughter off to you,

It seems to me that you would be the ox
And I the donkey. What if I was teamed with you
And couldn't pull my fair share of the load,
I, the donkey, would flop down in the mud
And you, the ox, would pay no more attention
To me than if I never had been born.
I'd find you quite unfair, and my own class
Of asses would laugh at me. Then, if it came   280
To a parting of the ways, I'd have no stable
Place to stand with either of the two groups.
The donkeys would sink their teeth into me,
The oxen would run me through with their horns.
It's very dangerous, this climbing up
From the donkey class into the oxen ranks.

MEGADORUS: The closer you join forces with good men,
The better. So, accept my offer, hear me,
And promise her to me.

EUCLIO: There's not a scrap
Of dowry I can give.

MEGADORUS: Don't bother. If a girl   290
Has character, she's well enough endowed.

EUCLIO: I had to say that so you wouldn't think
I'd found some hidden treasure.

MEGADORUS: I know that,
You don't need to say that, just tell me that
You promise me her hand.

EUCLIO: All right: it's done.
(Aside, hearing a noise)
Jupiter! What was that? My funeral?

MEGADORUS: What's the matter?

EUCLIO: That noise, that banging sound
Of something hitting iron, what is it?

(Rushes off into the house)

MEGADORUS: I'm having
Some digging done in my garden. . . . Where did he go?
He went off without telling me. He loathes me   300
Because he sees I want his friendship. He's acting
The way men do: just let a wealthy man attempt
To win a poorer man's regard, and the poor man
Fears to return the favor; and this very fear
Works against his own interests. Then the same man,
When the opportunity has slipped away, is eager for it,
After it's too late.

EUCLIO: *(Reenters, calling back to* STAPHYLA *inside the house)*
                                                    By Hercules,
If I don't have your tongue torn out by the roots
I myself authorize you to hand me over to anyone
You wish, to be castrated.

MEGADORUS: Good Lord, Euclio,   310
I see you think I'm the sort of man, with my years,
To be made a spectacle of when I don't deserve it.

EUCLIO: Heavens, Megadorus, I'm not putting you in a show;
Even if I wanted to, I couldn't finance it.

MEGADORUS: What about my offer? Will you still give me your
daughter?

EUCLIO: On the conditions stated, with the dowry I mentioned.

MEGADORUS: Well, then, you promise her?

EUCLIO: Yes, I promise her.

MEGADORUS: May the gods look kindly on us.

EUCLIO: May they, indeed.
Make sure you remember our agreement that my daughter
Conveys not a whit of dowry to you.

MEGADORUS: I remember.   320

EUCLIO: I know the way you people have of complicating
An agreement. It's agreed, then it's not agreed;
It's not agreed, then it's agreed, as you please.

MEGADORUS: You'll find no grounds for quarreling with me.
And as for the wedding—is there any reason
We cannot go ahead with it today?

EUCLIO: Heavens, no! That would be excellent.

MEGADORUS: I'll go and get things ready, then. Unless
There's something else you want of me?

EUCLIO: Nothing
Else but that. You run along. Goodbye.   330

MEGADORUS: (*Calling into his house*)
Hey, Pythodicus, come on with me to the market
And make it fast.

(*He exits*)

EUCLIO: So there he goes. Great gods!
What power gold has! He's gaping at it, and that's why
He's so intent on this liaison with me.
(*Calling at the door of his house*)
Where are you there, blabbing to all the neighbors
That I'll give a dowry to my daughter?
You, Staphyla, I'm calling you. Can you hear me?

Scene 3

(STAPHYLA *enters*)

EUCLIO: Hurry and see that the dishes are good and clean
  In there. I have promised my daughter to Megadorus
  In marriage today.

STAPHYLA: May the gods bless them. But, heavens,   340
  It's impossible. Too sudden.

EUCLIO: Be quiet and get back inside,
  and make sure that everything's ready by the time
  I'm back from the forum. And lock the doors, I'll be
  Right back.

(*He exits*)

STAPHYLA: What will I do now? Ruin is coming
  Closer for us, my master's daughter and me,
  And her shame and her pregnancy will soon
  Be public knowledge. It's impossible now
  To conceal it and keep it hidden any longer.
  I'll go in and see that everything the master told me
  To do is taken care of when he returns.   350
  My stars, I'm afraid I'll be draining to the dregs
  A drink compounded of trouble and of sorrow.

(*She exits*)

Scene 4

STROBILUS: My master bought the best groceries, hired the cooks
  And these flute-girls, down at the forum, and gave me an order
  To divide the banquet stuff into two equal shares.

CHARCOAL: You'll not divide my stuff up the middle, you won't:
    If you want me to serve ass a whole, I'm at your disposal.

EEL: Pretty proper popular people's pushover:
    If anyone wants dessert, you won't want to spread
    Your favors around, eh kid?

STROBILUS: Now, Charcoal kid,   360
    I meant share out in another sense, not the figure
    You fancied you might cut. A wedding day
    Is what my master is planning.

CHARCOAL: To marry whose daughter?

STROBILUS: The next-door neighbor's, Euclio's. And so,
    Half the stuff goes on over there to his house,
    And one of the cooks, and one of the two flute-girls.

CHARCOAL: And the other half stays back here in the house
    with us?

STROBILUS: Right you are.

CHARCOAL: What's wrong with the old father
    there?
    Can't he foot the bill for a feast for his own daughter's wedding?

STROBILUS: God, what a question!

CHARCOAL: What's the matter with that
    question?   370

STROBILUS: The question is whether you know what you're
    asking. That skinflint
    Is as stingy as a stone and twice as porous.

CHARCOAL: You don't say.

EEL: You don't say so.

STROBILUS: Yes, I do say so.
He sends up an anguished cry to the gods and to men
And claims he's being robbed of his sum and substance
If the smoke from his kitchen fire escapes out of doors.
When he lies down to sleep he fastens a bag at his neck . . .

CHARCOAL: A bag?

STROBILUS: Not to lose the breath exhaled in his sleep.

CHARCOAL: And plugs his lower windpipe, as well, I suppose,
So the air will not get away when he's asleep?   380

STROBILUS: Take my word, I'll take yours: is that fair?

CHARCOAL: Well no, it doesn't square with my gullibility.

STROBILUS: Well, would you believe a drachma a drop? When he
washes
He cries his eyes out at having to throw out the water.

CHARCOAL: You suppose we might hit him for one thousand
smackers
Down payment on our freedom from this old spender?

STROBILUS: Look, you ask him to starve you, and he'll begrudge
The gift of famine. The other day a chiropodist
Cut his toenails: he took the parings home with him.

CHARCOAL: That's a picture of a parsimonious person you're
painting.   390

STROBILUS: Want to know how self-denying the poor fellow is?
Other day a hawk carted off a morsel of his porridge:
He went to the praetor to file a complaint—that
Hawk was a culprit, he cried, and carried on

About how the court ought to let him sue the hawk
For redress of breakfast losses. Six hundred stories
I've got to tell—if we only had time today.
But which of you is the faster fellow? Remind me again.

CHARCOAL: I'm faster on my feet.

STROBILUS: I mean at cooking.
I'm not looking for a thief with a fast getaway.   400

CHARCOAL: That's why I call me a cook.

STROBILUS: Well, fellow, *et tu?*
What do you say?

EEL: I'm just what I look like I am.

CHARCOAL: Such luck! An off-day cook: when the cook's away,
This guy is brought into play.

EEL: So, a three-letter man
Like you is spelling me out, eh? Slow down, speedy.
You're just a thief: *the − e − f.* You are.

CHARCOAL: You're the triple-threat thief, with a yoke-sized neck.

STROBILUS: Okay, Charcoal, lay off, and size up these lambs.
Take the fatter one over to our place.

CHARCOAL: Chop, chop, sirry.

STROBILUS: Eel, you take this lamb and lug it away   410
To Euclio's place. You kids, go along with him.
You others, come over here with us.

EEL: No fair!
We lost out on that deal. They got the fatter lamb.

STROBILUS: Yes, but you're getting the fatter flute-girl.
Now just go along with him, Helen of Troy.
You come with me, Susan of Syracuse.

EEL: Strobilus, thou Subtlest! Shoving me off on that worst
Excuse for a host! The old crab wouldn't toss me a crust
Of bread if I cawed like a crow for it. Some rooking I'm taking.

STROBILUS: You are so dumb, and so darned difficult to
    please.   420

EEL: I'm supposed to be pleased?

STROBILUS: Of course you are. How can
    you ask?
The house you're assigned to is lonely and quiet. Take
whatever you want home with you. Don't waste time
Asking for it. Our place is crammed full of guests,
Full of family, and furniture, and gold-plated dishes,
Silverware, closets jammed full of costly cloth.
If anything's missing, they'll blame the cooks and yell,
"Catch those thieves, lock 'em up, bash in their brains,
Drop 'em way down a well!" You won't hear words
Like those in your ears, so you ought to be grateful to me.   430
There's nothing to lay your hands on, by the way,
So I trust your powers of restraint. There's nothing in sight
To steal. Come along now, let's go.

EEL: Oh, all right.

Scene 5

STROBILUS: Staphyla! Hey there! Emerge. And open the door!

STAPHYLA: (*From the house*)
Who's calling?

STROBILUS: Strobilus.

STAPHYLA: (*At the door*) What is it?

STROBILUS: It's a cook.
   And it's a flute-girl, and it's all the good food
   For the wedding feast. Come out and get it from me.
   Megadorus told me to bring all this stuff to Euclio.

STAPHYLA: Who's being married? Must be the daughter of
    Demeter.

STROBILUS: You're not Cereous.

STAPHYLA: No, I'm Staphyla. Cocus
   I see.   440
   But I don't see no wine what so evah. No *mead,* I mean.

STROBILUS: Do you have a code? Himself will bring on the mead
   When he comes on home from the forum.

STAPHYLA: We don't have no
   wood
   To cook with.

EEL: Has your house got beams in the roof?

STAPHYLA: Yes, yes, they's reams of beams.

EEL: There's your wood for
    the fire;
   You don't have to forage around for it.

STAPHYLA: Some nerve. You think
   Just because you got all the food for the feast
   You can come around here and order our house burned down.

EEL: I wasn't ordering it.

STROBILUS: Take him on in.

STAPHYLA: Follow me.

Scene 6

STROBILUS: (*Calling after them*) Look after things here. I want
   to go and see   450
  What the cooks are up to. My big job today
  Is to look after those cooks. If I don't they'll raise hell
  And end up cooking in the punishment pit, in the cellar,
  In solitary. If they did, we could haul up the servings
  In baskets when they're ready. But they'd take a taste in
   advance
  Down there, and the dwellers in the upper air would go
  Without dinner, while those denizens of the lower world
  Dined down there in style, if somewhat remotely.
  But here I stand, describing it, as though there were nothing
  To do in the house, gorged with a greedy gang of guests.   460

Scene 7

EUCLIO: (*Entering from the forum*)
  I wanted to show my generous intentions today
  To do things right for the marriage of my only daughter.
  So I went to the butcher's and priced some fish. Expensive.
  The lamb was expensive, the beef was expensive, the pork,
  The swordfish steak. Everything terribly expensive.
  Cost more than I could pay, especially since
  I really don't have any money. I was fed up,
  And came on home since there wasn't anything to buy.
  Well, I guess I turned the tables on those lousy merchants.

Well, walking home I began to say to myself,   470
"Feast today, and fast tomorrow, if you don't
Watch out what you spend." My stomach sympathized
With this argument, and my heart accorded with it.
Then I had the good idea of gracing my daughter's wedding
With the least expense. I bought this nice wreath of flowers,
And the piece of incense to place on the shrine of Lar,
To ask him to make our hearth and home happy,
On the wedding day of my daughter.
                              Do I see the doors open
At our house? There's a racket. Is a poor man like me
Being robbed?

EEL: (*Bawling out from inside*)
                   A big pot, a much bigger pot, go get it!   480
From next door. The pot in here is much too small
For what we need to put in it.

EUCLIO: Oh, death and disaster!
That's my swan song he's singing, all about the *aula*,
My precious pot of gold. I'll bet he'll carry her off,
My *aulul aria*. Oof! Why am I just standing here?
I'm done for for sure if I don't hurry up and hasten to hustle.
Apollo, come to my aid, I beseech you. Do help me!
Pierce those treasury thieves with a thousand arrows!
In times of yore, I mean: you've helped me before!
But I'm still standing around when I ought to be sprinting,   490
Gasping out my last breath in one mad dash.

(*Rushes off*)

                              Scene 8

CHARCOAL: Dromo, scale these fish. Machaerio, you
Skin this eel and bone the lamprey. Make it quick.
I've got to go get the baking pan I need to use

From Eelie Boy next door. And listen, I want
That cock plucked balder of its feathers than a boy's cheek.
What the hell noise is that they're making in there?
The cooks, I guess, boiling over as usual.
I'd better retreat, and make sure our kitchen staff
Doesn't start stirring up some disturbance in our place.   500

ACT III

Scene 1

EEL: (*Running out, making a trumpet-like call*)
Ta duh duh dah duh dah!
Friends, Romans, citymen, countrymen, natives,
Foreigners, tourists, everybody! Clear the track!
I need an escape route; flush everyone off the streets!
This is the first time I ever went to a brawl
In the kitchen in the daytime. Stirring up trouble, those
    women,
Debutantes of Dionysus! Me and my boys
Have been taking some Bacchic beating.
Those Bacchic bitches made my back ache.
In fact, I'm aching all over, I'm finished up.   510
The old man is using me for his gymnasium.

Holy invasion!
The female occasion
For raising ridges on my back and all—
Well, the party's begun, the fun progresses.
Now I know how to play, too.
The old master showed me the way.
I never saw a piece of wood handled more handsomely.
He drove us all out with that stick,
Me and my helpers. We've been struck, blow by blow.   520

Scene 2

EUCLIO: Come back here, you! Hold it, hold it!

EEL: Pipe down, you
  dope.

EUCLIO: I'm reporting your name to the triple constabulary.

EEL: What's the charge?

EUCLIO: I charge you with having a knife.

EEL: What good is a cook without his carving knife?

EUCLIO: How dare you point that knife at me?

EEL: More's the pity
  I don't fricassee your titty.

EUCLIO: You're just about the worst
  Sort of criminal type floating around the streets today.
  I wouldn't mind doing the worst I could to you.

EEL: Oh, pipe down. It's plain you feel pretty wrought up,
  And I get caught up in it. The fact of my back   530
  Squeaks for itself. I mean, I'm loose as a pulp.
  All drubbed limp like one of those beat ballet boys.
  Why put the touch on us, you poor panhandler?

EUCLIO: I beg your pulpy pardon. Was I not acting
  Quite within my rights? I was in my own house.

EEL: Now, lay off. You acted well within your wrongs,
  So far as my brains testify.

EUCLIO:　　　　　　　　　　　　Your brains and my bongs
　　Are in agreement. Of course, yours may be addled.
　　What business was it of yours to be in my house
　　When I wasn't there? And hadn't given permission?　　　　540
　　That's what I want to know.

EEL:　　　　　　　　　　　　　Oh, pipe down, then.
　　We rallied around to prepare the wedding meats.

EUCLIO: What the hell do you care whether I want to eat
　　My food raw or have it cooked? Are you my keeper?

EEL: I'd like to know if you're planning to let us cook
　　This dinner? Or aren't you?

EUCLIO:　　　　　　　　　　　I want to know whether you
　　Are planning to put your paws on my possessions,
　　Or are you?

EEL:　　　　　I only hope I get back home
　　With what I brought with me. I'm happy enough
　　With what I've got and I don't want nothing of yours.　　　550

EUCLIO: I have your message. Don't give me any instructions.

EEL: But what's your reason for refusing us the rights
　　To dish up your dinner? What have we done or said
　　That differs from your desires?

EUCLIO:　　　　　　　　　　　Well, you were hired
　　To poke into every corner of my house, were you?
　　And look into every locked room? Is that how your contract
　　Read? Some question from you, you loose-fingered looter.
　　Your business was standing right there at the stove.
　　You'd have developed less of a leak if you had.
　　You got what was coming to you. Now please take note　　　560
　　Of the orders I'm dishing out. If you budge an inch
　　From the stove, nudge your way over toward the door,

Without my telling you to, I'll turn you into a type
Of terribly troubled person on close terms with disaster.
You have your answer.

(*Rushes back in*)

EEL: Where are you going? Come back!
Hey, come here again. Oh, well. Robert the Obscure,
Patron saint of all thieves! Hear me, I pray:
If you don't order him to bring back my potties to me,
I'll scream and spread it around in front of the house.
What can I do? I sure came here under poor . . .   570
Well, auspices, I guess. A drachma a day:
And look at the huge doctor's bill I'll have to pay.

Scene 3

EUCLIO: (*Entering with the pot of gold concealed under his cloak*)
This is going to go wherever I go,
And not be so easy a prey to perils like these.
(*Calling inside*)
Now listen, you cooks and flute-girls, all of you.
Get back inside, you herd of hirelings, get cooking.
Start being good-looking: bustle about your business.
Make haste while the fire burns.

EEL: All in due time!
After your club's had its fill of holes in my head!

EUCLIO: Get in! You're being paid to cook, not splutter.   580

EEL: Old boy, I'll take my wages in money, not blows.
Earlier today, I was hired to cook, not cringe.

EUCLIO: Well, then, take it to court. Now don't be a pain.
Go in and cook dinner. Or get the holy hell out of here.

EEL: Why don't you get the holy hell and go . . . ?

(*He exits*)

Scene 4

EUCLIO: Well, he's gone. Immortal gods, what a risk I'm running,
A poor man like me, having anything to do with a rich man,
Or making a deal with him. Megadorus floors me,
Trying to do me a favor by sending these cooks
To grace the occasion. And what he actually sent   590
Was people to purloin this pot from poor old me.
It's just like that crazy old cook of a rooster the old woman
Let loose. Nearly cooked my goose, that rooster did,
Scratching around and scraping his spurs in the ground,
Right where I had the pot buried. Why make a long story
Of a short one? My heart contracted. I grabbed a club
And knocked the head off his cocky old shoulders. The thief,
I caught him in the act. Come to think of it, I bet those cooks
Promised a rake-off to the rooster to show them the treasure.
But I took the life of the enemy leader in combat.   600
So why make a long story of it? A battle was fought,
With a cocky old poultry cock. Ah, here's Megadorus,
My good neighbor, strolling home from the forum. I'd better
Stay clear, or I'll have to stand around and chat with him.

(*Steps aside*)

Scene 5

MEGADORUS: I met many friends and told them about my
    decision.
They all praised Euclio's daughter and said I had done

A sensible thing, and made a wise move. My view is,
That if other rich men followed suit and married the daughters
Of poorer people, and never mind about the dowry,
The civil state would be a good deal more stable.   610
And we would be a lot less vulnerable than we are now
To suspicious envy. The wives would be more concerned
About their behavior, we husbands less disturbed
By the household expenses than we are at present.
It would do the most good for the greatest number of people.
Of course, a greedy minority will still object:
Their spirits are galled by the need to acquire possessions.
There's no limit set by law; there isn't a cobbler
Who's solely content to keep in step with his needs.
You may say, "Wealthy women won't marry, will they,   620
If the law puts them in the hands of poor men?"
I say, they'll marry more gladly, not needing dowries.
And when they do, they'll watch their behavior more closely,
Furnishing themselves, as it were, instead of the dowries.
My plan would make good mules, which cost more than horses,
At present, cheaper than Gallic geldings in the long run.

EUCLIO: (*Aside*) Well, I'm getting a kick out of listening to him.
    It tickles me to hear a speech about lowering prices.

MEGADORUS: A wife won't say "I conferred a dowry on you
    Far greater than the money you had to offer,   630
    So it's only fair that I be given the gold
    And the crimson cloth I need, and the maids and the mules,
    And the mule-drivers, and the attendants for my carriage,
    And messenger boys, and carriages to ride in."

EUCLIO: (*Aside*) Isn't that the perfect picture of a Roman matron?
    I'd vote for him as prefect of feminine morals.

MEGADORUS: Wherever you go nowadays, you see more carts
    In the courtyards of town houses than you see in the country
    When you go to a villa to visit. But what takes the cake,
    The first prize for costs, can be learned from the following   640

Bills of particular, when they come and want to be paid:
There's the fuller, the goldsmith, the jeweler, the linen-
    dressmaker,
Retailers, hemstitchers, underwear-designers, sleevemakers,
Purple-pellon-dyers, wax-yellow dyer-fellows,
Flame-colored bridal veil designer-fellows,
And people that put myrrh on women's shoes to make them
    smell oh
So sweet on their feet. Linen weavers, brandishing clippers;
Sitting there are sandal-makers, shoemakers, sellers of slippers;
Standing around are the hush-puppy hawkers, and then the
    fellows
Who specialize in dyeing things marshmallow.   650
The fullers want their money; so do the seamstresses and
    menders;
The brassière developers are standing around, and the
    benders-
Over-backwards for their money, the guys who sell girdles.
You'd think that would exhaust the list, when I've hurdled
These claimants for cash. But just when they leave,
There come three hundred more to replace them, to receive
Their overdue installments. Crowding the atrium
Are fringe-benefiters, the belt makers and hem-designers,
And the architects of jewelry boxes. Their money is paid them.
But no sooner are they off the scene than it discloses   660
Saffron dyers, and dozens of others of theses and thoses.

EUCLIO: (Aside) I'd call him over if I weren't afraid of interrupting
His "owed" to the wonderful ways and means of women.
I'll let him finish.

MEGADORUS: When the cash has all been found
For these petty petitioners, they fade out, to reveal
A soldier still standing in line, more or less at attention.
It seems he wants to collect his army tax.
You go and consult your banker for help in computing
The amount owed the military. The soldier just stands there.
He hasn't had dinner, but he thinks he's going to be paid.   670

When the banker adds up his figures, he also discovers
You owe him some money. The soldier has to be put off
And pins his hopes on some other day in the future.
And that's just a sample of the way these wealthy women,
With their towering dowries, can put us all out of pocket,
And run up expenses that are bound to burden us down
To where we can't bear it. The woman without a dowry
Is under her husband's control. The woman with one
Slaughters her husband, makes his whole life a mess
And him a much worse off man. Oh, there's my neighbor   680
Standing in front of his house. How goes it, Euclio?

Scene 6

EUCLIO: My ears were lapping up your fine little talk.

MEGADORUS: You heard it?

EUCLIO: All of it, right from the beginning.

MEGADORUS: Still and all, I think you might spruce up a bit more
In honor of your daughter's wedding.

EUCLIO: A splendid outlay
In accord with his means, or a magnificent display
Indicating his resources, is the rich man's way
Of reminding himself of how much he owns. Megadorus,
For me, or any poor man, the setup at home
Is no better than people imagine.

MEGADORUS: Oh, but I trust
The gods will see to it that your substance increases.   690
More and more every day.

EUCLIO: (Aside)   My substance, is it?

I don't like the sound of that word. He seems to know
What I'm worth as well as I do. The old woman told him.

MEGADORUS: Why are you conferring with yourself apart from the
    senate?

EUCLIO: Just wondering how I might lodge my complaint against
    you.

MEGADORUS: What complaint?

EUCLIO: How can you ask? You installed
    A battalion of thieves to sack every corner of my house,
    Infiltrated five hundred cooks into my domicile
    With six hands apiece, to spider all over der place,
    Like Geryon, the Spanish king with three corporations.   700
    If Argus had tried to watch them, whose thousand-faceted
    Eye sockets made his body one great big eye,
    The fellow Juno put in charge of watching over Io,
    He couldn't have kept track of them. And that isn't all:
    That darn little flute-girl is drinking me out of wine
    All by herself. She could sop up the Spring of the Muses
    In Corinth, if it flowed wine. Then there's the banquet . . .

MEGADORUS: but I bought enough food for a regiment. And I had
    conveyed
    A lamb for the feast.

EUCLIO: That's some damned fine lamb!
    I never saw a creature like that for being emaciated.   710

MEGADORUS: Emaciated, you say? Care worn, or carefully
    picked?
    I'd like to hear your version.

EUCLIO: All skin and bones.
    Flourishing on undernourishment. The sunlight picks out

Its inside with perfect clarity. They glow and sparkle
Through the skin that's transparent as a Japanese lantern.*

MEGADORUS: But I bought the lamb for the slaughter.

EUCLIO: You'd have
    done better
To pay its funeral expenses; it was already dead.

MEGADORUS: Come, Euclio, I want to join you in a drink.

EUCLIO: I never touch the stuff.

MEGADORUS: But I told my men
    To trundle a tun of good wine from my place to yours.   720

EUCLIO: Thanks anyway. My rule is: drink only water.

MEGADORUS: I'll send you home soused today, if I can,
    You with your rule for water.

EUCLIO: (Aside)   I know what he's up to:
    Muddle me well with wine, that's his technique
    For making me change my place of habitation.
    I'll fox him and find a hole for it outdoors.

MEGADORUS: Well now, I'll go wash up. I have to perform
    The sacrificial rites. There's nothing else, is there?

(He exits)

EUCLIO: O my pretty little pot! How the enemy plots
    To get the gold nestled there in your stomach!   730
    The best thing is to put you, pretty little pot,
    In the hands of the Temple of Trust.† I'll hide you there,

*Plautus writes "lanterna Punica" ["Carthaginian lantern"].
†Punning on the meaning of Fides as commercial credit.

That's what I'll do for sure. O Goddess of Trust,
You know your servant, and I'm familiar with you.
Please be most careful not to change your name, Trust,
As I entrust my treasure to your safekeeping:
I'm totally indebted to your time-honored credit.

ACT IV

Scene 1

SOBERSIDES: This is the way your very good slave
    Should behave. Here's my prescription:
    Take Master's word for law, and give him   740
    No trouble of any description.

The slave who wants to obey
Master in just the right way
Must hasten to be at his service all day,
Or all night for that matter. If he must sleep
He's supposed to dream he's still a slave and keep
Awake to Master's needs, even in his dreams.

If you slave for a master like mine, who seems
So head over heels in love, your obligation
Is to engineer your driver's salvation   750
And steer him clear of damnation.

When boys are learning to swim we wrap them in bands
Of bulrushes, round their waists, to free their hands
And let them move and propel themselves through the water.
Well, your slave should be a life raft, just enough smarter
Than Master in love to buoy up his lively libido
So he doesn't pirouette down to the bottom, torpedoed.

Let him look quick and sharp to every wish of the master
And his eyes should get the message, that frown of disaster
On the forehead, for instance, and let him hurry faster   760
Than four-horse-power chariots. That way he won't be lashed,
    sir,
Or watch his leg chains take on a polished luster.

My young man's in love with the daughter of Euclio
But she'll marry Megadorus—they told him so.
He sent me out to take a good look around
And barge in on things. I guess I'll be altar-bound,
And spring up here on Faith, and above suspicion
Peer all about, this way and that, and condition
My mind to pounce on a more master-minded decision.

Scene 2

EUCLIO: (*Addressing the goddess*)
    Guaranteed Trust, be sure not to tell anyone   770
    That my gold is in your safekeeping. Not that I fear
    Anyone can find it so cleverly hidden away
    In a dark corner. But if someone did he'd transact
    An easy piece of business for himself, stumbling on this booty,
    A filled-to-the-brim pot of gold. So I ask you sincerely,
    Goddess of Trust, don't let that happen. Well, now,
    I'll go wash up to perform the sacrificial rites,
    And not keep my neighbor waiting to send his escort
    To bring him his bride, my daughter. Now Trust, see to it
    That my pot is safe in your care and that I get it back   780
    Just here in your trusting care,
    Entrusting it to your tiny temple in this gloomy grove.

(*He exits*)

SOBERSIDES: Immortal gods, what's this I've just been told?
  The nerve of him, hiding a pot chock full of gold
  Right here in the Temple of Trust.
  Listen to me, good Goddess, must
  You keep your word with him, or give it to me?
  I'm your servant and he's the father, isn't he,
  Of the girl my master loves? I'll go inside
  And consult the shrine for a place it may have to hide   790
  Gold in, while the old man's otherwise occupied.
  If I find it, O Goddess, my cup
  Overfloweth with faith, right up
  To the brim, a five-gallon slop-
  Bucket of bountiful gold. And I'll drink a toast
  To you for putting me in the hands of a host
  Who has driven me to drink for a better reason than most.

Scene 3

EUCLIO: (*Returning suddenly*)
  A raving raven on the left hand! Not the sort of sign
  To go unregarded. And raking the ground with his claws
  At the same time, and cawing in his most raucous tones!   800
  No wonder my heart started beating so fast, and doing
  That dance in my stomach, and rattling to make its way
  Up into my throat. But why am I just standing here?

Scene 4

EUCLIO: (*Discovering* SOBERSIDES *in the shrine*)
  Out of there, you nightcrawler, you daytime worm, you creep!
  Wriggling up out of the ground! There's something waiting for
    you
  You didn't bank on bumping into, up here.

I'll give you a hand, you prestidigitator,
With a fistful of heavy-handed head-spinners.

SOBERSIDES: What the hell's wrong with you? I've got no
    business
To conduct with you and your hands, you derelict!   810
Why are you socking me? Take your paws off my neck!
Why should I be your punching bag?

EUCLIO: Big bag of wind,
That's what you are, just asking to be tattooed,
And you can puff out a question like that, you light-fingered,
Triple-threat thief?

SOBERSIDES: Did I take something of yours?

EUCLIO: You give it right back.

SOBERSIDES: Give what right back?

EUCLIO: You ask?

SOBERSIDES: Information, please. I didn't take something of
    yours.

EUCLIO: I want what you took given back. You think you can get
    Away with it?

SOBERSIDES: Get away with what?

EUCLIO: You can't get away with it.

SOBERSIDES: What's got into you?

EUCLIO: Drop your load right here.   820

SOBERSIDES: Aren't you the one who lets loose a load in the road?

EUCLIO: Come on, drop it here. And drop your jokes along
  with it.
  I'm not in the mood.

SOBERSIDES: Well, what are you in? Drop what?
  Can't you call whatever it is by its right name?
  I didn't take a thing from you, didn't touch a drop.

EUCLIO: Show me your hands, then.

SOBERSIDES: Take a good look at them
  both.

EUCLIO: All right. Now show me the third.

SOBERSIDES: He seems to be
  mental,
  This sharp old temperamental, confused, accidental-on-
  purpose.
  I wonder if you're violent?

EUCLIO: You're driving me mad, I'll say
  that,
  By not hanging up on some tree, but you'll be there soon,   830
  If you don't confess to your crime.

SOBERSIDES: Confess to what crime?
  And to you?

EUCLIO: What did you take out of there?

SOBERSIDES: I'm damned
  If I took anything of yours.
  (Aside)
                      And also damned
  If I didn't want to.

EUCLIO: Now, just shake out your cloak.

SOBERSIDES: As you wish.

EUCLIO: I bet you've got it under your tunic.

SOBERSIDES: Feel free: have a look.

EUCLIO: You disgusting crook,
  Just so I won't think you took anything! Once again,
  Now, show me your right hand.

SOBERSIDES: There.

EUCLIO: And now show the left.

SOBERSIDES: Why, of course. Here they both are.

EUCLIO: Oh well, I
     suppose
  I might as well stop looking. Just give it back.   840

SOBERSIDES: Give what back?

EUCLIO: Oh, don't kid around. You've got it.

SOBERSIDES: I've got it, have I? What is it I've got?

EUCLIO: Pretty tricky!
  You want me to say what it is, eh, so you can hear?
  Oh, no! I say, give me back what you took.

SOBERSIDES: You must be out of your mind. You looked me all
     over,
  Anywhere you wanted, and didn't find anything of yours
  Anywhere in my possession.

(*Starts to leave*)

EUCLIO: Wait, something else . . .
Who's your accomplice in there?
(*To himself*)

                                                     I'm caught in a trap:
The other one's making some noise inside. If I go
Searching him over at least; this one hasn't got it.   850
(*To* SOBERSIDES)
You can go if you want.

SOBERSIDES: May Jupiter and the gods jump on you!

EUCLIO: That's a nice way to thank me. I'll hurry on in there
And strangle that accomplice of yours. And meanwhile you,
Will you please get out of my sight? Are you leaving or aren't
    you?

SOBERSIDES: I'm leaving.

EUCLIO: Well I'd like to see you run through it
    once.

                                   Scene 5

SOBERSIDES: (*Alone*) I'd rather die some painful, lingering way
Than not set a trap for old foxy pop today.
Of course, he won't dare leave it here in the shrine,
He'll cart it off with him and change the place of confine-
Ment, in a moment . . . oh, there's the door, it's the man   860
Old Himself, Gold He Lugs out to hide where he can.
I'll duck behind this door and listen in on him.

(*Hides in* MEGADORUS's *doorway*)

Scene 6

EUCLIO: I counted on Trust to be my trustworthy tool
    And she almostest made the worstest old fool of me.
    Lucky that crow cawed in, or I'd have been caught!
    I wish the old crow would fly by again, the same one
    Who gave me the high sign. I'd like to express my thanks.
    He gave the raucous word. I'd reciprocate
    As soon as waste my words on the air. Now, where
    Shall I hide my pot? In what lovely spot, I wonder?   870
    There's the grove of Silvanus, outside the city walls,
    Very hard to find, enclosed in a thicket of willows:
    That's the place to bury it. I'm sure Silvanus's wood
    Is boxier and safer to apply to than the goddess of Trust.

(*He exits*)

SOBERSIDES: Excellent! Very fine! Good! The gods want me
    Safe and solvent—so I'll run there and climb a tree
    In Silvanus's wood to perch on and look out to see
    Where the old man puts his gold in its hideaway.
    Trouble is, my master told me for certain to stay
    Right here; his orders were clear. And so I may   880
    Get more trouble than gain with my effort to profit.

Scene 7

LYCONIDES: I've told you, Mother; you know everything in my
        heart
    As well as I do, my feelings for Euclio's daughter.
    So please, Mother dear, I implore you, I ask you again
    As I have before, take the matter up with my uncle.

EUNOMIA: Be assured I only want you to have what you want,
   And I'm certain I can prevail on my brother to do it.
   Your reason is honest enough if, as you say,
   You took advantage of the girl the night of the revel
   When you were the worse for wine.

LYCONIDES: It's only the truth: 890
   I wouldn't tell you a lie to your face, Mother, would I?

PHAEDRIA: (*Offstage*) Help me, Nurse! My labor pains are
   beginning!
   Juno, goddess of light and life, oh, help me!

LYCONIDES: Well, Mother, facts speak louder than words: she's
   crying.
   She's in the throes of birth.

EUNOMIA: Come to my brother's
   With me, my son, and you will win his consent
   To the request you have made of me.

LYCONIDES: You lead the way,
   Mother dear, I'll follow. Now, where is old Sobersides,
   My trusty slave? I posted him to guard duty
   Hereabouts somewhere, didn't I? Let me see: 900
   If he's doing his job it's not fair for me to scold him.
   I'll go in where the committee is considering my case.

Scene 8

SOBERSIDES: (*Strolls on carrying the pot of gold*)
   I've struck it rich
   Richer than the songbird Pitch
   Who guards the golden mountain.
   The others aren't worth counting:
   Royal names of rich old birds

Like the Silver Eagle and Golden Hawk,
I'm as rich as a sheik with a shawl full of shekels,
A duke with a deckload of ducats,   910
A crowned head with a pocket full of crowns,
A gold-crested rich old bird.

It's been a good day for me.
I slipped off and scaled a tree
To take up my watch. My program, you see,
Was to get a good view of what the old man would do
And follow his schedule. He buried his loot, and then
When he disappeared I swooped right down again
From my nest and dug up the pot of gold, the best
Haul I ever made. Here he comes now. He's afraid   920
Of a friend with a spade, no doubt. I'd better clear out.
I'm out of sight, old undercover me
But I'll race home and hide my discovery.

Scene 9

EUCLIO: Done for! Done in! Done up! Where shall I hurry?
Where shall I not hurry? Catch him, hold on to him!
Him whom? He who? I don't know who he is!
I can't see anyone, I'm going blind,
I'm going around in circles. Oh, where am I?
Who am I? I don't know. I can't calm down
Long enough to try and find out.
(*To audience*)
                                        All of you people   930
Out there in front, won't you please lend me a hand?
I didn't say give me a hand, I'll pay for your interest.
I beg of you, serve as witnesses, show me the man
Who took away my treasure. You, sir, sitting right there,
You're the sort to be trusted, I can tell you are
From looking at your face. But why are you laughing
At me, all of you, what's the reason? Oh yes, I know:

Of course, you're all of you thieves, every last one,
All dressed up in your nice white holiday gowns,
To keep your true nature covered, sitting so sedately,   940
As if you were reliable, thrifty people.
(*Slowly*)
I don't suppose someone of you has got it?
You've ruined me. Just tell me, please, who has it?
You don't know?
I'm a wreck, then,
Plunging straight to the bottom,
Rack and ruin, shabbily treated:
Such grief and misfortune and sorrow
This day has brought me! And famine
And poverty. I'm the most unhapppiest fellow   950
On earth. Why should I go on living
When I've lost such a lot of gold
Which I took such pains to bury
So deep in the ground? I fooled myself,
I guess, and tricked my own mind,
And cajoled my own character,
So other men could get a big laugh
And lots of pleasure, just looking on
At my misfortunes, profiting from my losses.
I can't bear to be the target of other men's laughter.   960

LYCONIDES: Who's this old coot clamoring out here, in front
     Of our place, telling the tale of his sorrows? Oh, I know
     Him: that's Euclio, surely. Oh, oh, I'm done for—
     The jig is more or less up. He knows that his daughter
     Has produced a child. That's my interpretation.
     I'm undecided as to just how I should proceed.
     Disappear, or shall I wait here? Should I go
     Up to him and confront him, or take to my heels?
     What to do, what to do? I wish I knew.

Scene 10

EUCLIO: Who is that man I hear talking?

LYCONIDES: (*Tragically*)   A lass! Poor me!   970

EUCLIO: Oh, no: poor *me*. I'm the powerfully depleted person
    To have such sorrow and trouble descend on me!

LYCONIDES: Come now, cheer up!

EUCLIO: How could I possibly do that?

LYCONIDES: This misdeed that darkens your mind—well, the
    fact is,
    I did it, and I admit to it.

EUCLIO: You mean, you say . . .

LYCONIDES: I'm telling you the truth.

EUCLIO: What did I ever do to you,
    Young man, to deserve such scandalous treatment from you
    Toward me and my children?

LYCONIDES: Some god impelled me to it:
    I was irresistibly tempted.

EUCLIO: But how could that be?

LYCONIDES: I admit I've done something wrong and deserve
    the blame   980
    For having done it. I'm in your presence, now,
    To ask your pardon and beg you to understand.

EUCLIO: How dare you touch something not belonging to you?

LYCONIDES: What's the use asking? The deed is done, and it can't
  Be undone again. I believe the gods impelled me:
  If they hadn't wanted it done, I know it wouldn't
  Have happened.

EUCLIO: Well, I believe that what the gods wanted
  Was to have me clap you in chest-irons, and take it out
  On your organ of sensation.

LYCONIDES: Don't talk like that!

EUCLIO: But what have I done to you, to make you lay
      hands on   990
  Something of mine, against my wishes?

LYCONIDES: It was wine—
  I was out my head, very much in love, and so I went wrong.

EUCLIO: You've got some nerve, you organ of sensation,
  Coming in here with a speech like that and casting it
  In my teeth! If there were any justice in your excuse
  We might as well steal a matron's gold in daylight
  And when apprehended offer as our excuse
  The fact: we were drunk; we were madly in love;
  That's why we did it. Pretty cheap way to get off
  You've found there—a jug of wine, a girl beside you.   1000
  Let any lover, or drunk, act any way he wants,
  So long as it's pleasant: he won't be called to account.

LYCONIDES: But I'm here of my own free will, to ask you to
      pardon
  My foolish behavior.

EUCLIO: I don't care much for men
  Who do something wrong and then apologize for it.
  You knew she belonged to me. You shouldn't have laid
  Your strange hands on her.

LYCONIDES: But I did dare touch her
  And I don't pretend I didn't take total possession.

EUCLIO: So you have something of mine without my permission?

LYCONIDES: I don't mean to stay in possession without your
       permission.   1010
  My possession is such that, well, I think it's mine,
  Not yours anymore. And you'll discover, Euclio,
  That it really belongs to me, as I say it does.

EUCLIO: If you don't give it back . . .

LYCONIDES: Give it back to you? What?

EUCLIO: What you stole of mine, I'll rush you right off to court
  And swear out a warrant . . .

LYCONIDES: What did I steal of yours?
  Where did I get it? What is it?

EUCLIO: How Jupiter
  Must favor you in your ignorance!

LYCONIDES: How can I know
  What you're talking about, unless you tell me yourself?

EUCLIO: I'm asking you back for the pot of gold, the
       treasure   1020
  You admit you took from me.

LYCONIDES: But I didn't say
  I took any such thing. Because I didn't.

EUCLIO: You deny it?

LYCONIDES: I deny it, most negatively. I never saw
  Any gold, or heard anything about any pot.

EUCLIO: Give her back! You stole her here in the grove of
    Silvanus.
    Come on, hand her over. I'll split the contents with you,
    Even though you've robbed me, I won't give you trouble.
    Come on, hand her over!

LYCONIDES: You can't be in your right mind,
    To call me a thief. I thought, Euclio, we were talking
    About something else you'd found was missing of yours   1030
    That I had to do with. It's a rather significant thing,
    And if you have time to discuss it, I'd like to talk
    The whole business over with you.

EUCLIO: Just tell me, honestly,
    You did not steal my gold?

LYCONIDES: Honestly not.

EUCLIO: You do not know who did?

LYCONIDES: Honestly don't.

EUCLIO: But if you do find out who stole it, you will
    Point him out to me, won't you?

LYCONIDES: Honestly will.

EUCLIO: Promise not to shelter the thief, or ask for a share
    When you catch whoever it is?

LYCONIDES: Promise not.

EUCLIO: But suppose
    You go back on your promise?

LYCONIDES: Great Jupiter   1040
    Can do to me what he will.

EUCLIO: That's good enough
For me. Tell me now what you were going to say.

LYCONIDES: Perhaps you're not acquainted with me and my
    background.
    Megadorus is my uncle; my father was named
    Antimachus; I am called Lyconides;
    My mother is Eunomia.

EUCLIO: Oh yes, I know your family.
What is it you want of me? I'd like to know.

LYCONIDES: You have a daughter . . .

EUCLIO: Yes indeed, right here at
    home.

LYCONIDES: You have promised her hand, I believe, to my uncle?

EUCLIO: You've got the right information.

LYCONIDES: He's instructed me
    to say   1050
    To you that he is now abrogating the contract.

EUCLIO: Going back on his word, and walking away from the
    wedding,
    When everything is ready? I hope the immortal gods
    And goddesses jump on his neck, good and hard, all of them!
    The man for whose sake today I have lost so much gold,
    Poor me!

LYCONIDES: Don't be dejected, and don't curse him out.
    This business will work out well for you and your daughter.
    So, rather ask the gods to turn it to your advantage.

EUCLIO: May the gods make it work out well!

LYCONIDES: I hope they will,
   And for me as well. Now listen to me. There's no one,   1060
   Not a man, who admits to having done wrong, who's so bad
   As not to excuse himself for feeling quite guilty
   About his misconduct. I beg of you, Euclio,
   That even though I have sinned against your daughter
   And you, you will grant me your pardon, and grant me your
      daughter
   To have and to hold as my wife in legitimate marriage.
   I confess it outright: I did violate your daughter,
   At the revels of Ceres, out of my head with wine,
   In an onrush of youthful passion.

EUCLIO: Oh God, poor me!
   You are reporting a crime, and I have to listen   1070
   To your larceny!

LYCONIDES: Oh, don't complain so, Grandfather!
   That's what I've made you on the festival day
   Of your daughter's nuptials. She's given birth to a child.
   It's ten months, counting the first, if you reckon back
   To the first festive day. And it's for my sake
   That my uncle has kindly relinquished his claim on the girl.
   Do go in and ask if what I say isn't true.

EUCLIO: Curtains, for certain. A gang of troubles ganging up
      on me.
   I'll go in the house and find out what the truth is.

LYCONIDES: I'll be right with you. Out of deep water at
      last—   1080
   I feel sure of that. But I don't see old Sobersides
   Anywhere around, to tell the news to. Perhaps I can wait
   Just a moment or two, before I follow my father.
   That will give him some time to make his inquiries
   About what I've done. His daughter's faithful attendant,
   The old nurse there, can explain the whole matter to him.

ACT V

Scene 1

SOBERSIDES: (*Entering*) Gods almighty and immortal,
  It was heavy! But I can chortle
  With glee for the burden that's fallen on me.
  What great gifts, and how heavy,   1090
  I have now to heave a happy sigh for:
  A four-pound pot of gold I didn't have to try for!
  Wherefor, and whyfor—for that matter, whofor
  Is richer today than I am? Is there a dearer
  Man in all Athens than me to the gods, or a nearer?

LYCONIDES: I seem to hear the voice of one crying out
  In bewilderment.

SOBERSIDES: Well, there, it wouldn't be my master
  I see before me?

LYCONIDES: Is that my servant I see?

SOBERSIDES: Yes, sir, it's he.

LYCONIDES: Yes, it's nobody else.

SOBERSIDES: I'll walk over to him.

LYCONIDES: I'll pick up my feet. I
  suppose   1100
  He's visited the maiden's old nurse, as I told him to.

SOBERSIDES: Why don't I say I found some treasure for him,
  (*Aside*)
  And speak right up? I'll humbly request manumission

From him on the spot. I'll go and plead my case.
(*Aloud*)
Finders!

LYCONIDES: You found her keepers?

SOBERSIDES: I've got a deeper
   Secret than kids say they have when they find a worm
   In a bean.

LYCONIDES: Oh, you: still at the same old game,
   I guess. You're joking.

(*Starts to leave*)

SOBERSIDES: Wait. Master. Let me explain.
   Wait. Listen.

LYCONIDES: Go ahead with your explanation.

SOBERSIDES: I have found a wealth of riches today, good
      Master.   .   1110

LYCONIDES: Where in the world?

SOBERSIDES: In a four-pound pot of gold.

LYCONIDES: What scandal is this I hear?

SOBERSIDES: I stole the stuff
   From old Euclio.

LYCONIDES: Where is the gold?

SOBERSIDES: In a chest
   In my room at home. I hereby request manumission.

LYCONIDES: Me, manumit you?
  That's the best request in your chest,
  You superfluity of criminal ingenuity.

SOBERSIDES: Come off it: I see what you're up to. Pretty clever
  Of me to plant the thought in your mind. You were about
  To latch onto it for yourself.

LYCONIDES: Enough fooling around: 1120
  Hand over the gold.

SOBERSIDES: Me? Hand over the gold?

LYCONIDES: Yes, you, I mean. And I'll hand it back to
  Euclio.

SOBERSIDES: From where?

LYCONIDES: From where you said it was, in the chest.

SOBERSIDES: Oh you know how I'm always fooling around!

LYCONIDES: Go get it, man: your mission is* to bring it
  Back here to me or end up worse than dead.

SOBERSIDES: You can pound me to a pulp but still you'll
    never
  Get that box from me . . . but if you unhand me . . .

(He exits)

*The manuscript of the play ends at this point. A few lines, apparently from the
concluding scenes, read:

      unassigned: for those fine saffron dresses, girdles, trousseau outlay
      unassigned: how he fleeced the man
      EUCLIO: I used to be digging ten ditches a day
      EUCLIO: I never had a bit of rest day or night
          watching it. Now I shall sleep.
      unassigned: People that serve me raw vegetables
          ought to add some sauce.

Scene 2

EUCLIO: (*Returning*) You described the case very well. I'm a grand
   popper,
   A poor pauper, and a papa-in-law, in one day.   1130
   I'll confer the poor girl on you, but you must remember,
   There's no dowry. In fact, now there's even less than nothing
   In the house.
                    You'll be in for additional expense, you know:
   Those saffron silk slips women dote on wearing,
   Those flimsy brassières: there's no end to the money they
      spend.
   It's enough to put the bite on a miser, or bleed
   A poor man to death.

LYCONIDES: I don't care about the cost:
   What matters the most to me is the girl. If she's shedding
   Her clothes, like an annual snake, it's still her wedding
   To me that makes the day as attractive as the night.   1140
   I love her dearly: that much troth I do plight.
   Truthfully and youthfully: well, even sonfully now,
   And no longer sinfully, now that I'm your grandson's father
   Duly, and wholly your own son-in-law solely.
   Oh, where's that good old slave? Don't leave, Euclio:
   I think there's another surprise here in store for you.

SOBERSIDES: (*Staggering in with the pot*)
   Clunk! I'm in your hands. Please take this junk
   Off my hands. And how about my manumission?

(*Gives the pot of gold to Lyconides*)

EUCLIO: (*Rubbing his eyes, then his hands*)
   A mirage, no doubt. I guess these poor old eyes
   Just can't see how myopic I've always been . . .   1150
   Getting my hopes up—like the dope I am . . .

(*Starts to go*)

LYCONIDES: Wait, Euclio! This is some sort of local yoke-
    Bucket my funny old slave is pulling up broke
    From the well of his sense of humor.
    He wants to be free today. The rumor
    Is: manumission is the price we pay
    When we give permission for something dear
    We love to go on its way. A tradition
    With us poor pagans, and worth the price of admission
    To one of their funny old plays. Wait!   1160
    (*Gives the pot of gold to* EUCLIO)
    With this pot he thee pays
    For the trouble to which you've been put.
    She goes, *Phaedria illa*
    But she stays, *olla illa*, the merrier *aulularia*,
    Right there in your two-room villa.
    How's that for turning the tables?

EUCLIO: I can't quite believe it. Can I have a lucky star,
    Or that little house of mine have room for a *Lar*?

LAR FAMILIARIS: (*Strolls casually out of the house*)
    Yes, Euclio. And I'll never be very far
    From you. But don't hitch your wagon to a jar   1170
    When you've got a Cinder like *illa*.
    Cheer up! Everything worked out rather well.
    Don't be dejected! This has all turned out
    Better than you expected. You are one person less,
    But have given your daughter a house full of happiness,
    And still have your treasure, a full four pounds' measure.

EUCLIO: But you know how I used to work, digging ten ditches
    A day, so no one could know I had such riches,
    And never got a bit of rest, either during the day
    Or at night, because I was always on my guard.   1180
    Well, all I want to do now is to award
    This hoard to the young couple, for them to keep:
    (*Hands them the pot of gold*)
    And I will get some sleep.

TWO SISTERS
NAMED BACCHIS
(*BACCHIDES*)
Translated by James Tatum

INTRODUCTION

The *Bacchides* has been esteemed more often for its parts than for its effectiveness in the theater. Through an unknown *florilegium* or medieval anthology of tags and quotable verses it inspired one of the most famous lines in European poetry: "Abandon every hope, you who enter here" ("Lasciate ogni speranza, voi ch' entrate"), the words written above the entrance to hell in Dante's *Inferno*. The idea of the abandonment of hope at the entrance to the underworld first appeared as a metaphor in a monologue of one of the characters in act 3, scene 1, of the *Bacchides*, in a very different setting. The tutor Lydus is seeking to flee, not the gateway to the pagan underworld, but the doorway of a whorehouse.[1]

> Ope' wide at once this door to hades!
> I beg you, unlock the door!
> Yes, a door to hell and nothing less:
> no one comes this way unless he has
> abandoned all hope who enters here.

The *Bacchides* has more recently attracted readers for what it reveals about Plautus's use of Greek sources and his originality in adapting Greek New Comedy to the Roman stage. The play had long been known to be based on Menander's lost comedy *The Double Deceiver* (*Dis Exapaton*). The discovery and publication of an extensive papyrus fragment from that play in 1968 made it possible to compare a sequence of seventy lines in Plautus (*Bacchides* III.3–

---

[1]With *Inferno*, canto 3.9, cf. *Bacchides* 368–70: "pandite atque aperite propere *ianuam hanc Orci* obsecro. / nam equidem haud aliter esse duco, quippe qui *nemo advenit*, / *nisi quem spes reliquere omnes* esse ut frugi possiet." The other famous line in the play is Chrysalus's quotation in IV.7 of an aphorism attributed first to Menander: ὅν οἱ θεοὶ φιλοῦσιν ἀποθνῄσκει νέος, "quem di diligunt adulescens moritur" ["He whom the gods love dies young"].

155

III.6) with the original scene in Menander.[2] Comparison shows that
Plautus is an exact or free translator, depending on his own dramatic
purposes. He aimed, of course, to write a play quite different from
the naturalistic comedy of Menander. Efforts to reconstruct the lost
opening scene have contributed a great deal to our understanding of
the play, since a clear sense of the entire comedy is required if one is
to write a performable and dramatically coherent opening.[3] But no
script can be seen in clear outline, nor is its theatricality easily
assessed, until it is produced; and in performance the *Bacchides* at
once comes into focus as a peculiar play. It appears to be willfully
eccentric in its dramatic structure, with a concluding scene that
seems at first sight to be gratuitously cynical, almost an afterthought
to the main action.

The *Bacchides* could be summed up as a play about two young
men willing to do anything for love who are passionately devoted to
two courtesans who will do anything for money. Thanks to the ma-
chinations of a clever slave, both pairs get what they want. The
audience gets a good deal more. The *Bacchides* seems to have two of
everything. Besides the sisters Bacchis (Bacchis of Athens and her
sister Bacchis visiting from Samos, here named Bacchis I and Bacchis II) and their young men (Pistoclerus and Mnesilochus), there
are two fathers (Philoxenus and Nicobulus) and two slaves (the tutor
Lydus and the mastermind Chrysalus). There also seem to be two
plays. The two sisters Bacchis who give their name to the *Bacchides*
are peripheral to most of its action; they appear only in the opening
and closing scenes. For nearly a thousand lines and all but twenty
minutes of performance time, the stage is given to the slave Chrysalus and his ingenious plots to unite the young men with the sisters
Bacchis. A more detailed summary is needed to appreciate the particular logic of this play, for it does have a logic that works in the
theater.

Bacchis I learns that her sister has returned to Athens, but
under contract for one year to the soldier Cleomachus. To free her
from this obligation, the two sisters call on young Pistoclerus. Since
Pistoclerus's best friend, Mnesilochus, is in love with Bacchis II,
Pistoclerus can do a double favor to his mistress and his friend. The

[2]See E. W. Handley, *Menander and Plautus: A Study in Comparison* (London, 1968).
[3]On *Bacchides* I.1.A (the reconstructed opening scene), see note to the translation.

sisters then retire. Pistoclerus first turns aside the warnings of his tutor Lydus about the evils of the Bacchis sisters, then commissions the slave Chrysalus to take care of the matter. Chrysalus does this by persuading the old man Nicobulus that the money he had entrusted to Chrysalus and his son Mnesilochus was stolen by a perfidious Greek at Ephesus named Archidemides. The entire sum is in fact untouched and under the guard of Mnesilochus. Chrysalus's scheme works perfectly until Mnesilochus arrives. Overhearing a long harangue by Lydus about Pistoclerus's affair with Bacchis I, he assumes that his best friend has betrayed him and stolen Bacchis II. In a fit of jealousy, Mnesilochus turns over all the money he was bringing from Ephesus. Chrysalus's plot is now exposed to Nicobulus.

Mnesilochus and Pistoclerus are soon reconciled and turn quickly to Chrysalus for another plot. This time his trick consists in appearing to offer sound advice and good evidence. By dictating several letters to Mnesilochus, Chrysalus successfully portrays himself as an injured innocent who is trying to save Nicobulus and his son from the boy's own foolishness. When the soldier Cleomachus suddenly appears, Chrysalus outdoes himself by persuading Nicobulus that Bacchis I is the *wife* of Cleomachus. Terrified for his son's safety, the old man guarantees repayment of Bacchis II's fee. Once Chrysalus has won his second game of deception, he celebrates his triumph, and walks off the stage and out of the play. Nicobulus discovers the truth too late, since he has paid the fee twice: once to his son and once to the soldier. He is joined by Philoxenus. Both old men charge in a rage to Bacchis I's door and summon the sisters outdoors. After a quick consultation, Bacchis I and Bacchis II decide to lure the old men inside so that their sons' expenses can be kept up. Philoxenus easily gives in, and after increasingly weaker protests, so does Nicobulus. Fathers and sons end the day in the same bed, with the two sisters named Bacchis.

Bacchis I and Bacchis II run an elaborate establishment that they support through the systematic seduction of their customers.[4]

---

[4]There are abusive terms in Latin for the profession of Bacchis I and II, and such words are sometimes used by angry male characters: for example, *scortum* (literally, "hide"), which I generally render as "whore" or "slut", and *illecebra* (literally, "allurement"), which comes across nicely as "hooker." But Plautus's regular word for the sisters Bacchis is *meretrix*, which can be translated variously as a "woman earning wages" (cf. *merere*, "to earn money, to draw

These men think of themselves as lovers (*amantes*), but in the eyes of
Bacchis I and II they are merely sources of income.[5] In the *Bacchides* the usual business of the courtesans, seduction, is supple-
mented by another way of making money: the elaborately staged
production of Chrysalus's double deception, and a production in no
figurative sense. Producers supervise the performance of a play, and
they profit from it, but they do not direct it or act in it. This is
precisely what Bacchis I and II do. They seduce Pistoclerus, then
commission him to get money; he in turn commissions Chrysalus to
contrive a plot. Although he is willing to play any role necessary,
Pistoclerus is like any actor in that he himself has no idea what that
role may be. Chrysalus is more obliging.

The *Bacchides* is thus the property of its producers, the sisters
Bacchis. They are the only players comparable to Chrysalus. Where
he uses his wit to manipulate others, they use their beauty; and his
wit is itself in service to that beauty. Every other character in the
play is only a person to be manipulated. Although Lydus at first
seems to be a vivid exception to the rule, he is finally ordered into
obedience by his masters. His moralizing convinces no one, least of
all Pistoclerus, who appears to have learned only rhetoric from his
teacher, not good sense. While Nicobulus may seem to be made of
sterner stuff and to have produced a better son, Mnesilochus is
distinguished mainly for his narcissistic soliloquies. Like theatrical
producers in real life, Bacchis I and her sister are able to withdraw
from most of the turmoil of the drama that the director Chrysalus
creates.

Chrysalus will remind many readers of Pseudolus, the clever
slave turned playwright in the later comedy *Pseudolus*, produced in

pay"), "kept woman," and, as it is usually rendered here, "courtesan." In contemporary usage
"courtesan" may seem too genteel compared with "prostitute," "harlot," or "whore," but in
most instances these words would serve as a harsh and misleading description of what the
meretrix does. She is not coarse enough to be called a harlot, nor does she conduct her
business in the streets, like a prostitute. Occasionally the context permits the translation
"whore," but in most instances that word brings with it too heavy a charge of immorality. The
meretrix is as much geisha as kept woman and courtesan is the word that comes closest to
conveying what cooly calculating characters Bacchis I and II really are.
    [5]This is also true of Phronesium and her lovers in the *Truculentus*. See *Truculentus* I.1–
II.1 and IV.4.

191 B.C.[6] Without the misapprehension of Mnesilochus, Chrysalus's first deception would have worked. His task was to invent a believable fiction. He fails because he is not at first fully in charge of the stage he attempts to control. Mnesilochus's indiscretion undoes everything, and because of the unreliable forces he works with, Chrysalus must move from a plot of innocent mariners threatened by pirates and swindled by Greeks to a plot characterized by an imagery of warfare. And war it is, since his task is far more difficult the second time around; his victim knows about the first plot and is on guard against further tricks. Hence Chrysalus becomes "General Chrysalus," *imperator Chrysalus* (IV.4):

> CHRYSALUS: Now, pay attention, Mnesilochus, and you too,
> Pistoclerus. Both of you go now into the dining room.
> Take your places on that twin-sized couch of yours. Once
> you're set up there, your job is to start drinking. That's an
> order.
> PISTOCLERUS: Any more orders?
> CHRYSALUS: One more: once you've taken your places, don't
> dare leave unless you get a signal from me.
> PISTOCLERUS: O noble general!

When Chrysalus no longer needs his not-too-competent soldiers, he orders them off stage and out of the play. The imagery of an army on the march culminates in the showpiece of the *Bacchides*, the "Song of Troy" (IV.9). Nicobulus is likened to Priam and besieged Troy, and Chrysalus is cast as the Geeks—Ulysses, Agamemnon, Menelaus, Ajax, and Achilles rolled into one. Like a Roman general leading his troops home, he offers a report of his conquests, modestly declines the honor of a triumph, and leaves the stage (IV.9).

Although Chrysalus congratulates himself on a well-run campaign, he in fact leaves behind some unfinished business that only the Bacchis sisters can complete. An audience may wonder why the sisters need to reappear. There are no threads left to tie up from the opening scene. Neither Mnesilochus nor Pistoclerus is a serious

---

[6]The *Bacchides* is customarily dated prior to 191 B.C., at some date earlier than the *Casina* and the *Truculentus*. For the slave-playwright Pseudolus, see John Wright, "The Transformations of Pseudolus," *Transactions and Proceedings of the American Philological Association* 105 (1975): 403–16.

romantic interest for Bacchis I or II. Recall, then, that money, not love, is essential to the courtesan; Nicobulus and Philoxenus unwittingly offer the sisters an unexpected source of further income. Nicobulus has paid twice, but he has not paid enough. He has also been tricked twice, but not enough. He has only discovered Chrysalus's plotting and trickery, but he and we have yet to discover what he really is. For all his indignation, he is a father not one bit better than his son. The epilogue spoken by the company is prim and to the point:

> If these two old men had not been worthless
> since boyhood, they'd not be snared in scandals
> today in their hoary manhood; nor would we
> much delight in our play's long survival,
> had we not often seen pimps made rich
> by greedy sons and fathers playing rivals.

The joke on Nicobulus is not only that he was tricked twice and paid twice, but that he thought he was a better man than other men and was not. For him, this is costly knowledge. Thus, the *Bacchides* is a traditional comedy of deception, and more. Although we revel in Chrysalus's plots, we realize at the same time that his brilliant imagination serves other ends than our entertainment. While we have had a good time, two sisters named Bacchis have made a good deal of money. This is a complex message to leave with an audience.

James Tatum

TWO SISTERS
NAMED BACCHIS

CHARACTERS

RUNNING SLAVE, servant of Bacchis I
BACCHIS I, courtesan of Athens
BOY, in service to Cleomachus
BACCHIS II, sister of Bacchis I and a courtesan arriving from Samos
PISTOCLERUS, young man of Athens in love with Bacchis I
LYDUS, pedagogue, slave of Philoxenus, and teacher of Pistoclerus
CHRYSALUS, slave of Mnesilochus and Nicobulus
NICOBULUS, old man of Athens
MNESILOCHUS, son of Nicobulus
PHILOXENUS, old man of Athens and father of Pistoclerus
PARASITE, in service to Cleomachus
ARTAMO, slave overseer of Nicobulus
CLEOMACHUS, soldier

SCENE: *A street in Athens with the houses of* BACCHIS I *and* NICOBULUS.

ACT I

Scene 1

I.1.A*

(RUNNING SLAVE *runs on stage; darts back and forth, finally comes to* BACCHIS I*'s door; bangs loudly*)

RUNNING SLAVE: She's here! She's here! Is anybody home?

BACCHIS I: (*Inside*) Who is here?

(*Comes out*)

RUNNING SLAVE: Bacchis is here.

BACCHIS I: You mean my sister?

RUNNING SLAVE: Yes, your sister.

BACCHIS I: My dear sister Bacchis from Samos?

RUNNING SLAVE: Yes, Bacchis from Samos.

BACCHIS I: The one who is as much like me as one drop of milk is like another?

---

*The continuous text of the *Bacchides* starts in the middle of a conversation between Bacchis of Athens and her sister, Bacchis from Samos (I.1.B). Exactly how much has been lost before this point remains a difficult problem for which no conclusive answer seems possible. Some twenty fragments of the opening scene have been preserved and are conveniently arranged in the Loeb edition with Paul Nixon's translation (*Plautus* I.330–33). The present version follows the plot Friedrich Leo constructed from the fragments. The opening to the *Bacchides* (I.1.A) is a free invention based on most but not all of the fragments, and not necessarily in the order proposed by Leo and others. It was composed by working backwards from the completed translation of the rest of the script.

RUNNING SLAVE: Yes, it's her.   10

BACCHIS I: The sister who has the same name as mine?

RUNNING SLAVE: The very same one.

BACCHIS I: (*Sends* RUNNING SLAVE *into house*)
All right, inside at once! Out with the pails and water! Bring on the
brooms! I want this house in order for the arrival of my dear, dear
sister.
(RUNNING SLAVE *dashes inside. Servants start running around,
cleaning, dusting, etc.* BACCHIS I *confides to audience.*)
Bless her heart. She's living in Ephesus and sent me a letter
saying that she had snared a rich young man from Athens. In fact,
he's the son of my next-door neighbor, Nicobulus.   18
(*Gestures toward* NICOBULUS's *house, next door*)
But then she found an even bigger catch: a stupid mercenary
soldier. You know, the kind that sells his life for gold. Too bad for
the boy next door, but business is business. She says the soldier is
all boasting and bellowing. The only reason she agreed to go with
him was that he offered to pay her a huge salary for one whole
year.
(*Laughs*)
What it must be like to be in his service! All huffing and puffing!
Banging in bed with him must be noisier than the banging in a
blacksmith's shop.

BOY: (*Enters leading train with* BACCHIS II *and slaves carrying her
baggage*)
Which house is it, you say?

BACCHIS II: Why, this house. Wouldn't I know the house of my own
sister? In fact, there she is, standing at the door! Oh, Sister dear!
Greetings! Here I am, back in dear old Athens again.   31

BACCHIS I: Greetings! Is it really you? Home after all this time?

BACCHIS II: Yes, home after a whole year abroad.

(*They embrace warmly*)

BOY: (*Unimpressed, to audience*)
  Abroad? Why are they so excited about being abroad?

BACCHIS I: I am *so* delighted at the news of the soldier, dear. I only
  regret you had to give up my neighbor's boy Mnesilochus to get
  him.

BACCHIS II: Yes, even though he doesn't have much money, his
  father does, and that's what really counts.   39

BACCHIS I: Indeed it does. If only there were some way to keep you
  here in Athens for a year. You would earn *far* more from Nicobulus
  and his son if you did.

BOY: (*Breaks in indignantly, to* BACCHIS II)
  What plot are you two plotting? Don't you know you're hired out
  to my master for a year? You're not supposed to take a fee from any
  man but him for one whole year! And no belly-bumping with
  anybody else, either.

BACCHIS II: (*Chases him away*) Shut up, you little slug! Go back to
  the harbor this instant! You're supposed to wait there until your
  master arrives. When he does, bring him here to my sister's
  house.   50

BOY: (*Slinks away, muttering to audience*)
  What good does it do to be a loyal slave? Curses if you're honest,
  the whip and the whipping post if you're not.

(*He exits*)

BACCHIS I: I wish there were some way we could keep you here,
  Sister dear. There's so much money in my neighbor's house.

(*Enter* PISTOCLERUS. *He does not at first notice the two sisters
standing in front of* BACCHIS's *house.*)

PISTOCLERUS: (*To audience, holding up a letter*)
    Just today I received a letter from my old pal Mnesilochus.
    He's the son of Nicobulus, the old man who lives here.
    He's been away in Ephesus on business for his father.
    He says that he's fallen in love with a woman from Samos,
    a woman named Bacchis, and *that's* quite a coincidence,
    because I happen to be in love with her sister Bacchis,   60
    the one from Athens. He asks me to do anything I can
    to free *his* Bacchis from some soldier named Cleomachus.
    He says this Cleomachus has hired her for a whole year
    and that this soldier Cleomachus is bringing her to Athens.
    He wants me to get *his* Bacchis away from the soldier,
    one way or another. I don't have any idea
    how I'll do that, but I know one thing
    for sure: I'd do anything for my old pal.

BACCHIS I: (*To* BACCHIS II) Look, dear! It's my latest catch, Pis-
    toclerus, the son of that rich old man Philoxenus! He's the one that
    will save us.   71

PISTOCLERUS:
    (*Catching sight of* BACCHIS I *and* BACCHIS II; *to audience*)
    Why, what's this I see? It's my very own mistress, Bacchis, and her
    sister . . . Bacchis . . . the one who has my old pal all aflame. I'd
    do anything in the world for her . . . for Bacchis . . . my Bacchis,
    that is . . . not her sister Bacchis.
    (*Runs over*)
    My honeybuns! My heart! My hope! My sweetie! My food! My
    joy!

(*Kneels, embraces* BACCHIS I *around the waist*)

BACCHIS I: Pistoclerus! Dear, dear Pistoclerus, how sweet you are!

(*Signals to* BACCHIS II *to step to one side*)

BACCHIS II: (*Steps to one side; to audience*)
    Ah! So this is the young man my sister has been working on! While

his friend Mnesilochus was off on business with me in Ephesus,
he stayed behind in Athens. If you ask me, he's strayed as far from
home as his friend. They say that Ulysses had a terrible time
wandering away from home for twenty years. But Pistoclerus has
outdone him, and all his wanderings have taken place right inside
the walls of Athens!   85

PISTOCLERUS: (*To* BACCHIS I) Honeybuns, you could charm the
heart of any man you pleased.

BACCHIS I: (*Peels off each hand, fastidiously*)
Yes, dear, I know. Now let me have a word with my sister.
(*Crosses to* BACCHIS II)
Sister, dear, do you see what I see?

BACCHIS II:
(*Surveying goggle-eyed* PISTOCLERUS *with a professional eye*)
H'm . . . why yes, dear sister, I think I do. He's the fellow who
will get me out of that contract with the soldier and into the house
of Mnesilochus and his father Nicobulus.   92

BACCHIS I: You're right, dear. And aren't you relieved we have *Plautus* now to help us play this play?

BACCHIS II: (*With relief*) Oh dear, yes! He's been kept out of it too
long as it is!

I.1.B

BACCHIS I: (*To* BACCHIS II) Just keep quiet and let *me* do most of the
talking.

BACCHIS II: Fine, go ahead.

BACCHIS I: If my memory fails me, do come to my aid, Sister dear.

BACCHIS II: Dear Sister, *me* sing *your* tune? I know I'll fail.   101

BACCHIS I: Why, Sister dear, you, our bedroom nightingale?

(*They go over to* PISTOCLERUS)

PISTOCLERUS: (*Aside*) What are those twin sisters with one name up to?
(*To* BACCHIS I *and* BACCHIS II)
What schemes have you been scheming?

BACCHIS I: Nice ones.

PISTOCLERUS: (*Aside*) I see.
(*To* BACCHIS I)
Not at all in your usual style.

BACCHIS I: (*Attempts the tragic style*)
Who is there more miserable than a woman?

PISTOCLERUS: Who would you say more deserves to be? 110

BACCHIS I: My sister here wants me to find some man to protect her, so that the soldier—
(BACCHIS II *signals worriedly to her; she catches herself*)
I mean that man can take her home when her rental time is up.
(*Leaning on him*)
Would you please look after her?

PISTOCLERUS: Look after her? How?

(*Again on his knees with arms around her*)

BACCHIS I: (*Again breaks the embrace;* PISTOCLERUS *falls to floor*)
By taking her home when she's finished her job. Then the soldier won't have her for his housemaid. You see, if he got back the money he paid for her, he'd be glad to let her go.

PISTOCLERUS: (*On all fours*) Where is he now? 119

BACCHIS I: I think he'll arrive at any moment. But it would be better for you to come to our house. You can sit there and wait until he comes. You'll have wine, and I'll give you a kiss with your drink.

PISTOCLERUS: (*Arising*) Your sweet words are pure birdlime.

BACCHIS I: What do you mean?

PISTOCLERUS: (*Striking a pose*) Because I know that two of you are after one pigeon.
(BACCHIS I *and* BACCHIS II *each take him by one arm*)
Damn!
(*Aside*)
Those birdlime twigs are brushing my wings!
(*He breaks free*)
Look, you, I don't see any profit for me in this crime.

BACCHIS I: Why, dear?   130

PISTOCLERUS: Why? Because I'm afraid of you bacchantes and your bacchanals, Bacchis.

BACCHIS I: What is it? What are you afraid of? You don't mean my *bed* is tempting you to do something naughty?

PISTOCLERUS: I'm more afraid of your *head* than your bed.
(*Aside*)
You're a wicked beast!
(*Resumes*)
Look, you, your dank, dark den is no profitable place for a young fellow like me.

BACCHIS I: You know I would stop you myself if you tried to do anything foolish at my house.
(*He grabs for her again; she glides away and shifts to a businesslike tone*)   140
Now, when the soldier comes, I want you to be at my house; that way no one will do her or me any harm, not as long as you're

around. You'll help us, and the help you give us will help your *old
pal*. When he comes, he'll think I'm your girlfriend.
(PISTOCLERUS *is already baffled by all this*)
Now, dear, why are you so quiet?

PISTOCLERUS: (*Strikes a moral pose*)
Your words are charming to listen to,
but test them and you'll find their thorns:
they pierce the heart, they squander fortunes,
they wound us and our reputation.

BACCHIS II: (*Interposes*) Why are you afraid of her?   150

PISTOCLERUS: Why am I afraid of her? Should a young man like me
go into a gymnasium like *this*, to sweat away his wealth into bank-
ruptcy?
(*Warming to his theme*)
Where I'd take on a debt instead of a discus? Ruination instead of
running?

BACCHIS I: (*Both sisters are resigned to this fit of eloquence*)
Oh, how charming!

PISTOCLERUS: (*Striding about*) Where I'd take up "*my turtle
dove*" instead of my *sword?*
A *goblet* instead of a *helmet?*
A *garland* instead of a *standard?*
Dice instead of a *spear?*   160
Sissy Greek garments
instead of the *reins of a stalwart steed?*
Ride a lover's couch instead of a horse?
Strap on a broad instead of a buckler?
Oh no! Not me!
(*In a frenzy*)
Away with you! Away I say!

(*Recovering himself, he stares nobly into the distance*)

BACCHIS I: (*Caressing him*) Oh, you're much too hard on us.

PISTOCLERUS: (*Responding to her hands*)
Not nearly as hard as I am on myself.

BACCHIS I: (*Fondles him*) I'll have to take you in hand myself. You
need to *relax*.   170

PISTOCLERUS: (*Draws back in shock*)
Ah, your handcraft costs too much.

BACCHIS I: Then make believe you're in love with me!

PISTOCLERUS: (*Falls on his knees again, embracing her*)
Should I make believe for a joke, or play like I mean business?

BACCHIS I: *Not now!* (*Peels him off and straightens her clothing; in
businesslike tone again*)
This is what I want to do: when the soldier arrives, I want you to
hug me.

PISTOCLERUS: (*Still on his knees*) Why should I do that?

BACCHIS I: (*Exasperated at his slowness*)
I want him to see you.
(*Interrupts his protest*)
I know what I'm doing.

PISTOCLERUS: God knows, I'm afraid you do. But look here . . .

BACCHIS I: Yes?   181

PISTOCLERUS: What if all of a sudden you happened to have a lunch,
or a round of drinks, or a dinner? You know, the sort of thing that
usually happens at little get-togethers like yours? Where would I
be then?

BACCHIS I: Next to me, my heart and soul: a nice boy and a nice girl, side by side. You'll always have a free place at our house, no matter how unexpectedly you show up. Whenever you need to have a nice time, just say to me,
(*She bends him over in an embrace; in rasping baritone*)
"Hey, Rosie . . . you got a nice place for me?"   190
(*She kisses him, then drops him to the floor; surveying his prostrate form*)
I'll be sure to give you a *nice place* to rest in.

PISTOCLERUS: (*Aside, from the floor*)
This is one rapid river! No quick and easy crossing here!

BACCHIS I: (*Aside*) And it's a river you're likely to lose something in, too.
(*Abruptly*)
Now, give me your hand and follow me.

PISTOCLERUS: Oh no! Absolutely not!

BACCHIS I: Why not?

PISTOCLERUS: (*Still on the floor*) Because there could be no combination more tempting than this: a night, a woman, wine, and a *young innocent* like me.   199

(*He stares, dewy-eyed, into the distance*)

BACCHIS I: (*Revolted by this narcissism; feigning resignation*)
Very well! I don't mind at all. Anything for you, dear. Let the soldier take her away. You don't have to be there if you don't want to.

PISTOCLERUS: (*Aside, still on the floor*)
So I'm worthless, eh? Got no will power at all, eh?

BACCHIS I: What are you afraid of?

PISTOCLERUS: (*Crawls over to her*)
Nothing, dear. A mere trifle. I surrender, dear. I am yours. I am at your service.

(*Clasps her around the middle*)

BACCHIS I: (*With a triumphant glance to her sister*)
What a nice boy!
(*Again peels his hand away and resumes her businesslike tone;* PISTOCLERUS *watches her with gaping mouth*)
Now, this is what I want you to do. I want to give a homecoming dinner for my sister. I'll order the servants inside to bring you some money. Then you go and get us the most gorgeous groceries you can find.   211

PISTOCLERUS: No, I'll pay for the groceries myself! It would be to my everlasting shame to have you, a mere woman, work for me and pay all the bills as well.

BACCHIS I: But I don't want a single thing from you!

(BACCHIS II *turns away giggling*)

PISTOCLERUS: Oh, do let me!

BACCHIS I: (*Feigning great reluctance*)
Well . . . if you want to . . . all right.
(PISTOCLERUS *starts to kiss her; she pushes him off*)
Please, do hurry along.

PISTOCLERUS: (*Starts to go; turns, with outstretched arms*)
I'll be back long before my love for you cools off.

(*Exits backward to forum, with arms outstretched*)

BACCHIS II: (*Collapses in laughter*) You've prepared a splendid entertainment for my arrival, my darling sister!   221

BACCHIS I: Indeed, why do you think so?

BACCHIS II: You've netted quite a little catch in your net, as I see it.

BACCHIS I: Yes, he is a nice catch. Now I'll have to help you with
Mnesilochus, Sister dear. You can make your money here instead
of having to go off with the soldier.

BACCHIS II: Exactly what I want.

BACCHIS I: (*Advances to house*) To work! The water's hot. Let's go
inside so you can take a bath. I imagine the ups and downs of a sea
voyage left you a little shaky for this kind of work?   230

BACCHIS II: Possibly a little, dear Sister. Let's go now.
(*Sounds of the approach of* LYDUS, PISTOCLERUS, *and their train*)
Listen! Someone is coming.

BACCHIS I: Follow me in, then. You need to relax after your journey.

(*They exit*)

Scene 2

(*Enter* PISTOCLERUS *with attendants carrying provisions, wine, and
flowers. He is followed by his teacher* LYDUS.)

LYDUS: (*In fussy manner*) Now, Pistoclerus, I've been following you
silently for some time to see what you're going to do with all this.
(*Gestures toward provisions*)
May the gods bless me! I think even a senator would be tempted
to naughtiness here! Where are you going with so much fancy
food?

PISTOCLERUS: Here.

(*Points to the house of* BACCHIS I)

LYDUS: Here? What do you mean "here"? Who lives there?   240

PISTOCLERUS: (*In ecstasy*) Who? Oh, Love, Pleasure, Venus, Grace,
Joy, Jest, Sport, Chatter, Smoochabella.

(*Smacks lips*)

LYDUS: (*Shocked*) What business have you with such god-awful
gods?

PISTOCLERUS: (*Striking moral pose*)
"Evil is that man who of good men does evil say." You're not
addressing these gods properly.
(*Wagging finger*)
That's *wrong*.

LYDUS: You mean to say there is a god named Smoochabella?

(*Smacking lips*)

PISTOCLERUS: You mean to say you thought there wasn't?
You really *are* a barbarian Lydian, Lydus.   250
You, the man I once thought knew more than Thales,
Why, you know less than a baby barbarian!
At your age! Not knowing the names of the gods!

LYDUS: (*Gesturing toward provisions*)
I don't like the looks of this.

PISTOCLERUS: Well, no one brought it here for you. It was brought
here for me, and I do like it.

LYDUS: So *now* you're starting to use smart talk with me? You, who
ought to keep silent even if you had ten tongues?

PISTOCLERUS: You can't play the lead in every game in life, Lydus. What I'm most concerned with now is whether the cook's concoctions will do justice to this food. 261

LYDUS: Now you've wasted yourself and me and my good works— *me*, who so often advised you so well. All, all in vain!

(*Raises arm to brow in tragic style*)

PISTOCLERUS: (*Unimpressed*) I wasted my "good works" the same place you wasted yours. Your brand of education was of no use to me or you.

LYDUS: (*In tragic style*) Oh what a heart hardened to hardness!

PISTOCLERUS: Oh what a bore! Keep quiet and follow me, Lydus.

LYDUS: (*To audience*) Just listen to that! He doesn't call me "teacher" now, just "Lydus"! 270

PISTOCLERUS: It wouldn't be right or proper to have "teacher" along when a man has gone to all the trouble of buying so much food, and is lying on his mistress's couch—especially not with all those other guests around, too.

LYDUS: (*Shocked again*) Good heavens! You mean you brought provisions here for *that* kind of party?

PISTOCLERUS: (*Again strikes moral pose*) "The heart hath hopes; their outcome lies in the hands of god alone."

LYDUS: So you're determined to have a mistress, then?

PISTOCLERUS: When you see her you'll get the answer to that question. 281

(*Goes to* BACCHIS I's *door*)

LYDUS: (*Blocking his way*) Oh no you don't! You'll not have her, nor will I allow it! You go home this minute!

PISTOCLERUS: Just drop it, Lydus. Save yourself the trouble.

LYDUS: What do you mean, "Save yourself the trouble"?

PISTOLERUS: I'm long past the age where I need your consent.

LYDUS: (*In supertragic style, to the audience*)
O infernal pit, where art thou now?
How gladly would I come to thee!
I have seen more here than I could have wished.
It were a far, far better thing to have died   290
than to have lived to see this.
That a pupil should so threaten his teacher!

(*Crumples dramatically to the floor*)

PISTOCLERUS: (*Stepping over him; straddling him*) I think I'll play the role of Hercules. You know, he *killed* his teacher Linus.

LYDUS: (*Jumps up*) And I'm afraid *I*'ll have to play the teacher Phoenix and tell your father of the death of his little Achilles!

PISTOCLERUS: (*Dryly*) That's enough Greek mythology for now, Lydus.

(*Starts again for door of* BACCHIS 1's *house*)

LYDUS: (*To audience*) He's beyond all shame.
(*Goes to block door; to* PISTOCLERUS)
This show of insolence is no credit to your years.   300
(*To audience*)
I'm destroyed.
(*To* PISTOCLERUS)
Have you forgotten that you have a father?

PISTOCLERUS: Who's the slave here—you or me?

LYDUS: Some wicked teacher taught you these ways, not me.
I see you're more teachable in these subjects
than in the ones I wasted my time trying to teach you.
That you could commit such crimes at your age!
That you could conceal them from me and your father!

PISTOCLERUS: (*Silences him with a wave*)
You've had enough free speech for now, Lydus. Just follow me in
and keep quiet.   310

(*They enter the house of* BACCHIS I)

ACT II

Scene 1

(*Enter* CHRYSALUS *solo*)

CHRYSALUS: Land of my master, hail! Two years ago I left you
for Ephesus, and now I gladly see you once again.
(*Turns to altar to Apollo*)
I salute you, Apollo, you who dwell neighbor to our house.
I pray, don't let my master Nicobulus see me
before I meet his son Mnesilochus's old pal Pistoclerus.

(*To audience*)

You see, Mnesilochus sent him a letter about his mistress
Bacchis.

Scene 2

(*Enter* PISTOCLERUS *from the house of* BACCHIS I)

PISTOCLERUS: (*Pushed onstage, he talks through door to* BACCHIS I)
It's odd that you keep nagging me to go so much when I couldn't
leave you even if I wanted to.
(*To audience, with a sigh*)
Fixed and fettered by love, that's me.   320

CHRYSALUS: (Rises) By the immortal gods, it's Pistoclerus! O Pistoclerus, greetings!

PISTOCLERUS: Why, greetings, Chrysalus.

CHRYSALUS: (PISTOCLERUS *starts to talk;* CHRYSALUS *stops him*)
I'm going to save you the trouble of making a speech. You are
delighted that I'm here, and I believe you.
(PISTOLERUS *tries to speak again;* CHRYSALUS *stops him again*)
You promise me entertainment and a meal, as is only proper for
someone returning from abroad.
(PISTOLERUS *tries to interrupt again*)
Why, how kind! I accept your invitation.
(*And again*)
Oh yes, very best wishes to you from your old pal.
(*Yet again*)
Then you ask, "How is he doing?" He's alive.   330

PISTOCLERUS: Is he really doing well?

CHRYSALUS: That's exactly what I wanted to find out from you.

PISTOCLERUS: How could I know that?

CHRYSALUS: Who would know better?

PISTOCLERUS: Well, how *do* I know?

CHRYSALUS: Here's how. If the woman he loves has been found, he's alive and well. If she hasn't been found, he's not so well, he's about to die. If she is here, then his money is lost and he's worthless anyway.   339
(PISTOCLERUS *gapes in wonder at all this*)
But what have you done about the instructions he sent you?

PISTOCLERUS: Do you think I'm the kind of man who would let him arrive without having done what his messenger told me to do? I'd rather live in Hades than do that.

CHRYSALUS: Then you have found Bacchis?

PISTOCLERUS: Yes, the one from Samos.

CHRYSALUS: Please be careful that no one handles her carelessly! You know how fragile Samian pottery is.

(*Guffaws*)

PISTOCLERUS: You're as witty as ever, I see.

CHRYSALUS: Now, please tell me where she is.   349

PISTOCLERUS: Here, in the house you just saw me come from.

CHRYSALUS: (*To audience*) Now that *is* good news! She lives right next door to us.
(*To* PISTOCLERUS)
Does she still remember Mnesilochus?

PISTOCLERUS: Does she still remember him? Why, she considers him her one and only man in the world.

CHRYSALUS: Amazing!

PISTOCLERUS: Why, you do believe her, don't you? And you know what else? The poor girl is pining away for love.

CHRYSALUS: That's nice to know.   359

PISTOCLERUS: And you know what else, Chrysalus? She doesn't let even one teeny-tiny moment pass by without saying his name.

CHRYSALUS: So much the better for her.

PISTOCLERUS: And you know what else?

CHRYSALUS: What else I know is that I'd rather be anywhere but here.

PISTOCLERUS: You don't object to hearing about your master's good fortune, do you?

CHRYSALUS: (*Aside, to audience*) It's not his good fortune that makes me sick! It's your bad acting! I can't even watch a comedy by Plautus when an actor like you is acting in it. And that's one playwright I love as much as I love myself.   371
(*To* PISTOCLERUS)
So you think Bacchis really is a good girl, eh?

PISTOCLERUS: Of course she is. If I didn't already have Venus herself, she would be *my* Juno.

CHRYSALUS: (*Aside*) Well, now, Mnesilochus, it looks to me as if you have already got the woman you love. Now you need to find out how to pay for her.
(*Turns back to* PISTOCLERUS)
Perhaps you need gold?

PISTOCLERUS: Yes! As many gold coins as we can get.

CHRYSALUS: And perhaps you need them now?   380

PISTOCLERUS: In fact, we need them sooner than that. The soldier is due any minute.

CHRYSALUS: Oh? There's a soldier too?

PISTOCLERUS: And he'll want gold for releasing Bacchis from her
contract.

CHRYSALUS: Let him come when he pleases. But he had better not
keep me waiting: there's plenty of gold at home. I'm not afraid of
any man. I don't have to beg for anything as long as I can come up
with a good lie. But you go inside now. I'll look after things here.
Once you're there, tell Bacchis that Mnesilochus will be here any
minute.   391

PISTOCLERUS: Just as you say.

(*He exits*)

CHRYSALUS: (*Solo*) I am in charge of this gold business. We've
brought 1,200 solid gold coins from Ephesus that a friend there
owed to the old man. Now to fabricate some fabrications to get that
gold for my love-struck master. Uh-oh, our door is opening! Who's
coming outside now?

Scene 3

(NICOBULUS *enters from his house*)

NICOBULUS: I'll go down to the Piraeus to see if any merchant ships
have come into port from Ephesus. I'm worried that my son has
stayed there so long and has not come home yet.   400

CHRYSALUS: (*Aside*) Now, if only the gods will let me, I'll fleece him
neatly! This is not time to go to sleep on the job. I'll make a
Croesus out of Chrysalus. Now for the ram and its golden fleece.
I'll shear the gold right down to the roots!
(*Goes up to* NICOBULUS *and salutes him formally*)
From slave Chrysalus to master Nicobulus: greetings!

NICOBULUS: Chrysalus! By the immortal gods, where is my son?

CHRYSALUS: (*Miffed*) Well, you could have at least returned my greetings first.

NICOBULUS: (*Impatiently*) Well, greetings. But where is Mnesilochus?   410

CHRYSALUS: He's alive, he's well.

NICOBULUS: Has he arrived?

CHRYSALUS: He has.

NICOBULUS: Thank the gods. I can breathe again! Is he still in good health?

CHRYSALUS: In Marathonically—no, *Olympically*—good health.

NICOBULUS: Now, then, what about the job I sent him to do in Ephesus? Did he get my money back from our friend Archidemides?   419

CHRYSALUS: (*Wringing hands*) Oh, woe! Nicobulus, my head and heart just split in two at the very mention of that person's name. Don't you realize that the man you call a friend is really a fiend?

NICOBULUS: What do you mean?

CHRYSALUS: I'm sure that none of the four gods—Moon, Sun, Daylight, or Fire—ever shone on a more wicked man than he!

NICOBULUS: No man more wicked than *Archidemides?*

CHRYSALUS: That's what I said: than Archidemides.

NICOBULUS: What has he done?

CHRYSALUS: What hasn't he done? Why don't you ask me that? First of all, he began to lie to your son and denied that he owed you so much as one coin. 431
(NICOBULUS *tries to interrupt;* CHRYSALUS *silences him*)
Then Mnesilochus at once called for your tried and true friend, the old man Pelagon. In his presence he showed him the token you gave your son to carry to him.

NICOBULUS: What happened when he showed him the token?

CHRYSALUS: He said it was a counterfeit and not his token at all. And what slanderous things he said to your innocent boy! He said that he had counterfeited other things, too.

NICOBULUS: Well, did you get the money? I want to know!

CHRYSALUS: Oh yes, after the law courts rendered a verdict against him, he was convicted and paid out a fine of . . . let me see . . . twelve hundred gold coins. 442

NICOBULUS: That's exactly what he owed!

CHRYSALUS: But there's more. Listen. He wanted to give us a fight.

NICOBULUS: There's more?

CHRYSALUS: (*Aside*) Now to swoop down for the kill.

NICOBULUS: (*Raging, to audience*) I've been tricked! I entrusted my money to a bigger thief than all the Greeks who plundered Troy!

CHRYSALUS: Will you please listen?

NICOBULUS: Obviously I never knew what a greedy character he was. 451

CHRYSALUS: After we went off with our gold, we boarded ship and eagerly set sail for home. By chance, while I was sitting up on the deck, I happened to look around and I saw a long, mean-looking galley being readied to sail.

NICOBULUS: Oh no! I'm done for! That galley will ram my side!

CHRYSALUS: Your friend was part-owner of the ship, along with . . . uh . . . pirates!

NICOBULUS: How could I have been such an idiot as to trust him? His very name makes it clear that he would rob me. Archidemides—just like a *Greek!*   461

CHRYSALUS: This galley pulled off, hoping to ambush our ship. I made sure to keep a watch to see what they were up to. In the meantime our own ship set sail from the harbor. Once we were out of port, they began rowing after us. Neither birds nor winds could have been faster. When that happened, we stopped our ship at once. When they saw us stop they began to slow down their own ship in the harbor.

NICOBULUS: Oh gods, what devils they are! What did you do then?

CHRYSALUS: We went back to port.   470

NICOBULUS: That was a wise move. Then what did they do?

CHRYSALUS: They went ashore at sunset.

NICOBULUS: By Hercules, they *did* want to steal our gold! That's what they were up to.

CHRYSALUS: They didn't fool *me*. I knew what they were up to, and it scared me to death. As soon as we saw that they were after our money, we laid our plans right there and then. The next morning we brought the money off the ship and carried it right in front of them in public, in the open, so they would see it.   479

NICOBULUS: That was clever! Come on, now, what did they do then?

CHRYSALUS: They looked extremely disappointed. As soon as they saw that we were taking the gold with us out of the harbor, they just shook their heads slowly and put their galley back in dock. Then we deposited all the gold with Theotimus, the priest of Diana at Ephesus.

NICOBULUS: Who is this Theotimus?

CHRYSALUS: Oh, *he's* the son of Megalobulus, the dearest man in Ephesus . . . to the Ephesians.

NICOBULUS: If he runs off with all of my gold, he'll be as dear *for* me as he is dear *to* them.   490

CHRYSALUS: Don't worry, the gold is stored in the temple of Diana. It's under public watch there.

NICOBULUS: You've ruined me! It would be much safer if it were in safekeeping here. Didn't you bring any of the gold home with you?

CHRYSALUS: We did. I don't know how much it was, though.

NICOBULUS: What? You don't know?

CHRYSALUS: Well, you see, Mnesilochus visited Theotimus at night, in secret, and he didn't want to trust me to anyone else on the ship. And so I just don't know how much of a tip he brought with him. But he couldn't have brought very much.   501

NICOBULUS: You think he could have brought half of it?

CHRYSALUS: Oh, I really don't know, but I don't think so.

NICOBULUS: A third of it?

CHRYSALUS: Oh, I don't think so, but I really honestly don't know. In fact, the only thing I *do* know about the gold is . . . that I *don't*

know. Now you'll have to sail there yourself if you want to get your
gold home from Theotimus.
(NICOBULUS *starts to go off*)
Oh yes!

NICOBULUS: (*Returns*) What is it? What do you want?   510

CHRYSALUS: Be sure you remember to take your son's ring along
with you.

NICOBULUS: Why do I need his ring?

CHRYSALUS: Because we arranged with Theotimus that he would
give the gold to the man who brought the ring.

NICOBULUS: (*Agreeably*) I'll remember. That's good advice.
(*Again starts to leave; pauses*)
But is this Theotimus rich?

CHRYSALUS: Is he *rich?* Why, he has gold soles on his shoes!

NICOBULUS: How can he afford to live so lavishly?

CHRYSALUS: He has so much money he doesn't know what to do
with gold.   521

NICOBULUS: I wish he would give it to me! Who else was there when
the money was given to Theotimus?

CHRYSALUS: The whole city. No one at Ephesus doesn't know about
it.

NICOBULUS: At least my son acted wisely in that: he gave the gold for
safekeeping to a rich man. You can get money from that kind
whenever you need it.

CHRYSALUS: *Why, indeed you can.* He won't keep you waiting the
least bit. You'll have it the very day you arrive.   530

NICOBULUS: I thought I had at last escaped a sailor's life, so an old man like me wouldn't have to set sail at this late stage in life. But I see now that I have no other choice, thanks to my dear friend Archidemides. So.
(*Starts to leave again*)
Where is my son Mnesilochus now?

CHRYSALUS: He's gone off to the forum to greet the gods and his friends.

NICOBULUS: Then I'll head that way and meet him as soon as possible. 539

(*He exits*)

CHRYSALUS: (*Solo*) There's one man who's weighted down and carrying an overload! Not at all a bad web I've started to weave. To supply my master's son in his love affair, I've seen that he'll have as much gold as he wants; he can return as much to his father as he likes. The old man will go off to Ephesus to get his money while we lead a plushy life here—that is, if the old man leaves us behind and doesn't take me and Mnesilochus with him.
(*Chuckling*)
What a mess I'll make!
(*Pauses*)
But what will happen when the old man finds out, when he learns that he went off on a wild goose chase while we spent all his money? What will happen to me then? He'll change my name for me when he returns! At once he'll turn me from Chrysalus into Crossalus! 552
(*Stretches out arms, as if on cross*)
I'll run away if that looks the better course. But if I am caught, I'll give him plenty of hard work. He may have whips in the country, but my back is here at home with me. Now I'll tell my young master about this trick to get the gold for him and his girlfriend Bacchis.

(*He exits*)

ACT III

Scene 1

LYDUS: (*From inside* BACCHIS I's *house*)
  Ope' wide at once this door to Hades!
  I beg you, unlock the door!
  (*Enters in a state of disarray; to audience*)
  Yes, a door to hell and nothing less: 560
  no one comes this way unless he has
  abandoned all hope who enters here.
  These sisters Bacchis aren't Bacchises, they're Bacchae!
  (*Wildly, in tragic style, now as if seeing Aeschylus's Eumenides*)
  Keep away from me, ye sisters who suck men's blood!
  The whole house is one great gaudy, bawdy trap!
  (*Again to audience*)
  As soon as I realized that, I delivered myself to the
  tender care of my feet.
  (*To an invisible* PISTOCLERUS)
  Am I one to keep all this a secret?
  Am I one to conceal it from your father, Pistoclerus?
  You're not the least bit ashamed of the deeds you've done?   570
  Deeds that make your father and me,
  your friends, your relatives, partners in your crimes?
  Well, before you can pile one more evil
  on top of what you've already done, I'll tell your father.

(*To audience*)

I'm going to clear myself of any blame for this by exposing it to the
old man. Then he can drag him as soon as possible out of this filthy
latrine.

(*Exits wildly to the forum*)

Scene 2

(Enter MNESILOCHUS *followed by slaves with baggage; during the following, they dutifully try to applaud each aphorism)*

MNESILOCHUS: *(With great calm, to audience)*
  After many a moment of meditation,
  I have an important announcement to make.
  "That man who is a friend to his friends,   580
  in the *real* sense of the word,
  is a man excelled only by the gods themselves."
  That's my experience.

(Polite patter of applause; he bows)

After I left Athens for Ephesus—this was nearly two years ago—I
sent a letter from Ephesus here to my old pal Pistoclerus, telling
him to find my mistress Bacchis. I learn now that he did find her,
or so my slave Chrysalus has just told me.
(Laughs)
You know, that's some scheme he's put together to get my father to
supply me with fuel for my fires. In my view, "Nothing is more
expensive than an ungrateful man."   590

(A weaker patter of applause from the slaves; he bows)

Yes,
"It's more profitable to pardon those who are against us
than to abandon those who are for us."
(Still weaker applause, but he bows again)
Yes, indeed,
"It's better to be known as a spendthrift than a miser:
good men praise the first sort, but even evil men
find fault with the second."
(One slave half-heartedly claps once, twice, then falls silent;
MNESILOCHUS *bows anyway)*
Now I must be careful and keep my eyes open.

(*Striking bold pose, as if in soliloquy*)
Yes, Mnesilochus, here's where you show yourself!
Here's the test of what kind of man you really are.
Bad, good—one or the other.   600
Just or unjust.
A miser or a spendthrift.
A comrade or a cad.
Just see that you don't let your own slave outdo you
in doing the right thing. Whatever kind of man you are,
you won't be able to hide it.
(*Looks down street*)
But look!
There's the father and teacher of my old pal!
I'll listen to what they say from here.

(*Stands to one side with his slaves*)

Scene 3

(*Enter* LYDUS *and* PHILOXENUS)

LYDUS: Now I'll find out what kind of stuff you're made of. Follow
     me.   611

PHILOXENUS: Follow you where? Where are you leading me now?

LYDUS: To the woman who has completely ruined and destroyed
     your one and only son.

PHILOXENUS: There, there, Lydus. "Those who most gently rage do
     knowledge more acquire." It would be more surprising if a boy
     that age weren't up to something like that than if he were.
     (*Aside*)
     I did the same sort of thing when I was a young man.

LYDUS: Oh, woe is me! Woe is me! This very *permissiveness* is what
ruined him. Why, if it were not for *you* I could have made him into
a man of fine, upstanding character. Now you and your trusting
nature have made Pistoclerus—a *degenerate!*   622

MNESILOCHUS: Immortal gods! He just said my old pal's name!
What's going on? Why is Lydus attacking his master Pistoclerus?

PHILOXENUS: Now, Lydus, every man has to give way to desire once
in a while. The time will come when he will hate himself for it.
Give him rein. As long as he's careful not to go too far, just let him
alone.

LYDUS: No, I won't let him alone! He will not be corrupted as long as
I'm alive! But you, *you* who offer excuses for a child so corrupted,
was this the same kind of education *you* had when you were a
young man?   632
(PHILOXENUS *starts to speak;* LYDUS *silences him*)
I say no! In your first twenty years of life you never had the chance
to stick so much as a finger outside the house without your teacher's permission. If you did not reach the exercise ground before
sunrise, the trainer made you pay a pretty price when you did.
Nor was that all. On top of that disgrace they piled another: the
teacher and his pupil were subject to equal shame.

(*Loses contact with surrounding world as he warms to his subject*)

Oh yes!   640
Then they got their exercise by running,
by wrestling, by throwing the javelin and the discus;
by boxing, playing ball, jumping—
(*Spits line out*)
not by working out with whores and their *kisses!*
(*Backs* PHILOXENUS *down the stage*)
That was how they spent their lives,
not in dank dens of darkness!
Then when you had returned home from the track
and the exercise ground,

you would sit there in your nice, *short* little tunic
before your teacher . . .   649

(*Stares into distance imagining the short little tunic; suddenly
comes back to the point*)

If you mispronounced so much as one syllable while you were
reading, your hide would be as striped as a zebra's coat.

MNESILOCHUS: (*Aside*) I can't stand it! My poor old pal has to put up
with this, and all on my account! He's suffering this for my sake,
the poor thing!

PHILOXENUS: Things are done differently today, Lydus.

LYDUS: Indeed they are! I doubt it not! In the days gone by, a pupil
actually held elected office even before he had ceased to listen to
his teacher like a good boy. But now even before he's seven years
old, if you so much as lay a finger on him, right away the boy
smashes his little writing tablet on his teacher's head. When you
go to complain to the father, he says to his boy,   661

(*Strutting about, imitating the father*)

"That's my boy! it takes a real man
to stand up to a teacher's abuse!"
Then he calls in the teacher:
"Hey, you worthless old bum,
don't you dare lay a finger on that boy.
He's only showing his spirit!"
That's the verdict. Case dismissed.

(*To audience*)

How can a teacher have any authority under these conditions if
he's the one who gets the whipping?   670

MNESILOCHUS: (*Aside*) Now *there's* a real complaint for you! It's a miracle Pistoclerus hasn't beat Lydus to a pulp for talking like this.

LYDUS: (*At last notices* MNESILOCHUS *standing to one side*)
Wait! Who is that standing in front of the house? Oh, Philoxenus! Here's one person whose favor I would as soon have as I would a god's.

PHILOXENUS: Who is he?

LYDUS: Mnesilochus. Your boy's old pal. And not at all of the same caliber as the one lying in bed in that whorehouse! Oh lucky Nicobulus! To have reared such a fine lad!   680

PHILOXENUS: Well, how are you, Mnesilochus? I'm delighted to see you safe and sound.

MNESILOCHUS: (*Trying to be as dignified as possible, under the circumstances*)
And may the gods bless *you*, Philoxenus.

LYDUS: (*Still carried away about the good old days and thrilled at this sudden incarnation of his ideals*)
Oh yes, *here's* the kind of offspring a father can be proud of!
(*Pushes* PHILOXENUS *to one side; embraces* MNESILOCHUS)
He goes off to sea. He takes care of family business. He looks after the household. He's obedient and attentive to his father's every wish and command. He's been Pistoclerus's *old pal* since they were both little boys. There's not more than three days' difference in their ages, but this boy is more than thirty years his senior in common sense.   690

PHILOXENUS: You'd save yourself a lot of trouble if you would stop ranting about him.

LYDUS: Hush! You fool, you! Why get angry about your son's bad reputation when he deserves it?

MNESILOCHUS: Lydus, why are you so angry at my old pal and your
  pupil?

LYDUS: (*Collapses on* MNESILOCHUS'*s shoulder*)
  Your old pal is dead and done for.

MNESILOCHUS: Oh, gods forbid!

LYDUS: It's just as I said. Why, I myself saw him die. I'm not reporting something I heard.   700

MNESILOCHUS: What happened?

LYDUS: He's dying of love for—oh, the shame of it—a courtesan.

MNESILOCHUS: (*Prudishly shocked*) You don't mean it!

LYDUS: She's an absolute whirlpool of a woman. Every man she
  comes in contact with, she sucks down out of sight.

MNESILOCHUS: Where does this woman live?

LYDUS: Here.

(*Points to* BACCHIS I'*s house*)

MNESILOCHUS: Where do they say she comes from?

LYDUS: From Samos.

MNESILOCHUS: What's her name?   710

LYDUS: Bacchis.

MNESILOCHUS: (*Much relieved*) Oh, well you're wrong, Lydus.
  ` I know all about this affair. You're wrong to charge Pistoclerus
  with wrongdoing. He doesn't love her himself. Don't believe it.

He's simply doing a favor for his friend and well-wisher. His *old pal*.

(*His eyes mist over at the thought of his "old pal"*)

LYDUS: (*Without a moment's hesitation*)
Oh, he is, is he? Does doing a nice favor for his friend and *old pal* include holding the woman in his lap and kissing her?
(*Lubriciously*)
Is there no way he can do this favor except by running his hands all over her breasts, and never taking his lips off hers . . . and . . . and . . .   721
(*Sputters*)
Why, I can't bring myself even to mention the other shameful things he did.
(*Long pause;* MNESILOCHUS *looks relieved*)
But . . . (MNESILOCHUS *winces*)
while I was there, I saw him slip his hand under Bacchis's dress. Why say more?
(*Drools, recovers*)
He's done for: my pupil, your old pal, his son. For I say "That man is dead in whom all shame has died." What need is there of more words?
(*Coyly*)
If I had wanted to watch a little longer, I should have seen more than was proper for either him or me.   731

MNESILOCHUS: (*Enraged aside*) Well, *old pal*, you've ruined me! Just wait till I get my hands on that woman! You think I won't ruin her? I'd rather die like a dog. It really is true. You can't know who to trust or believe.

LYDUS: (*Gleefully, to* PHILOXENUS)
See there! Observe what agony your son's corruption has brought to his *old pal*.

PHILOXENUS: Mnesilochus, please try to help him control his passions. Save your *old pal* for your sake and my son for mine.

MNESILOCHUS: *(Grimly)* I intend to do just that.   740

PHILOXENUS: *(To* MNESILOCHUS*)* I entrust the entire burden to you.
This way, Lydus.

LYDUS: *(Reluctantly)* Very well, I'm coming. But it would be better
to leave me here with him.

PHILOXENUS: He can handle this.

LYDUS: *(Pauses for one last word of advice)*
Mnesilochus, watch over him, make him pay for the disgrace he's
brought on me, on you, on all his other friends.

(PHILOXENUS *drags* LYDUS *off*)

Scene 4*

MNESILOCHUS: Now, I don't know who to believe is my worst ene-
my: my *old pal* or Bacchis. So she wanted him more than me?
Well, let her have him. Fine. I'll see that this causes plenty of
trouble for . . . me.   751
(Tries again to be indignant)
May no one ever again believe my sacred oath if I don't use
everything in my power to . . . to love her.
(Tries again to be angry)
I'll show her she's got one man she can't make a fool of! Why, I'll go
home right now and steal something from . . . my father. And I'll
give it to her.

---

*This scene and the following are parts of the play for which we have fragments from
Menander's *The Double Deceiver*. Plautus changed the names of the young men from Mos-
chos and Sostratos to the more exotic Pistoclerus and Mnesilochus, and that of the clever slave
Syros to Chrysalus (for its potential for wordplay). Lydus remains Lydus for the sake of puns.
Mnesilochus's monologue is twice as long as the speech of Sostratos (Mnesilochus) in Menander, and all the business about begging his father to forgive Chrysalus is not in Menander at
all.

(Making one last effort)
Oh, yes, I'll get my revenge in all kinds of ways. I'll drive her right
into the street begging . . . drive my father, that is.   758
(Pauses, head in hands)
But wait. Can I really be acting in my right mind, forecasting what
will happen in the future? You see, I think I *do* love her—in fact I
know I do. But I'd rather outbid a beggar in begging than let her
get so much as one fraction of a feather heavier with my money.
No, you'll see, she won't make a fool of me and live! I've decided
right now to give back every bit of gold to Father. Then just let her
try all her wiles on me. With me penniless and empty it won't do
her any more good to coax me than it would to tell ghost stories to
a corpse in a tomb.
(In a brighter mood)
That's it. Fixed and final. I'm returning that money to Father. And
I'll beg him not to harm Chrysalus . . . for my sake. I'll beg him to
be angry for being made a fool of . . . for my sake. It's only fair
that I protect the man who told him a lie . . . for my sake.
(With insufferable self-satisfaction, he turns at last to attendants)
You! Follow me!   772

(They exit)

Scene 5

(Enter PISTOCLERUS *from* BACCHIS I*'s house)*

PISTOCLERUS: *(To* BACCHIS I, *inside)* I'll postpone everything, Bac-
    chis, until I've done what you ordered me to do: I'll find Mne-
    silochus and bring him to you.
    (Starts toward NICOBULUS*'s house)*
    But I find his delay very strange. Did my message reach him? I'll
    look for him here. Maybe he's home.

Scene 6

(*Enter* MNESILOCHUS *from* NICOBULUS's *house*)

MNESILOCHUS: I've given Father back every bit of his money. I'd like to see her now that I don't have a coin left. How Father hated to pardon Chrysalus! But I finally got him not to hold it against him.*   781

PISTOCLERUS: (*Aside*) Isn't this my old pal?

MNESILOCHUS: (*Aside*) Isn't this my enemy I see?

PISTOCLERUS: (*Aside*) Why, it certainly is.

MNESILOCHUS: (*Aside*) It certainly is.

PISTOCLERUS: (*Aside*) I'll go right up to him.

MNESILOCHUS: (*Aside*) I'll head there now.

PISTOCLERUS: Greetings, Mnesilochus.

MNESILOCHUS: Greetings.

PISTOCLERUS: We must have a dinner to celebrate your safe arrival home from overseas.   791

MNESILOCHUS: I have no desire for a dinner that would upset my appetite.

PISTOCLERUS: Oh dear, has some trouble spoiled your homecoming?

*These lines of misunderstanding between the two friends are not in Menander; they were added by Plautus for their heavy dramatic irony.

MNESILOCHUS: Yes, the worst possible trouble.

PISTOCLERUS: What caused it?

MNESILOCHUS: A man I thought was my friend up to now.   798

PISTOCLERUS: (*Indignant, he launches into a* LYDUS-*like tirade*)
There are quite a few people around like that now, the kind you
think are your friends until they are found out to be traitors
steeped in treachery. Lying, ready of tongue! Yes, lazy in work,
faithless. There's no one whose good fortune they don't envy.
Their slothful ways ensure that no one envies them.

MNESILOCHUS: (*Dryly*) Well, I see you have a clear idea of their
character. But add one more fault: out of their evil ways they
create their own evil. They have no friends, all men are their
enemies, and when they deceive themselves, the fools think
they're deceiving others. That's exactly the behavior of the man I
thought was as much a friend to me as I am to myself. He worked
as hard as he could to do me as much harm as he could and take
every bit of money I had.   811

PISTOCLERUS: (*Shocked*) He must be an absolute villain!

MNESILOCHUS: My opinion exactly.

PISTOCLERUS: I beg you, tell me who it is!

MNESILOCHUS: A man on excellent terms with you. If it weren't for
that, I'd ask you to get back at him any way you could.

PISTOCLERUS: Just tell me his name. If I don't get back at him one
way or another why, you can call me the most cowardly man on
earth!

MNESILOCHUS: He's a scoundrel, but he's also your friend.   820

PISTOCLERUS: All the more reason to name him! The friendship of a scoundrel means nothing to me.

MNESILOCHUS: I see I have no choice but to say his name.
(*Backs up*)
Pistoclerus, you have completely destroyed your old pal.

PISTOCLERUS: What did you say?

MNESILOCHUS: What do you mean, "What did you say?" Didn't I write you from Ephesus telling you to find my mistress for me?

PISTOCLERUS: Of course you did, and I found her.   829

MNESILOCHUS: Well, weren't there enough courtesans for you in Athens? Did you have to make love to the very girl I had entrusted to you? Did you have to betray me?

PISTOCLERUS: (*Incredulous*) Are you in your right mind?

MNESILOCHUS: I got the whole story from your teacher. Don't deny it. You've ruined me.

PISTOCLERUS: (*Angrily*) Are you saying all this to get me angry?

MNESILOCHUS: Don't you love . . .

PISTOCLERUS: Bacchis? Yes. But listen, there are *two* Bacchises inside here.

MNESILOCHUS: What? Two . . .   840

PISTOCLERUS: And they're sisters.

MNESILOCHUS: You're talking nonsense now and you know it.

PISTOCLERUS: That's enough! If you continue to insult me, I'll throw you over my shoulder and carry you inside.

(*Starts to advance*)

MNESILOCHUS: (*Backing away*) I'll go! I'll go! Just wait.

PISTOCLERUS: I won't wait, and I won't have you accusing me without proof.

MNESILOCHUS: I'm coming, I'm coming.

(*They enter* BACCHIS I's *house*)

ACT IV

Scene 1

(*Enter* PARASITE *with* BOY *of* CLEOMACHUS)

PARASITE: (*To audience*) I am the parasite of that worthless, wicked scoundrel, the soldier who brought his girlfriend with him from Samos. Now he's ordered me to go to her and find out whether she's going to give him his money or go home with him.   852
(*To* BOY)
Whatever house she's in, knock on the door.
(BOY *is timid*)
Well, go to the door!
(BOY *gives a timid knock*)
Back off, out of the way!
(*To audience*)
See how the little rascal knocks?
(*To* BOY)

You know how to eat a loaf of bread three feet long, but you don't
know how to knock on a door!
(*Pushes* BOY *aside; knocks loudly on the door*)
Is anyone home? Hey, is anybody inside? Will someone open the
door? Is anyone coming?   860

(BOY *joins in; there arises a horrendous racket*)

Scene 2

(PISTOCLERUS *enters*)

PISTOCLERUS: What is this? Why all this knocking? Why, you little
  wretch! Why are you wearing out your knuckles on our door?
  You've nearly knocked it down! What do you want?

PARASITE: (*Calmly*) Hello, young man.

PISTOCLERUS: Hello. Who are you looking for? Who do you want?

PARASITE: Bacchis.

PISTOCLERUS: Which one?

PARASITE: (*In a superior way*) All I know is, Bacchis. To make a long
  story short, the soldier Cleomachus sent me to her with the order
  that she either return his two hundred gold coins or else return
  with him today to Elatea.   871

PISTOCLERUS: She's not going. She isn't allowed to go. Go back and
  deliver that message. She loves another man, not him. Now, off
  the premises!

PARASITE: (*Calmly*) You seem to be upset.

PISTOCLERUS: And you know why I'm so upset? That face of yours is about one instant away from a beating. See how this dental demolition is twitching?

(*He thrusts both fists in* PARASITE's *face*)

PARASITE: (*Turns aside, to audience*) If I grasp his meaning correctly, I had better be careful he doesn't knock my teeth out. That would mean my dinner's demolition.   881
(*Crosses stage; turns back to* PISTOCLERUS)
Very well, then. I'll tell him. It's you who's in danger.

PISTOCLERUS: What did you say?

(*Advances*)

PARASITE: I'll tell him what you said.

PISTOCLERUS: "Him"? Tell me, who are you?

PARASITE: (*Self-importantly*) I am the armor plating of his body.

PISTOCLERUS: He really must be worthless to have a wretch like you for his armor plating.

PARASITE: He'll be in a soufflé of a rage when he gets here.

PISTOCLERUS: Fine, I hope he collapses.   890

PARASITE: (*Going*) Anything else you need?

PISTOCLERUS: Yes, go! And you'd better be quick about it.

PARASITE: Good day, Dental Demolator.

PISTOCLERUS: And you, Armor Plate, good-by.
(PARASITE *and* BOY *scamper off*)

Now things have gotten to the point where I don't know what advice I should give my old pal about his girlfriend. He got all angry and paid back all the money to his father, and now he doesn't have one coin to pay back to the soldier.

(*The door of* NICOBULUS's *house opens*)

But I'd better step to one side here: someone's coming out.

(*Enter* MNESILOCHUS, *dejected*)

Why, look! It's poor old Mnesilochus himself coming out.   900

Scene 3

MNESILOCHUS: (*Croons*)
   Here am I,
   Oh so hasty in my heart,
   petulant,
   Oh so reckless, oh so mad,
   with a head out of control,
   not in tune, not in style,
   here am I.
   Here I am,
   without honor, without right,
   without trust, in a fight,   910
   no one else to love,
   no one to love me,
   my love affair gone sour,
   here am I.

(*To audience*)

Can you believe all this?

(*Resumes character; rapidly*)

I'm everything I wish someone else was!
There's not a more worthless man alive
not one less worthy of the gods' kindness,

not one less worthy of anyone else's company or love.
Enemies are what I should have, not friends;   920
bad people should help me, not good people.
No man on earth deserves a worse reputation;
it's the only fair reward for a fool like me.
Love made me give my father all his money back,
all that gold I had in my hand.

(*To audience*)

Have you ever seen a worse fool than me? I ruined myself
and I undid everything Chrysalus did for me.

PISTOCLERUS: (*Aside*) I should console him. I'll go to him now.
(*To* MNESILOCHUS)
Mnesilochus, how are things?

MNESILOCHUS: I'm ruined!   930

PISTOCLERUS: Oh gods! Say it's not so!

MNESILOCHUS: I'm ruined!

PISTOCLERUS: Will you be quiet, you fool?

MNESILOCHUS: (*Shocked at an idea he finds incomprehensible*)
Be quiet? Me?

PISTOCLERUS: You're clearly not in your right mind.

MNESILOCHUS: I'm ruined! You can't imagine how many woes are
crowding in on me, each one sharper and nastier than the last. To
think that I could have believed those charges! I had no right to be
angry at you.

PISTOCLERUS: (*Wearily*) Oh, cheer up.   940

MNESILOCHUS: (*Clearly relishing the self-pity*)
How can I cheer up? A dead man is worth more than me.

PISTOCLERUS: (*Making one last effort*)
The soldier's parasite was just here asking for his money. I drove
him away from here, away from the house and the woman. I
kicked him out with plenty of tough talk.

MNESILOCHUS: What good does that do *me?* Poor *me!* I can't do a
thing. He'll take her away, I just know it.

PISTOCLERUS: (*In exasperation*) Well, if I had the money, I wouldn't
give it to *you!*   948

MNESILOCHUS: Oh yes you would! I know you. If you weren't in love
yourself, I wouldn't trust you so much. As it is, you have more
than enough of your own troubles to worry about. I have nothing,
but what kind of help can I expect from a man who has nothing?

PISTOCLERUS: Oh, shut up! Some god or other will look out for us.

MNESILOCHUS: Nonsense!

PISTOCLERUS: Wait a minute.

MNESILOCHUS: What is it?

PISTOCLERUS: I see your banker Chrysalus!

Scene 4

(*Enter* CHRYSALUS, *very pleased with himself*)

CHRYSALUS: Here is one man worth his weight in gold, a fellow
worth setting up a gold statue to. I've done a double deed this day,

and I'm off with double spoils. I made my old master play the fool.
What a game he played!   961

Clever though the old man be,
more clever snares have snared him,
impelled him and compelled him
to trust every word I say.
I've won a royal ransom,
I've rained a golden shower
on the old man's son. You know,
the young boy in love?
the one I eat with?   970
the one I drink with?
the one whose indoor wherewithal
supports his next-door whorewithall?

Oh, you timid slaves in Greek comedy, you're not for me!
You only earn two or three minas of gold for your masters.
What could be more worthless than a slave without a plot?
You're no good unless you have a powerful brain.
If you need a plot, find it in your head.

No man's worth his salt
unless he knows how to be good *and* bad.   980
He has to be wicked with the wicked,
be a bandit with bandits.
He has to steal where he has to.
The man who knows his trade
knows how to change his skin.
Let him look good to good people
and bad to bad people.
Whatever the moment calls for,
he's ready and willing and able.   989

(*Returns to the business at hand*)

Well, now, I would like to know just how much gold Mnesilochus
skimmed off for himself and how much he returned to his father. If

he has sense, he'll treat Nicobulus like Hercules: give one part
and keep the other nine for himself.
(*At last he sees* MNESILOCHUS *and* PISTOCLERUS)
Well, well! Here's the very fellow I was looking for. O Master . . .
(*They say nothing*)
Why are you two staring at the ground? Did you drop some mon-
ey?
(*Both continue to mope and moon*)
What are you so sad and gloomy about?
(*Aside to audience*)
I don't like this. There has to be a reason for this.
(*Still no reply*)
Why don't you answer me?

MNESILOCHUS: Chrysalus, I'm a dead man!   1000

CHRYSALUS: Oh, is that all? Maybe you didn't keep enough of the
gold for yourself?

MNESILOCHUS: You're damned right I didn't keep enough; in fact, I
kept a lot, lot less than enough.

CHRYSALUS: What? You nitwit! When it was *my* courage that let you
skim off as little or as much as you pleased? Well, what did you do?
Did you carry off only what you could hold by two teeny little
fingertips? Didn't you know that an opportunity like this one
doesn't often come your way?

MNESILOCHUS: That's not the problem.   1010

CHRYSALUS: Then the problem is that you didn't skim enough off.

MNESILOCHUS: You'll have even more to blame me for once you
know what else happened. I'm a dead man.

CHRYSALUS: (*Aside, to audience*) Those words tell me there's something worse to come.

MNESILOCHUS: I'm ruined.

CHRYSALUS: Why?

MNESILOCHUS: Because I handed back every bit of the money to my father.

CHRYSALUS: *You gave it back?*   1020

MNESILOCHUS: I gave it back.

CHRYSALUS: (*Voice breaking*) Not all of it . . . not . . . every . . . bit of it?

MNESILOCHUS: Every . . . bit of it.

CHRYSALUS: *We're all dead men!* How did it ever come into your head to do such a horrible thing?

MNESILOCHUS: Well, Chrysalus, I heard a false charge that Bacchis and Pistoclerus were plotting against me. I was angry about that, and that's why I gave back all the gold to my father.   1029

CHRYSALUS: (*In tears of frustration*)
What did you tell your father when you gave him the gold?

MNESILOCHUS: I said I got the gold directly from his friend Archidemides.

CHRYSALUS: These words will get Chrysalus criss-crossed on a cross this very day. As soon as he sees me, the old man will drag me off to the public executioner!

MNESILOCHUS: Oh, I persuaded my father . . .

CHRYSALUS: (*Stepping on line*) . . . to do what I just said he'd do, right?

MNESILOCHUS: No, no, not at all: *not* to harm you or be angry with
you about it.   1040
(*Instantly turns sweet*)
I barely managed to do it, too. Now *you* have to do something
about all this, Chrysalus.

CHRYSALUS: What do you want me to do?

MNESILOCHUS: I want you to lay down another highway to the old
man. I want you to lie, create whatever plot you please, concoct
some clever fabrication to trick my clever father and make off with
his gold.

CHRYSALUS: I don't see how it can be done.

MNESILOCHUS: Oh, go on! *You* can do it. No problem.   1049

CHRYSALUS: *No problem?* Damn it all! Make a fool of a man who just
caught me in a lie? He wouldn't believe a word I said. The only
way he'll believe me is if I tell him *not* to believe me.

MNESILOCHUS: (*Picking up this line with interest*)
Ah, well . . . if only you could hear what he said about you.

CHRYSALUS: What did he say?

MNESILOCHUS: (*Points up to the sky*)
He said that if you told him that the sun was the sun, he'd believe
it was the moon, and that if you told him it was daylight, he'd know
for sure it was really night!

CHRYSALUS: Then I will swindle him again today!
(*Aside, calmly*)
I don't want him to be accused of exaggeration.

MNESILOCHUS: Now what do you want *us* to do?   1060

CHRYSALUS: Absolutely nothing but make love. And that's an order. One more thing: tell me how much gold you need. I'll give it to you. What's the good of having a golden name like Chrysalus if you can't live up to it? Now, tell me, Mnesilochus, just what teeny sum do you need?

MNESILOCHUS: I've got to have two hundred gold coins now to buy Bacchis back from the soldier.

CHRYSALUS: Consider it done.

MNESILOCHUS: (*Eyes glazing over as all his troubles recede*)
Well . . . then we'll need an expense account.   1069

CHRYSALUS: No, I'd rather do one thing at a time. First this plot, then the next one. I'll train my catapult on the old man for the two hundred. If I can shatter his towers and breastwork with that charge, then I'll go through the smashed gate into the old, ancient city. Once it's fallen, you and your friend can carry off his gold by the basketful, as much as your heart desires.

PISTOCLERUS: Our lives are in your hands, Chrysalus.

CHRYSALUS: Now, Pistoclerus, go inside to Bacchis and bring out . . .

PISTOCLERUS: (*Salutes*) . . . what?

CHRYSALUS: . . . a stylus, wax, tablets, and string.   1080

PISTOCLERUS: I'll do it right now.

(*Salutes; runs into* BACCHIS I*'s house*)

MNESILOCHUS: What are you going to do? Tell me!

CHRYSALUS: Is dinner ready? How many are coming? Pistoclerus, you, and your girlfriend?

MNESILOCHUS: That's right.

CHRYSALUS: There's no woman for Pistoclerus?

MNESILOCHUS: Oh, yes. He's in love with one sister Bacchis, and I'm in love with the other; that adds up to two Bacchises.

CHRYSALUS: What's this?

MNESILOCHUS: Just the lay of the land.   1090

CHRYSALUS: Then where is this twin-sized dining couch of yours?

MNESILOCHUS: Why do you want to know?

CHRYSALUS: It's my business to know. You have no idea what I'm going to do; you don't know what a huge scheme I've got underway.

MNESILOCHUS: (CHRYSALUS *follows*) Very well, give me your hand and follow me to the door.
(*They stand outside* BACCHIS I's *house*)
Now look inside.

CHRYSALUS: (*A leg dangles out the door*)
Wow! Too sweet for words! Just what I've always wanted!

(PISTOCLERUS *reenters with tablets, etc.*)

PISTOCLERUS: As you ordered, sir.   1100
(*Salutes*)
A good order carried out by a good man.

CHRYSALUS: What do you have here?

PISTOCLERUS: Everything you commanded me to bring.

CHRYSALUS: (*To* MNESILOCHUS) You there, take the stylus and the tablets.

(PISTOCLERUS *holds the tablets while* MNESILOCHUS *writes*)

MNESILOCHUS: Then what?

CHRYSALUS: Write down exactly what I tell you to. I want you to do the writing so your father will recognize your hand when he reads it.

MNESILOCHUS: What should I write?   1110

CHRYSALUS: Greetings and good health to your father, but in your own words.

PISTOCLERUS: Wouldn't it be better for him to write "sickness and death"? That would be more to the point.

CHRYSALUS: No interruptions!

MNESILOCHUS: (*Labors away, mindless and diligent*)
I've got that order down now.

CHRYSALUS: How does it go?

MNESILOCHUS: (*Stands up; reads proudly*)
"From: Mnesilochus. To: Father. Subject: Greetings."

CHRYSALUS: (*Winces*) Now quick, add this: 1119
(*In a huge rush*)
"Chrysalus keeps nagging me all the time, Father. He's not nice because I gave your gold back to you and I didn't swindle you."

PISTOCLERUS: Give him time to get it down.

CHRYSALUS: A lover's hand should be quick.

PISTOCLERUS: His hand should be faster at spending money than at writing about it.

MNESILOCHUS: All right, that's down.

CHRYSALUS: (*Continuing to dictate*)
"Now, dear Father, be on your guard. He's putting together a regular Greek swindle to cheat you out of your gold. *And* he's admitted openly that he'll take it." Now, write that out plain and direct.   1130

MNESILOCHUS: (*After a moment*) All right, go on.

CHRYSALUS: "*And* he promises that he's going to give it to me so I can give it all to whores and gobble it up like a degenerate Greek, Father. *But,* Father, watch out: don't let him make a fool of you today. Please, *please* be careful."

MNESILOCHUS: (*Finishes*) Go on. What next?

CHRYSALUS: Just add . . . h'm . . .

(*Pauses*)

MNESILOCHUS: Tell me what to write.

CHRYSALUS: Ah! "But, Father, *please* remember what you promised me: don't beat him. Just tie him up and keep him at home under guard."   1141
(*To* PISTOCLERUS)
You, give us the wax and string.
(*To* MNESILOCHUS)
Come on, fasten it and seal it, quick!

MNESILOCHUS: (*Looks blank*) Now, will you please tell me what good all of this is going to do? Why are you telling him not to trust you and to tie you up and stand watch over you at home?

CHRYSALUS: Because I want to tell him, that's why. You mind your own business and leave mine alone! My solid references got me this job. I'm the one taking all the risks.

MNESILOCHUS: Fair enough.   1150

CHRYSALUS: Hand over the letter.

MNESILOCHUS: There you are.

CHRYSALUS: Now, pay attention, Mnesilochus, and you too, Pistoclerus. Both of you go now into the dining room. Take your places on that twin-sized couch of yours. Once you're set up there, your job is to start drinking. That's an order.

PISTOCLERUS: Any more orders?

CHRYSALUS: One more: once you've taken your places, don't dare leave unless you get a signal from me.

PISTOCLERUS: O noble general!   1160

CHRYSALUS: You're still here? You could have had *two* drinks by now!

PISTOCLERUS: We're *running!*

CHRYSALUS: You tend to your business. I'll busy myself with mine.

(*They both double-time into* BACCHIS I's *house*)

Scene 5

CHRYSALUS: (*Solo*) What a monstrous concoction of a plot I've got brewing! My only worry is that I may not be able to make the plot work. The first thing I've got to do is get the old man mad and

raging at me. It wouldn't be a proper Greek swindle if he saw me
in a tranquil, gentle mood. I'll have him turned inside-out today,
stake my life on it. I'll roast him dry as a parched pea.   1170
Now to stroll to his door! When he comes out, I'll be well placed to
put the letter in his hand.

Scene 6

(NICOBULUS *comes rushing out of his house*)

NICOBULUS: What an outrage to me and my dignity! That Chrysalus
has got away from me!

CHRYSALUS: (*Aside*) I'm saved! The old man is angry. Now's the time
for me to go up to him.

NICOBULUS: Who is that talking over there? Why, I believe it's
Chrysalus!

CHRYSALUS: Here goes.   1179

NICOBULUS: (*Sarcastically*) O excellent slave, greetings. How are
things? How soon should I set sail for Ephesus to bring back my
gold from Theotimus?
(CHRYSALUS *does not respond*)
Nothing to say? I swear by all the gods that if I didn't love my son
so and want to give him anything he asks for, your hide would have
been well whipped by now. You could spend the rest of your life in
chains at the mill. I've learned all about your crimes from Mnesilochus.

CHRYSALUS: (*Innocently*) He's charged me?
(*Aside*)
That's perfect! *I'm* the one that's wicked and the scoundrel. You
just watch what happens! I won't say another word.   1190

NICOBULUS: You cut-throat! Are you making threats?

CHRYSALUS: You'll know soon enough what kind of person *he* is. He
ordered me to bring you this letter. He asked that you do whatever is written here.

NICOBULUS: Hand it over.

CHRYSALUS: Notice the seal.

NICOBULUS: I do. Where is he?

CHRYSALUS: I don't know.
(Aside)
The only proper thing for me is to know nothing. I've forgotten
everything.   1200
(To NICOBULUS)
You know that I'm a slave. I don't even know what I do know.
(Aside)
Now the little birdie has seen the worm and walked into the trap.
With the noose I've set, I'll have this fellow hung up nicely.

NICOBULUS: Just a moment.
(Reads the letter)
Aargh! I'll soon come back to you, Chrysalus.

(Goes back into his house)

CHRYSALUS: As if he were playing the trick on me! As if I didn't know
what he's going to do! He's gone inside to get some slaves to tie me
up. But it's his ship of state that's floundering nicely; my little bark
is sailing along fine. Now I'll quiet down. I hear the door opening.

Scene 7

(*Enter* NICOBULUS *with his slave overseer* ARTAMO *and other slaves*)

NICOBULUS: Now, Artamo, seize that fellow there and tie him up.

(ARTAMO *and company do so*)

CHRYSALUS: (*feigning innocence*) What have I done?   1211

NICOBULUS: (*To* ARTAMO) Smash him in the face if he lets out a peep!
(*To* CHRYSALUS)
What does this letter say?

CHRYSALUS: Why are you asking me? I took it from him and brought
it all sealed to you.

NICOBULUS: Oh, you rascal, you! You've been berating my son because he gave the gold back to me? And you said that you would
use some Greek swindle to get the money from me?

CHRYSALUS: (*All innocence*) I said *that?*

NICOBULUS: Yes.   1220

CHRYSALUS: Who is it said that I said that?

NICOBULUS: Quiet!
(ARTAMO *hits* CHRYSALUS)
No man said it. The letter you brought here indicts you.
(*Points to the letter*)
See! These words order you to be tied up.

CHRYSALUS: (*Takes letter, pretends to read very carefully*)
Aha! Your son has made me the courier of my own death warrant,
just like Bellerophon. So I brought the very letter that orders me
to be tied up? Very well. So what?

NICOBULUS: I'm only doing this to make you persuade my son that
    he ought not to live like a degenerate Greek, you wretched swine.

CHRYSALUS: Oh, you fool, you fool! Here you are, standing on the
    block, the slave dealer is calling out your name, and you don't
    even know that you're on sale.   1232

NICOBULUS: Tell me, who is selling me?

CHRYSALUS: (*To audience*)
    As the poet says,
    "He whom the gods love dies young,
    while he still has his strength, sense, and wit."
    (*Points to* NICOBULUS)
    If any god loved this man, he would have died more than ten years
    ago—no, more than twenty years ago. This burden on the earth
    walks around and knows nothing, feels nothing. He's as worthless
    as a rotten mushroom.   1240

NICOBULUS: (*To* CHRYSALUS) So, I'm a burden on the earth, you
    say?
    (*To* ARTAMO)
    Take him inside and string him up tight to the whipping post.
    You'll never take my gold away from me!

CHRYSALUS: Ha! You'll soon give it away.

NICOBULUS: Give it away?

CHRYSALUS: Yes, and you yourself will beg me to take it away, when
    you find out the deadly danger my accuser is in . . .
    (*Ominously*)
    . . . Oh how much deadly danger. Then you'll shower liberty all
    over Chrysalus, but I'll never take it.   1250

NICOBULUS: Tell me, you piece of trash, what kind of danger is my
    son Mnesilochus in?

CHRYSALUS: Follow me this way and you'll find out soon enough.

NICOBULUS: (*Following Chrysalus*) Where in the world are we going?

CHRYSALUS: Just three steps.

NICOBULUS: More like ten.

(*They go over to* BACCHIS I's *door*)

CHRYSALUS: Come now, Artamo, open this door just a teeny little crack. Softly! No squeaks!
(*The door is opened a crack*)
Now, that's enough.   1260
(*To* NICOBULUS)
Come here, you. You see the banquet going on inside?

(*Sounds of drunken orgy*)

NICOBULUS: (*Peers in; door is closed*) I saw Pistoclerus lying opposite Bacchis!

CHRYSALUS: And who is on the other couch?

NICOBULUS: (*Peers in again*) Oh no! I'm destroyed!

CHRYSALUS: You know the fellow?

NICOBULUS: I know him.

CHRYSALUS: Now, please give me your opinion: isn't she beautiful?

NICOBULUS: Very much so.

CHRYSALUS: And do you think she's a courtesan?   1270

NICOBULUS: What else?

CHRYSALUS: You couldn't be more wrong.

NICOBULUS: Then, for God's sake, who is she?

CHRYSALUS: (*Mysteriously*) You'll find out soon enough . . . but not
   from me . . . and not today.

Scene 8

(*Without warning, the soldier* CLEOMACHUS *enters. At first he does
not see the crowd at* BACCHIS's *door.*)

CLEOMACHUS: (*To audience*) So! It's Mnesilochus, son of Nicobulus,
   who keeps my woman here by force? What are his intentions?

NICOBULUS: (*To* CHRYSALUS) Who is *that?*

CHRYSALUS: (*Aside*) The soldier has come just in time for me.

CLEOMACHUS: (*Continues to speak to audience*)
   May he think me not a soldier but a woman   1280
   who cannot defend myself and those who are mine.
   May neither Bellona nor Mars ever again trust me
   if I don't render him lifeless when I meet him,
   if I don't disinherit him from his living estate!

NICOBULUS: Chrysalus, who is that man who's threatening my son?

CHRYSALUS: Him? Oh, just the husband of the very woman your son
   is in bed with!

NICOBULUS: *What!* Her husband!

CHRYSALUS: That's what I said, her *husband.*

NICOBULUS: Oh no! She's married!   1290

CHRYSALUS: You'll learn for sure soon enough.

NICOBULUS: Poor me! I'm ruined!

CHRYSALUS: Now, then, does Chrysalus seem such a villain to you? Go ahead, keep me tied up! Just listen to your son. Didn't I tell you you would find out what kind of man he is?

NICOBULUS: Now what will I do?

CHRYSALUS: Order me to be untied at once. If I'm not untied soon, he'll catch your son in the act.

CLEOMACHUS: (*Continues to address audience*)
Nothing, no sum of money, would give me as much pleasure as catching him in bed with her! Then I could kill them both!

CHRYSALUS: Did you hear what he said? Are you going to order me untied or are you not?   1302

NICOBULUS: (*To* ARTAMO) Untie him! I'm scared to death!

CLEOMACHUS: (*Brandishing sword*) I'll show her, that woman who sells her own body to the mob! This is one man she won't be able to say she made a fool of.

CHRYSALUS: (*To* NICOBULUS) P-p-p-p-possibly you could pacify him with a pittance from your pocket?

NICOBULUS: (*Startled; recovers*) Well, pacify him any way you please, just so he doesn't catch my son *in flagrante* and kill him!

CLEOMACHUS: (*Continues to address the world at large*)
Unless exactly two hundred gold coins are returned to me at once, I shall instantly squeeze the breath of life out of both of them!

NICOBULUS: There! Pacify him now, if you can.   1313

CHRYSALUS: I'll do exactly that.
(*Goes over to* CLEOMACHUS; *shouts*) *Why are you shouting?*

CLEOMACHUS: (*At last notices others on the stage*)
Where is your master?

CHRYSALUS: (*for* NICOBULUS*'s benefit*)
Nowhere. I don't know.
(*Whispers to* CLEOMACHUS)
Do you want two hundred gold coins right now, on the condition
that you don't make a noise or uproar here?

CLEOMACHUS: There's nothing I would more prefer.

CHRYSALUS: (*Aside only to* CLEOMACHUS)
And on the condition that I can use harsh language with you?

CLEOMACHUS: (*Nods assent*) As you think best.   1321

NICOBULUS: (*Completely misreading their gestures*)
See how that murderer is giving in!

CHRYSALUS: (*Whispers*) That's the father of Mnesilochus. Follow
me. He'll promise it to you. Ask for your gold. As for the rest,
(*Loudly so* NICOBULUS *hears*)
A word to the wise is sufficient.

NICOBULUS: Well? Now what?

CHRYSALUS: I've made a settlement for two hundred gold coins.

NICOBULUS: O my salvation! You've saved me! How soon should I
say "I'll pay"?

(*Embraces* CHRYSALUS*'s knees*)

CHRYSALUS: (*Lifts* NICOBULUS *up; turns to* CLEOMACHUS)

You make your demand.   1330
(CLEOMACHUS *kneels; to* NICOBULUS)
And *you* swear your oath.

(NICOBULUS *kneels*)

NICOBULUS: All right, I swear.
(*To* CLEOMACHUS)
Now make your demand.

CLEOMACHUS: Will you give me two hundred genuine gold coins?

CHRYSALUS: (*To* NICOBULUS, *raising him*)
Now answer him. Say, "I do."

NICOBULUS: I do.

(CLEOMACHUS *rises also*)

CHRYSALUS: (*Turning on* CLEOMACHUS *for a mock tirade*)
Now what, you scurvy dog? Is anything else due you?
(*Backs* CLEOMACHUS *across the stage*)
Why are you upsetting him? Why are you threatening him with
death? He and I will see that you pay for this! You have a sword
here, but we have a spit inside. You get me mad enough at you,
and I'll puncture you with more holes than a mouse in a mouse-
trap. So help me, I know what's been bothering you so. You think
Mnesilochus is inside with that woman!   1343

CLEOMACHUS: *Think* he is? I *know* he is!

CHRYSALUS: (*Raising his hands in prayer to heaven*)
So help me
Jupiter, Juno, Ceres, Minerva, Latona,
Spes, Opis, Virtus, Venus,
Castor, Pollux, Mars, Mercury, Hercules,
Summanus, Sol, Saturn
—and any other gods that happen to be around—   1350

he's not lying down with her,
he's not walking alongside her,
he's not listening to her,
he's not doing anything to her
they said he was doing to her!

(*Collapses in a faint in* NICOBULUS's *arms*)

NICOBULUS: (*Thrilled, to audience*) What an oath! He's saved me by
his perjury!

CLEOMACHUS: Then where *is* Mnesilochus?

CHRYSALUS: His father sent him to the country. As for Bacchis, why,
she's gone up to the Acropolis to look at the Parthenon. It's open,
you know. Go and see if she's not there.   1361

CLEOMACHUS: Well, then, I'll go to the forum.

CHRYSALUS: (*Aside*) Or to hell.

CLEOMACHUS: (*Turns back*) I do get the gold today, right?

CHRYSALUS: Get it and be hanged! Don't think he's going to beg you
for anything today!
(CLEOMACHUS *and attendants exit*)
He's off, and good riddance.
(*To* NICOBULUS) By the gods, sir, let me go inside to your son.

NICOBULUS: Inside? Why do you want to go inside?

CHRYSALUS: I intend to give him a good dressing down, in detail, for
putting us to all this trouble.   1371

NICOBULUS: Oh, please *do*, Chrysalus! Don't spare him a single
word!

CHRYSALUS: *You're* telling me what to do? When he's going to hear
more mouthing from me today than Socrates ever heard from
Xanthippe?   1376

(*Runs into* BACCHIS I*'s house*)

NICOBULUS: (*To audience*) That slave is exactly like a sore eye: if he's
not there, you don't want him and you don't need him; if he *is*
there, you can't keep your hands off him. If he hadn't had the good
luck to be here today, that soldier would have caught Mnesilochus
with his wife. He would have hacked him into little pieces for his
adultery. It's as if—in a manner of speaking—I've bought my own
son for the two hundred coins I promised the soldier. But I won't
pay them rashly until I've had a chance to see my son. I'll never
put rash trust in Chrysalus. Still, I think I might read this letter
over again. You can always trust signed and sealed letters.

(*Goes off toward the forum but pauses; remains onstage throughout
the following scene*)

Scene 9

(*Enter* CHRYSALUS *from* BACCHIS I*'s house*)

CHRYSALUS: (*Declaims in epic style*)
   Of Atreus's two sons, those brothers who name
   Did most immortal win, when last was razed
   Proud Priam's patriotic Pergamum
   Destroyed though fortified by hand divine—   1390
   Through fell swords, horse, and Hellas's warriors all
   Illustrious, with a thousand ships besides,
   In siege permanent full ten years . . . I sing.

(*Briskly, cheerfully*)

All that was no more than a stubbed toe compared with the siege
I've laid on Nicobulus: a siege without ships and army, without a
single soldier.
(*Looks around the stage; does not see* NICOBULUS, *who is present
during the entire "Song of Troy"*)
Ah, I have time for one dirge before he returns.

(*Falls to one knee; sings*)

O Troy my enemy,
My country 'tis of thee,
O Pergamum,   1400
O Priam 'bout to die,
In twinkling of an eye,
Old man who lost four hundred coins,
Of thee I sing.

(*Stands up. As he gestures with the letter, he becomes a lecturer in
a lecture hall.*)

Now for a lecture in Greek mythology. You see, this letter that I
signed and sealed is no letter: it's the wooden horse the Greeks
left at Troy. Pistoclerus is its architect Epeos, Mnesilochus is the
traitor Sinon, left behind to trick the Trojans. Instead of Achilles'
tomb, there's Bacchis's bed: no signal fires here to summon
Greeks, just fires of passion. This Sinon is burning *himself* up.
And I'm the Ulysses who concocted the whole scheme. So the
words written here aren't really words, but Greeks armed and
hiding inside the Trojan horse. That's where our plot stands at the
moment. Our horse will make its charge on a strongbox instead of
a stronghold: an exquisite equestrian extinction for the old man
and his gold.   1416
(*Points to the door of* NICOBULUS's *house*)
   Now, think of the old fool Nicobulus as the city Troy, and say
the soldier Cleomachus is Menelaus; that leaves the roles of Agamemnon and Ulysses to me alone. Then Mnesilochus plays Paris,
the boy who caused his country's ruin. He ran off with Helen, see,
and that's why I had to lay siege to Troy. Now about Ulysses.

From what I've heard, he was as bad and bold as me. I was nearly
tricked by my own tricks, and so was he when he went on a re-
connaissance tour of Troy. But he tricked his way out of Troy,
and so did I: I was tied up, but my tricks untied me the same day.

(*Staggers backward as the Muse's inspiration strikes again*)

Three epic portents of Troy's doom were told:
If the citadel of a goddess statue
Was bereft; if Troilus, Priam's son,
Did die; if Phrygian gate by Trojan horse
Was from its hinge discharged . . . I sing.   1430
Well, that was that.

(*Returns to the lecture platform*)

That's good. Very good. Now for the commentary. There are three
portents that apply to our Troy, too. A little while ago, when I told
the old man that lie about his girlfriend and the gold and the
galley, that was stealing Athena's statue from the citadel. That left
two portents to go—I didn't have the town yet. When I took the
letter to the old man, that was killing Troilus. He thought that
Mnesilochus had been with the wife of the soldier. After that, I
locked in struggle with the soldier Cleomachus, the kind who
takes a city with words instead of arms. I beat him back. Then I
closed for a fight with the old man. With one lie I beat him to his
knees, with one quick blow I stripped him of his spoils. Now he's
given two hundred gold coins to the soldier, as he promised, but I
need two hundred more. After all, our soldiers need wine and
honey to celebrate the fall of Troy. But *this* Priam is a lot better
than the one in Homer. He had only fifty sons, but ours has four
hundred, and each one is in absolutely mint condition. I'll dis-
patch every one of them today, with just two blows.
(*Advances to audience*)
Is there any buyer for this Priam of mine? A real bargain. I'll sell
him as soon as I take the town by storm.   1450
(NICOBULUS *turns back toward his house*)

But look! There's Priam himself in front of his house! I'll go over and talk to him.

NICOBULUS: (*Looks furtively about*) Someone's speaking nearby. I wonder who?

CHRYSALUS: Oh, Nicobulus . . .

NICOBULUS: What's going on? Have you done what I sent you to do?

CHRYSALUS: You ask? Come over here.

NICOBULUS: Here I am.

CHRYSALUS: Outstanding orator, that's me. I reduced the boy to tears. I pointed out all his faults. I cursed him. I used everything I could think of.   1461

NICOBULUS: What did he say?

CHRYSALUS: (*Sighs heavily*) Oh, he didn't say a word. He stood there silent . . . weeping . . . listening to everything I had to say. He wrote out a letter . . . still silent . . . he sealed it . . . gave it to me. He ordered me to give it to you, but I'm afraid you'll sing the same song you sang before. Look at that seal. Is it his?

NICOBULUS: That's it. I'd like to read this.

CHRYSALUS: Oh, please *do*.   1470
(*Hands it over; aside*)
Now the Phrygian gate is down. Now for the fall of Troy! My Trojan-horse trick is working nicely.

NICOBULUS: Chrysalus, stay here while I read this letter.

CHRYSALUS: Why do I need to stay with you?

NICOBULUS: I want you to know what the letter says so that you can do what I order you to.

CHRYSALUS: I'm not going to stay, and I don't want to know.

NICOBULUS: No matter. Stay here.

CHRYSALUS: Stay here? What's the need?

NICOBULUS: The need is that you keep quiet and do what I tell you to.   1481

CHRYSALUS: I'm here, I'm here.

NICOBULUS: (*Opens letter*) Oh, what tiny little letters!

CHRYSALUS: They're small for someone whose eyesight is poor, but they're big enough for anyone who can see well.

NICOBULUS: Then pay attention.

CHRYSALUS: I said I don't want to!

NICOBULUS: And I said I want you to!

CHRYSALUS: (*As before*) What's the need?

NICOBULUS: The need is for you to do what I order you to.   1490

CHRYSALUS: It's only right that your servants serve at your command.

NICOBULUS: Pay attention now.

CHRYSALUS: Read when you are ready. My ears are at your disposal.

NICOBULUS: Gods, he didn't spare the wax or the stylus. But whatever it says, I'm bound to read it through.

(*Reads letter*)
"Father: please give Chrysalus two hundred gold coins. If you want me safe and sound, that is." Oh no! It's as bad as I thought!

CHRYSALUS: You know . . .

NICOBULUS: What?   1500

CHRYSALUS: He didn't even say "Dear Father" first!

NICOBULUS: (*Looks hard at letter*)
I don't see it anywhere.

CHRYSALUS: (*Indignantly*) You won't pay him a thing, if you're smart; but if you do decide to pay, let him find himself another messenger if *he's* smart. I'm not carrying anything anywhere, to anybody, no matter how much you order me to. I'm already under enough suspicion as it is, and I haven't done a thing wrong!

NICOBULUS: Listen! There's still more to read here.

CHRYSALUS: And it's an outrageous letter from the very beginning.

NICOBULUS: "I am ashamed to come into your sight, Father. I've heard that you know all about my horrible crime, about my sleeping with the wife of a foreign soldier." He's not joking there! I've saved you from your own sins with two hundred gold coins.

CHRYSALUS: There's nothing new there. You haven't said a thing *I* didn't say to him.   1515

NICOBULUS: (*Continues*) "I confess I acted foolishly. *But* please don't desert me in my foolishness, Father. Passion governed my heart; my eyes were not my own to control; I was persuaded to do that which I now am ashamed to confess I have done." Ha! The proper thing would have been for you to have avoided it, rather than be ashamed about it now!

CHRYSALUS: Why, I said the very same thing to him just a while ago!

NICOBULUS: (*Continues*) "*Please,* Father, I beg you to be satisfied with the endless, sound scoldings I got from Chrysalus. His instructions have made a better man of me, so you really ought to be grateful to him for that."

CHRYSALUS: (*Feigning surprise*) Why, is *that* what he says?

NICOBULUS: Here! Look! See for yourself.

CHRYSALUS: How easily a guilty man turns suppliant to everyone he meets!   1530

NICOBULUS: (*Continues*) "Now if I still have the right to ask you for something, Father, give me two hundred gold coins . . . please . . . pretty please?"

CHRYSALUS: If you're smart, you won't give him a single one!

NICOBULUS: (*Exasperated*) Let me finish! "I took an oath in no uncertain terms to give that money back to the woman before nightfall, before she leaves me. Now, Father, please see that I don't perjure myself and get me away from here as soon as you can and see that I escape the clutches of that woman who made me commit so many sins and crimes. Don't be upset over a trifling two hundred gold coins: I'll pay you back six hundred—if I live, that is. I remain, Sincerely yours, your disobedient son Mnesilochus. P.S. Take care of all this right away." Well! What do you think, Chrysalus?   1544

CHRYSALUS: (*Outraged*) Oh no, I'm not about to give *you* any advice today! I'm not about to take a chance of having you say you did something on my advice that later went wrong. *But* . . . if you want my opinion, if I were in your place, I'd give him the money rather than let him be completely ruined. There are two possibilities; the choice is yours: Either you lose your money or he loses

his good word. *I'm* not about to order you, or forbid you, or
persuade you to do anything.   1552

NICOBULUS: (*Weakening*) I *do* feel sorry for him.

CHRYSALUS: He's your son. Nothing strange in that. If there must
be more losses, it's better to accept them than to have his scandals
spread all over town.

NICOBULUS: By the gods, I'd rather have him in Ephesus, where
he's safe, than have him here at home. But what else is there to do?
I'll go ahead and lose what has to be lost. I'll bring out the four
hundred gold coins now, both the two hundred I've promised the
soldier—poor me—and the other two hundred. Wait here,
Chrysalus: I'll be right back.   1562

(*He rushes into his house*)

CHRYSALUS: (*Solo*) Troy is laid waste! The marshals of the host are
razing Pergamum! I knew I'd be the ruin of Troy! Whoever says
I'm worthy of the worst kind of punishment—well, I wouldn't
dream of disagreeing. What a confusing little plot I'm weaving!
But the door's opening! The booty is being carried out of Troy. I'll
keep quiet now.

(*Enter* NICOBULUS *with two bags of gold*)

NICOBULUS: Take this gold, Chrysalus. Go on, take it to my son. I'm
off this way to the forum to pay back the soldier.   1570

CHRYSALUS: Oh no, I absolutely won't take it! You go and find someone else to do it. I don't want this to be entrusted to me!

NICOBULUS: Take it! Don't annoy me.

CHRYSALUS: Oh no, I absolutely won't have it.

NICOBULUS: *Please.*

CHRYSALUS: I said that's that. And that's *that*.

NICOBULUS: Stop stalling.

(*Hands bags over*)

CHRYSALUS: (*Begins to relent*) I said I don't want the gold entrusted
to me! Well, at least get somebody to keep guard on me.

NICOBULUS: Aargh! You're getting me angry again.   1580

CHRYSALUS: (*Seeming to give way reluctantly*)
Give it here, then, if you have to.

NICOBULUS: Now, see to this. I'll be back shortly.

(*Runs off toward forum*)

CHRYSALUS: I'll see to it—
(*Pauses until* NICOBULUS *is offstage*)
—see that you're the most wretched old fool alive!
(*To audience*)
This is the way to finish: end with a flourish. How nicely things are
going! What a Roman triumph! What a load of spoils! To make it
official:
(*As if giving an official decree*)

The public safety having been established,
The town having been captured through guile,
I lead our army unharmed and whole back home.   1590

But don't be surprised if I don't celebrate a triumph now. They're
far too common these days, spectators. My troops will have all the
wine and honey they need. Now to carry this booty straight to our
quartermaster!

(*Exit into the house of* BACCHIS I)

Scene 10

(*Enter* PHILOXENUS)

PHILOXENUS: The more I ponder the turmoils my son is toiling in, the more the ignorant simpleton sinks into his life of hedonistic habits, the more I worry and the more I fear that he'll be compromised and corrupted. I know, I was his age once and I did all those things . . .   1599
(*Pauses*)
. . . but in a restrained way. I got married, I knew whores, I had too many drinks, I knew all about sex, I paid for all that—but not too often. In fact, I don't much care for the attitude most parents display these days toward their sons. I decided that I would give my son whatever his heart desired. I think that's only fair. Of course, I don't want to give *too much* play to his playing around.
(*Goes to* NICOBULUS's *door*)
Now I'll see Mnesilochus about my instructions to him, see whether or not his labors have contrived to drive Pistoclerus over to virtue and a rewarding life. I know he would have done that, given the chance. To do so is the nature of the boy.

ACT V

Scene 1

(NICOBULUS *enters in a rage from the forum. He does not see* PHILOXENUS *throughout the following.*)

NICOBULUS: (*To audience*)
Whoever and wherever they are,   1610
Whoever they have been or will be,

Of all the foolish, fatuous, fungus-covered,
   dunderheaded,
Stupid, driveling, dehydrated dolts!
In stupidity and mindlessness I outrun the pack.
I'm ruined! I'm disgraced!   1616

How could I be tricked *twice* like this, and at my age? The more I
think about the mess my son made, the hotter I get! Ruined and
ripped and wracked this way and that! Pursued by every evil
known to man, I've died each death there is to die. Chrysalus has
chopped me all to bits, and stripped the spoils from poor innocent
me. That devil has fleeced me of my gold, and with his anything
but innocent ways has done just as he pleased with me! You know
what happened? The soldier tells me that the woman is really a
courtesan, the woman Chrysalus called his wife! He told me everything else that happened, too. He had hired her out for a year,
so the money I paid him—stupid idiot that I am—was only the
gold that was the balance due on his account! *That* is what galls me
the most of all! The worst torture of all is to be made to play the
fool at my age! For me, with my white hair and my snow-white
beard, to be picked clean of all my money! I'm ruined. My own
slave treats me like dirt! If only I had lost my money some place
else! I'd at least be able to endure that better than this!   1633

PHILOXENUS: I'm sure I thought someone was speaking nearby.
(*At last he notices* NICOBULUS)
But who is this? Why, it's the father of Mnesilochus!

NICOBULUS: Oh, just what I needed! There's my partner in toil and
   trouble. Greetings, Philoxenus.

PHILOXENUS: Same to you. Where are you coming from?

NICOBULUS: The place any wretched, penniless old man should be
   coming from.   1640

PHILOXENUS: Yes, wretched and penniless men like us deserve to
   be there.

NICOBULUS: I see. We're as alike in our fortunes as we are in our years.

PHILOXENUS: Just so. But what's *your* trouble?

NICOBULUS: The same as yours.

PHILOXENUS: So! Does your malady have anything to do with your son?

NICOBULUS: You might say so.

PHILOXENUS: I have the same malady.

NICOBULUS: Chrysalus, that excellent fellow, ruined my son, me, and all my wealth. 1651

PHILOXENUS: Please tell me what your son has done to upset you.

NICOBULUS: I'll tell you. He's ruined your son! They both have mistresses!

PHILOXENUS: (*Recoils*) How do you know?

NICOBULUS: I saw them.

PHILOXENUS: Oh no! Ruined again!

NICOBULUS: Well, what are we waiting for? Let's both go and knock on the door.

(*Gestures toward* BACCHIS I's *house*)

PHILOXENUS: Excellent idea. 1660

NICOBULUS: Hey! Bacchis! Open this door at once! You'd better open the door now if you don't want to lose your door and doorpost to axes!

(*They both bang*)

Scene 2

BACCHIS I: (*From inside*) What's the meaning of this uproar? Who is it? Who called?

(BACCHIS I *and* BACCHIS II *enter*)

NICOBULUS: This fellow and me.

BACCHIS I: (*To* BACCHIS II) What's going on? Goodness, dear, who drove these sheep here?

NICOBULUS: The bitch is calling us sheep!

BACCHIS II: Their shepherd must be taking a nap to let them stray bleating like this away from the flock.   1670

BACCHIS I: Oh dear, they *are* trim and neat, aren't they? They don't seem a bit dirty.

BACCHIS II: Yes indeed, they've both been very well shorn.

PHILOXENUS: Look at them making fun of us!

NICOBULUS: Let them carry on as much as they like.

BACCHIS I: (*To* BACCHIS II) How often would you say they get fleeced? Three times a year?

BACCHIS II: (*Points to* NICOBULUS) I think this one was sheared twice today.

BACCHIS I: They are both fleeceless, aren't they?   1680

BACCHIS II: And they used to have such *nice* wool.

BACCHIS I:
> (*Sees that* PHILOXENUS *and* NICOBULUS *are more interested than indignant*)
> Now, I ask you, just look at those sidelong stares.

BACCHIS II: I don't think they mean anything nasty by it.

PHILOXENUS: (*To* NICOBULUS) This is just what we deserve for coming here!

BACCHIS I: They ought to be driven inside.

BACCHIS II: What good would it do? They don't have any milk or wool. Let them stand here. They've given as much as they can. All the fruit has dropped from their branches anyway.   1689
> (*Stares suggestively at the two men*)
> Don't you see how they're wandering around untended? Why, I believe they're dumb with age. They don't let out so much as one bleat when they're apart from their flock. They just seem stupid, not bad.

(*Laughs*)

BACCHIS I: Let's go back inside, Sister.

(*They turn to go*)

NICOBULUS: Both of you stay right there! These *sheep* want you.

BACCHIS II: This is indeed a miracle! These sheep are addressing us in human speech!

PHILOXENUS: This is *one* pair of sheep that's going to bite the hand that sheared them!

BACCHIS I: (*Briskly*) If you have a debt, I hereby cancel it. Keep the money, I'll never ask for it. What possible excuse could you have to threaten us in so unsheeplike a fashion?   1702

PHILOXENUS: Because you have our two little lambs fenced inside your house.

NICOBULUS: Besides those lambs, you have my watchdog too! Unless you lead them outside this instant, we'll turn into rams and butt you right down.

BACCHIS I: Sister, there's something I must say to you in private.

BACCHIS II: Do tell me what it is.

(*They draw to one side*)

NICOBULUS: Where are they going?   1710

BACCHIS I: (*With* BACCHIS II, *off to one side of the stage*)
I'm putting you in charge of that old man.
(*Points to* PHILOXENUS)
You calm him down. I'll take the one that's angry, and we'll both see if we can't persuade them to come inside.

BACCHIS II: I'll play my part as well as I can, but it is revolting to lie in the arms of a dead man.

BACCHIS I: Well, get to it.

BACCHIS II: Hush! You see to your job and I'll do mine.

NICOBULUS: What plot are those two hatching in secret over there?

PHILOXENUS: Uh . . . Nicobulus.

NICOBULUS: Yes?   1720

PHILOXENUS: There's something embarrassing I've got to tell you.

NICOBULUS: What is it that's so embarrassing?

PHILOXENUS: (*Pauses, then goes ahead*)
All right, here goes. I'm going to confess, my loyal friend. I'm worthless.

NICOBULUS: Oh well, I've known that for some time. But why are you worthless? Come on, tell me.

PHILOXENUS:
(*Straining toward* BACCHIS I *and* BACCHIS II, *in romantic tones*)
I'm adrift on a swelling tide of passion . . .
my heart's pierced through and through . . .

NICOBULUS: (*Disgusted*) It would be more in your fashion
to have your old *ass* pierced, too.   1730
(PHILOXENUS *is shocked out of his reverie*)
What do you mean? Even though I already probably know what you're going to say, I'd prefer to hear it from you.

PHILOXENUS: (*Points to* BACCHIS II, *who is parading alluringly*)
See her?

NICOBULUS: Yes.

PHILOXENUS: She's really not so bad . . .

NICOBULUS: Oh yes she is, and you *are* indeed worthless!

PHILOXENUS: Why say more? *I'm in love!*

(*Dashes over to her*)

NICOBULUS: *You? In love?*

PHILOXENUS: (*Clutching* BACCHIS II) Madly.

NICOBULUS: You disgusting old fool! You dare to fall in love at your age?   1741

PHILOXENUS: Why not?

NICOBULUS: Because it's disgraceful!

PHILOXENUS: There, there. No need for talk like that. I'm not angry at my son, and you shouldn't be angry at yours. If they are in love, they're acting wisely.

BACCHIS I:
(*To* BACCHIS II, *who has been watching all this in fascination*)
Now follow me.

NICOBULUS: Look! Here they come, those proven perpetrators of petty lace and persuasion.
(*To* BACCHIS I)
Well then? Are you going to return our sons and my slave? Or do you want me to use force?   1751

(BACCHIS I *embraces him*)

PHILOXENUS: Will you get away? You're certainly no gentleman addressing such a charming little girl with such uncharming words.

BACCHIS I: (*To* NICOBULUS, *as she makes advances*)
Oh, you nicest little old man in the whole wide world. About your naughty son's doings . . . don't fight it.

NICOBULUS: (*Still in her embrace*)
If you don't get away from me—why, no matter how pretty you are, I'll make you plenty sorry!

BACCHIS I: I can take it. I'm not one bit afraid of how hard you hit.

NICOBULUS: (*Aside*) What a talker! Oh me, I'm the one that's afraid!

BACCHIS II: (*To* BACCHIS I, *with* PHILOXENUS *in her lap*)
This one is much more . . . how shall I say . . . at peace.   1760

BACCHIS I: (*To* NICOBULUS) Do come inside with me. If you want to, you can punish your son there.

NICOBULUS: Won't you keep away from me, you shameless creature?

BACCHIS I: Oh, you noble thing, do let me persuade you.

NICOBULUS: *You* persuade me?

BACCHIS II: I shall certainly persuade *this* one.

(*Passionately embraces* PHILOXENUS)

PHILOXENUS: I don't need any more persuading! Let's go inside!

BACCHIS II: Oh, you charming thing!

PHILOXENUS: What are the terms for going inside?   1770

BACCHIS II: Being with me.

PHILOXENUS: (*Lyrical again*) You are . . . everything I've longed for . . .

NICOBULUS: I've seen worthless men in my time, but never have I seen one worth less than you.

PHILOXENUS: (*Agreeably*) You're so right.

BACCHIS I: (*To* NICOBULUS) Do come inside. There is lovely food, wine, perfumes . . .

NICOBULUS: Enough of your banquets! I don't care how much you entertain me! Chrysalus and my son have already tricked me out of four hundred gold pieces. I wouldn't pass up punishing that slave even if it costs another four hundred.   1782

BACCHIS I: But if he gives you back half of the gold, will you come in then? And won't you pardon him?

PHILOXENUS: He'll do it.

NICOBULUS: I will *not!* I don't want to! I won't stand for it! Leave me alone. I prefer to make those two pay for this.

PHILOXENUS: So! You're as worthless as me! Try this moral on for size: "Those goods that the gods have given take heed you through your own fault do not lose."   1790
(*A wince of recognition from* NICOBULUS)
Here's half your gold back. Now go in, have a drink, go to bed.

NICOBULUS: Me? Drink in the same house where my own son is debauched?

PHILOXENUS: *You* need a drink!

NICOBULUS: (*Begins to slip*) Well, come on, then. I'll force myself to do this, even though it's a disgrace to do it. You mean *I*'ve got to watch while she lies next to him on the couch?

BACCHIS I: (*Interposes*) Oh no, dear! Quite the contrary! *I*'ll be next to you. I'll make love to you and hold you in my arms.

NICOBULUS: Well, I *am* a little tense. I'm finished. I can scarcely keep on saying no.   1801

BACCHIS I: Now, dear, even if you do enjoy yourself, this life we live is not at all a long one. What you've lost today will never come again once you're dead.

NICOBULUS: (*Desperately, to* PHILOXENUS)
What should I do?

PHILOXENUS: What should *you* do? At your age, you're asking that?

NICOBULUS: I want to . . . but I'm afraid to.

BACCHIS I: What are you afraid of?

NICOBULUS: Of humiliating myself in front of my son and my slave.

BACCHIS I: Honey baby, please dear, even if that happens, he *is* your
son. How do you think he's going to pay for everything without
your help? Oh, please do forgive them!   1812

(*Kisses him*)

NICOBULUS: (*Aside*) How she drills through me! Has she convinced
me to do what I had sworn I would not?
(*To* BACCHIS I) Very well, thanks to you and your hard work, I'm a
scoundrel.

BACCHIS I: (*Aside*) How I wish it had been anyone's hard work but
mine!
(*To* NICOBULUS)
Do I have your guarantee now?

NICOBULUS: Once I've said something, I never change.   1820

BACCHIS I: (*To both* NICOBULUS *and* PHILOXENUS)
The day is almost gone. Both of you, go inside, lie down. Your sons
are waiting for you there.

NICOBULUS: (*Bitterly*) Yes, waiting for us to die, I would expect.

BACCHIS I: It's evening now. Follow me.

NICOBULUS: Lead us where you please. Just pretend we're your
slaves.

(NICOBULUS *and* PHILOXENUS *start to go into* BACCHIS I's *house*)

BACCHIS I: (*To audience*) Two men who tried to trap their sons are
   themselves trapped, victims of our charming plot.

(*Entire company enters*)

THE COMPANY: If these two old men had not been worthless
   since boyhood, they'd not be snared in scandals   1830
   today in their hoary manhood; nor would we
   much delight in our play's long survival,
   had we not often seen pimps made rich
   by greedy sons and fathers playing rivals!

   Spectators all, farewell, we wish you well!
   What you wish for us, your applause will tell.

THE ENTREPRENEUR

(*MERCATOR*)

Translated by George Garrett

INTRODUCTION

If, always allowing for those rare and perfect exceptions (Wilbur's Molière, for example, or Slavitt's Virgil and Ovid), poetry is what is lost in translation, then comedy is in even more trouble. Comedy, almost all of it, is like politics—it's local, topical, dependent on deep and deeply shared assumptions, set in its own context as if it were poured concrete, and, on top of everything else, blessed with a memory briefer than that of a mayfly. Last year's jokes in last year's words are already quaint at best. Go back a little in time, to other alien times, and quaint becomes almost incomprehensible. Our great comic dramatists, writing more or less in our own language, Shaw and Shakespeare, in spite of their superbly funny central plot situations, in spite of their complex and recognizable characters, are served up by our best contemporary actors and directors with the dubious benefits of much mugging and sight gags and directorial italics and grammar. Just so, the great comics of our century— Harold Lloyd and Buster Keaton, Chaplin and Fields—already require an introduction and footnotes when presented to the latest generation of students, punchy as they are from standup comics on TV and the amphetamine attention span of MTV. Comic in and of itself, the act of explicating jokes for the uninformed and uninitiated is a classic no-win proposition.

And yet. We are likely to know others, to know each other, better and more truly by what makes us and them laugh than we are able to in extreme situations, common enough but mysterious, of crisis. And we can gain at least an imaginative glimmer, a hint of the reality of the alien beings of ages past by what they found funny. Sometimes it is close to our own assumptions; sometimes it is far from our understanding, let alone the letting go of laughter.

Add to that the language problem. Even a living language, one freely and easily spoken by many people (and all the comedy we know of, be it elegant or crude, is based on the music of the spoken vernacular), has enormous obstacles, as much as poetry, to transference by translation. Leap backward in time to Latin and Greek, languages that are well known, at least in texts, by a few and still spoken by a *very* few, if any, and it would seem to be impossible to span the gulf of time and possess again any more than bits and pieces, shards only, of the nuances, references, allusions, and elements of style that dressed out comedy to advantage. Shakespeare is closer to us than Chaucer, needs fewer footnotes (though more and more, year by year); and we know, from his huge success, that his comedies were powerfully popular. Recent scholarship indicates that at heart his language was mostly based not on the big city fashions of the university and other urban wits, but was basically a generation or more behind that, rooted in the English country language, its rhythms and figures, which he heard and learned in Stratford, a language changing and moving as slowly as the unhurried Afton between its green banks. Marlowe was hip and with it in his thunderous plays. So was Ben Jonson in both comedy and tragedy. But it was Shakespeare, a wild young verbal adventurer with an older idiom, who lived to pick up all the marbles and go home.

What has all this got to do with anything? It has to do with Plautus, who lasted long enough, in a condition of some familiarity and fluency, to be hugely influential in the comedies of William Shakespeare among many others. Plays of Plautus were among the first things, certainly the first forms of drama, Shakespeare (and everybody else) studied as a schoolboy (which, of course, would guarantee mixed feelings about Plautus). The plays were, anyway, known to him, and to practically everyone else in England by the end of the century, when the queen's persistent and passionate concern for the education of her people paid off handsomely just at the time Shakespeare was moving to the forefront of the English dramatists. The plays were there and he cannibalized them, in fact and spirit, and found good use for their parts in his own radically different theater.

That would be reason enough to want to know more about Plautus and his work. He has lasted on into our age as much by influence as anything else. All these years later his comedies survive everything, even well-meaning "translation," to remain part of our consciousness. That this is so may be taken as good proof that there is at least a thread of comedy in the network of God's Providence. I can't seriously believe that Plautus himself, let alone his audience, allowed themselves the mad and madly comic thought that his works and words would still be alive, if old and feeble, in the final years of the twentieth century A.D. Of course, somebody must have liked them a lot or they wouldn't have been preserved in manuscript and copied down again and again on precious parchment or paper, using up precious time and storage space.

Now I have to tell you that there is a whole lot about the comedy of Plautus, specifically as it is shown and told here in the *Mercator*, that I don't understand. There's the language which, in and of itself, seems rich with punning and echoes and all sorts of verbal fun and games, ripe with the eccentric attitudes and inappropriate juxtapositions that surely could conjure up laughter even when the dramatic situation might not on its own. The only way for me to represent this was not by trying to duplicate Plautus's method, ways and means, but to come up with a mix of contemporary lingo that, one hopes, would have its anarchic moments worthy, at times, of the expense of laughter. I aimed to be as true to the spirit of his lines as I could. The letter was often expendable.

I found myself fascinated, as I humped along, by the things that Plautus and, evidently, his Roman audience found wonderfully funny—Greeks in general, sassy slaves in particular, and rebellious wives (premature feminists), passive and horny husbands, young men who could strike theatrical poses and stances, and a general milieu that seemed to present a focused picture of what a student of mine, reared on TV and not by books, referred to as "a doggie dog world." Even so, I did not at the outset really understand how this play worked, what it was *like* in my own experience, where (again in the words of students) Plautus was coming from. And then, as these slap-happy types stood in pairs, sometimes in trios, in their exterior street scenes, trading quips, playing parts with each other, cracking wise or dumb, memory came to my rescue. In the late 1940s I and others from Princeton went up to Newark on the train and from the station took a short walk to the celebrated Empire Burlesque Theater, where I saw about all that was legally to be seen of stars like

Georgia Southern and Winnie Garrett, the Flaming Redhead. And in between these fantastic and ritualized exposures of fantastic femininity—long before *Playboy* or even bikini bathing suits or coeducation at Princeton—there were the comedy routines. Closer, as I think and remember them now, to the art of circus clowns than standup comics; yet, except for the funny hats and baggy or shaggy costumes, the comedy was a largely verbal sparring, *shtick* before I had heard that word, something akin to Abbott and Costello in the movies, not far from the forms of vaudeville where my uncle worked for a time as a tireless tapdancer. There it was. There it is, I could tell myself now, Plautus still cooking and smoking in our time; and it was probably old enough already in his era.

Some things don't change a whole lot. The Princeton professor I admired most, the great medievalist D. W. Robertson Jr., calmly swore that he had never heard a joke he couldn't find a classical source for, that all our jokes seem to be as old as our languages, living and dead.

One thing more. One thing you can't take away from Plautus is his neat sense of plot and of a comic situation that, for all its foolery, could turn serious and messy enough at any minute. He comes on as a cheerful, lighthearted playmaker, so gifted that you tend to forget the truth that things could really get ugly any time, as they usually do in real life and never really do in comedy, except for black comedy. As for the little, lightweight morals at the end of things, they are unexceptional, just enough of a dose of down-home wisdom to save you from the notion (perish the thought!) that you have wasted your time watching some people, not so different from yourself, make fools out of themselves.

George Garrett

THE ENTREPRENEUR

CHARACTERS

CHARINUS, a young man of Athens
ACANTHIO, his slave
DEMIPHO, his father
LYSIMACHUS, a friend of Demipho
SLAVE, belonging to Lysimachus
EUTYCHUS, son of Lysimachus
PASICOMPSA, a courtesan
DORIPPA, wife of Lysimachus
SYRA, old slave of Lysimachus
COOK

SCENE: *A street in Athens where the houses of* DEMIPHO *and* LYSIMACHUS *stand.*

(*Enter* CHARINUS, *somewhat the worse for wear*)

CHARINUS

Two things, okay? Can you handle that all by yourself?
Okay. First off, I'm fixing to explain the plot of this play
And next I'm planning to tell you all about love,
My love, ladies and gentlemen, my grand and personal passion.

Usually lovers come stumbling out onto stages like this,
Howling at the inconstant moon, talking trash to the trees
(And even the trees don't bother to listen).
But I'm going to make my case to you folks who
Paid good money to be here and may still be paying attention
This early in the game. Okay . . .   10
In the Greek the play is *Emporus* by Philemon.
In living Latin it's *Mercator* by Maccius Titus,
Plautus, that is, me, myself, and I,
In a brand-new version by George Garrett
Which he, out of lazy irony, elects
To call *The Entrepreneur.*
Let's get on with it.
See . . . Yonder stands my father's house.
He sent me off to Rhodes on business
A couple of years ago, where I proceeded   20
To fall head over heels in love
With this incredibly beautiful girl.
And I'll tell you all about it, all
In due time if you still feel like listening.
But for the time being please accept my apology.
I started out trying to talk about love,
But lovers can't get their act together or the show
On the road. What happens is, see,
You flat fall in love and the next thing you know
You can't get to sleep or you can't wake up   30
And here comes trouble—the heartbreak of
Heartbreak, psoriasis, paranoia, seborrhea,
Not to mention the other multiple plagues,
Outward and visible, inward and spiritual,
Which drive true lovers to distraction.
Besides which we tend to talk too much,
As some of you may have noticed already.
Well, I can't blame myself. It's the curse,
The blessing of Venus, world without end.
In the beginning, which is to say,   40
Back when puberty blew childhood away,
I foolishly fell for a classy call girl and then

Spent a bundle on bundling, so to speak.
Most of which went to support the champagne taste
Of her rapacious pimp.
Needless to say, it was the business angle
That bugged my father the most,
The very idea of that pussy merchant living
High off of our assets led my old man
To wander all over town like the ancient mariner   50
Telling the world about his profligate son,
An albatross if there ever was one,
And giving my credit rating a classical beating.
When he was my age back on the farm,
He didn't mess around, he worked his ass off;
And his reward was maybe a peek at the city
Every four years. And all the time
His old man was telling him how it was
All for his own good, how he was humping to please
Himself. And when his father died,   60
Even before the old boy cooled and stiffened,
Daddy unloaded the farm and bought a boat
And hustled cargoes everywhere,
Buying cheap and selling dear until he was,
Let's face it, rich enough to afford even me,
Though he was losing patience fast
With my costly indifference to his example.
Okay. I got the message.
I pulled myself together and boldly announced
That I would personally go off on a trading journey   70
If that's what he had in mind for me.
I would call it quits with my call girl cutie
If that would make him happy.
He thanked me kindly for my good intentions
And to my dismay took me up on them.
He bought a new boat and filled it with goods,
Coughed up good money and sent along
A trusty slave to keep an eye on me.
And away we went riding a fair wind.
Arrived safe at Rhodes and promptly sold   80

My cargo at a better profit than even Daddy expected.
So I had time on my hands and a little extra money all my own.
When I ran into an old buddy who invited me
To a party. Where one thing led to another
And I ended up in the sack with the beautiful stranger
Who has changed my luck and my life.
Next day I begged my friend to be
My friend forever and sell her to me.
Which he did. And I brought her back.
But I don't want Daddy to know   90
So I left her back at the harbor on the ship
Along with my trusty servant
And, uh-oh, there he comes now
Running up from the harbor and I told him
Not to leave the ship no matter what.
But here he comes. What's happening?

ACT I

Scene 1

ACANTHIO: (*Puffing and blowing*) Feet, don't fail me now.
     Keep on keeping on, you just gotta save
     The young master. Come on, man,
     Don't quit til quitting time.   100
     Lemme catch my breath a minute here.
     You can be running for your life in this town
     And nobody pays you no attention.
     They just walk on and won't get out of the way.
     They run you right off the sidewalk.

CHARINUS: It's gotta be serious to get him out of slow motion.

ACANTHIO: I better get moving. More time I waste
    The more dangerous things get.

CHARINUS: It's got to be bad news.

ACANTHIO: Lord, I'm not fixing to break any Olympic
    records . . .   110
    The spirit is willing but the flesh is weak as a kitten . . .
    I wonder if Charinus is here . . .
    Knock Knock . . . Open up the door. Where's my master?

CHARINUS: Here I am, Acanthio. In person.

ACANTHIO: (*Still knocking, not seeing him*)
    Talk about lazy, no-account folks!

CHARINUS: What seems to be the problem here?

ACANTHIO: It's a problem all right. For you and for me too.
    Both of us.

CHARINUS: Tell me what's the matter.

ACANTHIO: In a word: the jig is up.   120

CHARINUS: For who?

ACANTHIO: For you.

CHARINUS: Make sense. For once tell me what's going down
    around here.

ACANTHIO: Easy, easy. I got to catch my breath.
    My feet are killing me. My head . . .

CHARINUS: Go soak your head in a chamber pot.

ACANTHIO: I'll give you some chamber music.

CHARINUS: This is the most sensitive slave I ever encountered.

ACANTHIO: Well, what can you expect with an insensitive lout for
    a master?

CHARINUS: Wait a minute. I'm just trying to be helpful.   130
    Like a friend.

ACANTHIO: With friends like that, who needs a master?

CHARINUS: Okay. Let's try again. No pain, no gain.

ACANTHIO: My pain, your gain. I know how it goes.

CHARINUS: Come on. Let's shake hands and start over.

ACANTHIO: Oh, all right . . .

CHARINUS: Now, then. Please and pretty please.
    Why won't you tell me what's wrong?

ACANTHIO: So you can blame me, huh?
    After I ran all the way across town to tell you.   140

CHARINUS: Freedom! I'll make you a free man . . . in a few
    months.

ACANTHIO: Fat chance *that* ever happens!

CHARINUS: Hey, I wouldn't try to fool a cool guy like you.
    It wouldn't work anyway.

ACANTHIO: Keep on talking while I fall asleep on my feet.

CHARINUS: Is this your idea of being helpful?

ACANTHIO: What do you want me to do?

CHARINUS: Good question.

ACANTHIO: Just tell me what you want.

CHARINUS: Okay. I'll tell you . . . 150

ACANTHIO: Don't just stand there. *Say something!*

CHARINUS: Could we maybe hold it down a little?

ACANTHIO: We wouldn't want to wake up the audience.

CHARINUS: Smart-ass!

ACANTHIO: You asked for it.
Are you ready for the latest news from the harbor?

CHARINUS: Speak up, man! What's the story?

ACANTHIO: Grief, misery, and woe. The baddest bad news you
can think of.

CHARINUS: Lord have mercy on me. I'm a ruined man.

ACANTHIO: Oh, I wouldn't say that. You're more like . . . 160

CHARINUS: Loser of the week. Bum of the month.

ACANTHIO: You said it, I didn't.

CHARINUS: Okay. Let's start back at the top. What's my problem?

ACANTHIO: It's the absolute worst, Boss. You should quit asking.

CHARINUS: Enough already!

ACANTHIO: Easy, easy.
  I need to work out some minor details before I end up getting
  whipped.

CHARINUS: Unless you speak up and spit it out right now
  I'll kick your bony ass around the block.

ACANTHIO: (*To audience*) Isn't he something else?   170
  Slick and smooth as silk.

CHARINUS: Okay. I take it all back.
  I beg you, man to man, friend to friend.

ACANTHIO: Master to slave.

CHARINUS: Yeah, but which is which?

ACANTHIO: You tell me.

CHARINUS: No, you tell *me*. Has my ship sunk?

ACANTHIO: No problem. Your boat is floating fine and dandy.

CHARINUS: How about the tackle?

ACANTHIO: All shipshape.   180

CHARINUS: Then why don't you share with us what made you
  come tearing after me?

ACANTHIO: I can't get a word in edgewise.

CHARINUS: I'll shut up. Right now.

ACANTHIO: If he's so eager to get bad news, just imagine
  how he would go for the good.

CHARINUS: Come on. Tell me. I'm ready.

ACANTHIO: Well, since you are so impatient, your father . . .

CHARINUS: What about him?

ACANTHIO: And your new love.

CHARINUS: What about her?   190

ACANTHIO: He saw her.

CHARINUS: How could he do that?

ACANTHIO: With his own eyes.

CHARINUS: He really saw her?

ACANTHIO: Just the same as I see you.

CHARINUS: Where did he see her?

ACANTHIO: On board the boat. He stood next to her
    and he talked to her, too.

CHARINUS: Wait a minute. Listen.
    Why didn't you hustle her away out of sight?   200

ACANTHIO: Everybody was busy on board getting things
    shipshape.
    And along comes your father in his dinghy
    and nobody noticed him til he was already on board.

CHARINUS: O tempestuous and treacherous sea! You wrecked me
    after
    I was safe on shore.
    (To ACANTHIO)
    Go on. What happened next?

ACANTHIO: As soon as he saw the girl he asked her whom she belonged to.

CHARINUS: What did she say?

ACANTHIO: I interrupted and told him you brought her to be your mother's maid.

CHARINUS: Did he believe that?   210

ACANTHIO: Sure. But then the old boy started groping.

CHARINUS: Her?

ACANTHIO: Not me, babe. He wasn't patting my ass.

CHARINUS: Oh Lord, what am I going to do?

ACANTHIO: Don't ask me.

CHARINUS: My father will never believe me if I say I got the girl for my mother. He'll never believe I bought such a beauty for somebody else.

ACANTHIO: Calm down, Boss. He already believed me.

CHARINUS: Not for long. He'll figure it out.   220

ACANTHIO: Maybe so, maybe not. I kind of doubt it.

CHARINUS: He wasn't even suspicious that she was my mistress?

ACANTHIO: I told him the story and he bought the whole nine yards.

CHARINUS: That's what *you* think.

ACANTHIO: That's what I think.

CHARINUS: And here I am pissing and moaning when I ought to
  be back at the ship. Come on.

ACANTHIO: Wait a minute, Boss. You're going to run right smack
  into your old man. He'll see how nervous and upset you are
  and will figure out what's going on.   230

CHARINUS: I'll go the other way. Do you think he's left the harbor
  yet?

ACANTHIO: Why do you think I ran all that way? Just so he
  wouldn't catch you.

CHARINUS: Way to go. Come on . . .

ACT II

Scene 1

(*Enter* DEMIPHO)

DEMIPHO: The gods play games with us in amazing ways.
  And one of those ways is by inflicting amazing dreams.
  Take me, for example. Only last night
  I tossed and turned, caught in a net of dreams.
  Seems like I had bought myself a beautiful goat.
  Next, so she wouldn't be hurt by another she-goat,   240
  I already had at home, I hired (believe it or not)
  A monkey to look after her.
  Pretty soon here comes aforesaid Mr. Monkey,
  Cussing and fuming and claiming that my goat
  Had ruined his life by eating up his wife's dowry.
  What would a good-looking goat do with a monkey's dowry?
  I ask you! Anyway, this crazy, sassy monkey

Said that unless I took my goat back right away,
He would lead her to my house and leave her with my wife.
So I felt simply terrible, trying to do the right thing   250
For my pretty little she-goat.
And next comes a smart-ass kid to report
He had (pardon the expression) kidnapped my goat
From the monkey. And he laughed a goat laugh
In my face. I woke up crying real tears.
Maybe Doctor Freud can figure it all out.
Any dream merchant can tell you
Goats and monkeys are symbols of lust.
But that doesn't apply to a solid citizen like me.
Anyway, I know now what some of it signifies.   260
This morning I went down to the harbor
To do some business, and I suddenly saw
The boat that brought my boy back from Rhodes.
So I jumped in a rowboat and went out to the ship,
Where, lo and behold, I saw a beautiful girl,
The girl my son brought back to be his mother's maid.
One look and I fell, ass over teakettle, in love.
Lord knows, I've been in love a few times before,
But never like this, just *blap!* and *blooey!*
I lost my heart and it looks like I lost my mind.   270
So I interpret my dream as a forewarning.
But what does that fucking monkey mean?
Look out! Here comes my neighbor out of his house.

Scene 2

(*Enter* LYSIMACHUS *and a* SLAVE)

LYSIMACHUS: Be sure and castrate that old goat who's so much
    trouble.

DEMIPHO: (*Aside*) Don't let my wife hear this and get any good
    ideas!

LYSIMACHUS: So, off to the farm and take care of business there.
　　And tell my wife not to expect me, I'll be
　　Busy in the city all day. Be sure to tell her.

SLAVE: Yes, sir. Anything else, sir?

LYSIMACHUS: That's it. Carry on.   280

(SLAVE *salutes and exits*)

DEMIPHO: Morning, neighbor.

LYSIMACHUS: Top of the morning, Demipho. How are you doing?

DEMIPHO: About as bad as can be.
　　Miserable, in fact.

LYSIMACHUS: What's wrong?

DEMIPHO: I'd like to tell you,
　　But you seem awfully busy.

LYSIMACHUS: Never too busy not to help an old friend.

DEMIPHO: I know. You are a truly generous man.

LYSIMACHUS: Well . . . ?   290

DEMIPHO: How do I look?

LYSIMACHUS: Not too bad for an old guy.
　　How old are you, anyway?

DEMIPHO: I'm only a boy, Lysimachus,
　　A seven-year-old boy.

LYSIMACHUS: Sounds like you've got a serious problem there.

DEMIPHO: It's the truth.
I'm not fooling around.

LYSIMACHUS: Oh, I get you.
Once you are really over the hill,   300
Once senility sets in,
You fall into a second childhood.

DEMIPHO: I never felt better in my whole life.

LYSIMACHUS: That's wonderful. I am glad to hear it.

DEMIPHO: I mean it.
I can see things clearer than ever before.

LYSIMACHUS: Excellent!

DEMIPHO: Of course, I can see all kinds of things
I'm not supposed to.

LYSIMACHUS: Like what kind of things?   310

DEMIPHO: Like, you know . . . naughty things.

LYSIMACHUS: That's not so good.

DEMIPHO: This is kind of off the record.

LYSIMACHUS: (*Aside*) More like kind of off the wall.

DEMIPHO: Lysimachus, I just started school today.

LYSIMACHUS: Oh yeah? So how's it going?

DEMIPHO: I already know five letters of the alphabet.

LYSIMACHUS: Five already?

DEMIPHO: *I- L - O - V - E.*

LYSIMACHUS: That's five, all right,   320
  You poor old bastard.

DEMIPHO: Old? Maybe.
  Poor? Not yet.
  I'm rich in love.

LYSIMACHUS: Enough already!
  Quit joking around.

DEMIPHO: Cut off my head if you think I'm kidding.
  Listen. You can cut off my finger or my ear or my nose.
  Cut off anything but the old you-know-what
  And I'll prove my love by not making a sound.   330

LYSIMACHUS: *(To audience)* Look at that silly old fart.
  You could put a frame around him
  And hang him on a museum wall
  As "The Foolish Lover."

DEMIPHO: You are probably going to speak harshly to me.

LYSIMACHUS: Why would I do something like that?

DEMIPHO: I can live without your lectures.
  I can name plenty of people who have done the same thing.
  Loving is human and so is desire . . .

LYSIMACHUS: You're the one who's making a lecture.   340

DEMIPHO: Well, I know what you are thinking.

LYSIMACHUS: You do?

DEMIPHO: You think a lot less of me.

LYSIMACHUS: God forbid I should think any less of you.

DEMIPHO: Promise me you never will.

LYSIMACHUS: Done. It's a done deal.

DEMIPHO: Are you sure about that?

LYSIMACHUS: Till death us do part
(*To audience*)
He's lost his marbles on the "Love Boat."
(*To* DEMIPHO)
Anything else I can do for you?   350

DEMIPHO: So long, good buddy.

LYSIMACHUS: I've got to hurry on down to the harbor.
See you around, neighbor.
Have a good day.

(*He exits*)

DEMIPHO: You, too. Have a good one.
Matter of fact, I've got business at the harbor, too.
But look. There's my son coming.
I've got to figure out a way
To con him into selling me that girl.
The main thing is to keep him from guessing   360
I've got the hots for her.

Scene 3

(DEMIPHO *hides. Enter* CHARINUS)

CHARINUS: If anybody alive is more miserable than I am,
I don't want to know about it.

Nobody could possibly have so many things
Turn out to be a bummer, turning against him.
I'm talking facts, not fancy here.
It is a fact that no matter what I do,
No matter how carefully I plan things,
Everything I care about goes to pot.
So I finally find the absolute girl of my dreams   370
And pay the price and bring her home
Planning to keep her a secret from my old man.
And first day home he sees her and finds out.
Meanwhile I haven't got the slightest idea
What to tell him when he asks me all about it.
My mind has turned into a parliament of fools,
All yelling at the same time.
The only plan on the table comes from my sassy slave.
And it won't work. My father will never
Believe I brought her to be a maid for Mother.   380
Suppose I tell him the truth? Then what?
Never mind what he'll do about me.
Worst case scenario is he grabs the girl
And sells her off to the highest bidder
At home or abroad. Bottom line
Is all the old man cares about.
So this is how it is to be a lover.
I'd rather be a shit-kicker on the family farm.
He already threw me out of the house
And sent me off on a business trip.   390
That's how I got into this whole thing
In the first place. It's no fun
When all I'm getting is aggravation.
It didn't do any good to hide her.
The old man's like a fly on the wall.
He doesn't miss a thing, no secret,
Nothing sacred or profane is safe from him.

DEMIPHO: (*Aside*) My boy seems to be a little twitchy.
    Wonder what could be bothering him?

CHARINUS: Oh shit!   400
    Here's my old man.
    Guess I better talk to him.
    Hi, Dad. How are they hanging?

DEMIPHO: You're looking a little peaked, my lad.

CHARINUS: Oh I'm fine, Dad.
    Fit as a fiddle . . .

DEMIPHO: Well, I should hope so.
    But you don't look so hot.
    Anything hurting?

CHARINUS: Well . . . I just feel a little fragile.   410
    I had trouble sleeping last night.

DEMIPHO: First night ashore.
    It's always that way.

CHARINUS: Maybe that's it.

DEMIPHO: Go home and go to bed.

CHARINUS: I can't. I'm in the big middle
    Of a lot of ongoing business.

DEMIPHO: Nothing that won't wait.
    Take care of it all tomorrow.

CHARINUS: But, Father, you always say   420
    Business comes first and foremost.

DEMIPHO: Whatever you think best
    Is fine by me.

CHARINUS: If he really meant that,
    I'd be home free.

DEMIPHO: (*To audience*) What do you suppose he's up to?
　　Walking around here having a debate
　　With himself? He can't know
　　About my feelings for the girl
　　Because I haven't even done anything yet.   430

CHARINUS: (*Also*) One thing for sure, he doesn't know
　　She's all mine, because if he did
　　He would be talking out of
　　The other side of his mouth.

DEMIPHO: (*Continues*) Why not ask him directly about the girl?

CHARINUS: (*Likewise*) Why not get out of here
　　While the getting is good?
　　(*To* DEMIPHO)
　　Well, sir, time for me to punch in
　　The timeclock. Idle hands are the devil's workplace.

DEMIPHO: Wait a minute!   440
　　There are a couple of minor things
　　I want to ask you about.

CHARINUS: Your wish is my command,
　　As they say.

DEMIPHO: Have you . . . been feeling well most of the time?

CHARINUS: Yes, sir. I mean
　　I was okay until we returned to port.

DEMIPHO: Post-traumatic voyage syndrome.
　　It won't last long.

CHARINUS: That's good.   450

DEMIPHO: Oh, by the way.
    Is it true you brought a new maid
    For your mother from Rhodes?

CHARINUS: Yes, sir.

DEMIPHO: What's your opinion of her?

CHARINUS: She's okay. Not bad . . .

DEMIPHO: How about her character?

CHARINUS: A fine girl. Never saw one better.

DEMIPHO: I would say exactly the same thing.

CHARINUS: Then you've seen her already?   460

DEMIPHO: I saw her, all right.
    Trouble is she won't do for us.

CHARINUS: Why not? What's wrong with her?

DEMIPHO: Nothing wrong, really.
    She just won't fit in.
    What we need is a real maid,
    Someone to do the cleaning and cooking,
    Someone who can do the heavy work.
    She's too pretty and delicate.

CHARINUS: You're right, sir.   470
    And that's why I bought her—
    To be a personal present for Mother.

DEMIPHO: Don't do it, son.
    Don't even say you bought her.

CHARINUS: (Aside) The gods are on my side!

DEMIPHO: (*Ditto*) Got the kid on the run!
   (*To* CHARINUS)
   Point is, son,
   She isn't the right kind of maid
   For your mother.

CHARINUS: Why not? 480

DEMIPHO: Picture it this way.
   The maid goes out on an errand
   And all the men give her the eye.
   They wink and whistle and pat and pinch.
   And pretty soon they're writing graffiti
   On my wall and doors and singing
   Love songs all night long.
   Next thing authorities think
   Our home is a whorehouse.

CHARINUS: By God, sir, 490
   I believe you are right.
   What can we do about it?

DEMIPHO: First, I'll go buy some big wench,
   Plain as a picket fence, for your mother.
   An Egyptian or some other kind of towelhead
   Who can work her ass off
   And never bring disgrace to our door.

CHARINUS: How about returning the girl
   To the man I bought her from?

DEMIPHO: Forget it! 500
   Out of the question.

CHARINUS: He said he would take her back
   If everything didn't work out.

DEMIPHO: No need for anything drastic.
   These things lead to misunderstandings
   And then to long-winded disputes.
   No, I would rather take a loss on the deal
   Than face a disgrace.
   Anyway, I am sure I can sell
   Her for top dollar.   510

CHARINUS: Please, you must not . . .

DEMIPHO: Must not what?

CHARINUS: Sell her for less than I paid.

DEMIPHO: No problem.
   I've already got an old man
   Looking for a girl just like that.

CHARINUS: And I know a young man
   Who wants to buy that kind of girl.

DEMIPHO: I believe my party
   Would pay eighty pounds for her.   520

CHARINUS: My client already offered
   A hundred and eight.

DEMIPHO: My guy says go for it.
   Go for a hundred and twenty.

CHARINUS: How?

DEMIPHO: How what?

CHARINUS: How does he say that?

DEMIPHO: Mental telepathy.
   Now he's talking one twenty-four.

CHARINUS: My client bids one twenty-eight.   530

DEMIPHO: How did he make that bid?

CHARINUS: Same way yours did.

DEMIPHO: He can't have her.

CHARINUS: It's good money.

DEMIPHO: I don't care. She goes
   To my man.

CHARINUS: My man bid more.

DEMIPHO: Hey, stop while you are ahead!
   You'll make a huge profit.
   My old man is out of his head   540
   With love and lust for her.

CHARINUS: But the young man I represent
   Is totally obsessed, dying of the hots.

DEMIPHO: My dirty old man is even more so.

CHARINUS: No old coot could be crazier in love than my client.

DEMIPHO: Shut up a minute
   And let me figure this out.

CHARINUS: Daddy?

DEMIPHO: Unh-huh.

CHARINUS: I don't have the legal rights to her.   550

DEMIPHO: No problem.
   He'll take her anyway.

CHARINUS: But it's against the law
  To sell her.

DEMIPHO: There's always a way.

CHARINUS: One other thing.
  I've got a partner,
  And I don't know if he wants to sell her.

DEMIPHO: He wants to. Take my word for it.

CHARINUS: How can you know that?   560

DEMIPHO and CHARINUS: Mental telepathy . . .

DEMIPHO: Let me get this straight.
  Your partner won't complain if your client buys her.
  Right? But he won't sell her to me
  For my client. That's a crock.
  Nobody can have her except my man.

CHARINUS: Is that final?

DEMIPHO: What else?
  I'm going straight to the ship
  And sell her myself.   570

CHARINUS: I better come with you.

DEMIPHO: You better not.

CHARINUS: I'm not happy about this.

DEMIPHO: Don't you have some business to take care of?

CHARINUS: I did.
  But all this argument with you . . .

DEMIPHO: So? Put the blame on me.
  Carry on and stay away from the harbor.

CHARINUS: Yes, sir.

DEMIPHO: (*Aside*) The way I see it is   580
  I'll get my friend Lysimachus
  To buy the girl on my behalf.
  Nobody will be the wiser.

                    Scene 4

CHARINUS: O Death, come close my eyes!
  Story is the Bacchantes tore Pentheus to pieces.
  The way I feel, I can believe it.
  I'd be a lot better off dead.
  I think I'll go buy some deadly poison.
  And see if that doesn't make me feel better.

(*Enter* EUTYCHUS)

EUTYCHUS: Hey wait.   590
  Hold it, Charinus.

CHARINUS: Who calls my name?

EUTYCHUS: *C'est moi!*
  Your pal, your buddy, your neighbor.

CHARINUS: You won't believe what's happening to me.

EUTYCHUS: I know all about it.
  I've been eavesdropping the whole time.

CHARINUS: You have?

EUTYCHUS: Your old man
    Wants to sell your new mistress.   600

CHARINUS: How do you know she's my mistress?

EUTYCHUS: You told me all about her yesterday.

CHARINUS: I did?
    How come I can't remember it?

EUTYCHUS: No big deal.
    Memory was never your strong suit.

CHARINUS: Well, I need your advice and counsel now.

EUTYCHUS: Yes?

CHARINUS: In your opinion
    What's the best way to commit suicide?   610
    What should I do?

EUTYCHUS: Shut the fuck up and forget it.

CHARINUS: Thanks a lot.

EUTYCHUS: How about it?
    Want me to run a number on your father?

CHARINUS: Go for it!

EUTYCHUS: Want me to head on down to the harbor
    And get the girl for top price?

CHARINUS: Offer her weight in gold.

EUTYCHUS: Sure   620
    But where's the gold?

CHARINUS: I shall beg Achilles
    For the gold of ransomed Hector.

EUTYCHUS: Get serious.
    You want me to buy her
    No matter how much he offers?

CHARINUS: Top his best offer
    By a hundred pounds.

EUTYCHUS: And then when your old man
    Comes for payment 630
    Where will you get the money?

CHARINUS: I don't know.
    How should I know?
    I'll figure out something or other.

EUTYCHUS: Swell. I'll tell him
    He can definitely count on something or other
    No matter what.

CHARINUS: Shut up while I'm thinking.

EUTYCHUS: Think of something else.

CHARINUS: No. Let's do it my way. 640

EUTYCHUS: Well, ciao, baby.
    I'm off to the harbor.

CHARINUS: Hurry! I'll be half-crazy
    Until you get back.

EUTYCHUS: Stay cool. I'll take care of everything.
    Wait for me at my place.

CHARINUS: Come back as quick as you can.

ACT III

Scene 1

LYSIMACHUS: I went and did it for my friend.
  I purchased this product
  just as he asked me to.   650
  Come along now, honey, you're all mine.
  And please don't cry your eyes out.
  Really you ought to be laughing instead.

PASICOMPSA: Tell me something, please, old man.

LYSIMACHUS: Go ahead, ask me anything.

PASICOMPSA: Why did you buy me?

LYSIMACHUS: Why did I buy you?
  Mainly to do whatever I want
  Just as I want to do the right thing for you.

PASICOMPSA: That's really sweet.   660
  I'll do my very best to please you.

LYSIMACHUS: You'll find I'm a very undemanding master.

PASICOMPSA: That's good because there are
  Lots of things I don't know how
  To do: toting and fetching,
  Child care and animal husbandry.

LYSIMACHUS: Not to worry. Just be good
  And you'll have a really good time.

PASICOMPSA: Lordy me, I guess I'm doomed.

LYSIMACHUS: Say what?

PASICOMPSA: Where I grew up
Only bad girls can have a really good time.

LYSIMACHUS: Meaning there's no
such thing as a good girl.

PASICOMPSA: Oh, I would never say that.
I try not to belabor the obvious.

LYSIMACHUS: It's worth the price
Just to listen to her talk.
May I ask you something else?

PASICOMPSA: You ask and I'll answer.   680

LYSIMACHUS: . . . Uh
Tell me . . . what shall I call you?

PASICOMPSA: Pasicompsa, sir.
It means "completely charming."

LYSIMACHUS: You can say that again.
Okay, Ms. Pasicompsa,
if you had to, could you do some delicate weaving?

PASICOMPSA: Sure.

LYSIMACHUS: And if you can do delicate work,
Why ordinary weaving will be easy.   690

PASICOMPSA: When it comes to weaving,
I am *numera una*.

LYSIMACHUS: Well, it all adds up.
You are a good girl, talented too,

And obviously you know how to do
The right thing when the time comes.

PASICOMPSA: You better believe it.
Nobody ever complains about my work.

LYSIMACHUS: I'm going to give you a sheep,
A nice one, sixty years old,   700
To have and to hold for your own.

PASICOMPSA: What will I do
With such an antique animal?

LYSIMACHUS: Don't knock it til you've tried it.
This old timer comes from the finest
Greek stock. Plenty good wooly wooly.

PASICOMPSA: I will always be deeply and sincerely
Grateful for anything I can get.

LYSIMACHUS: No point in fooling around
Anymore. I have to admit   710
You don't actually belong to me.

PASICOMPSA: Lordy me, who owns me then?

LYSIMACHUS: I bought you, myself,
But I did so in behalf
Of your own master.

PASICOMPSA: (*Aside*) Wow! I am home free
If he keeps his word to me.

LYSIMACHUS: Don't be sad. He'll set you free.
He's mad for you. And today
Is the first time he ever even saw you.   720

PASICOMPSA: Truth is, sir, we have been
　Together for two years now.

LYSIMACHUS: Wait a minute!
　You say you've known him for two years?

PASICOMPSA: Sure. And we made a solemn commitment
　Not to be unfaithful or fool around
　With anybody else in the world.

LYSIMACHUS: You mean to tell me he can't
　Even make love to his own wife?

PASICOMPSA: What wife?   730
　He isn't married
　And isn't going to be, either.

LYSIMACHUS: (*Aside*) He's a world-class liar.
　That's for sure.
　Well, come with me, please.
　Since my wife has gone to the country,
　He asked me to look after you.

Scene 2

DEMIPHO: The time has come to let it all hang out.
　I have bought myself a wonderful young mistress.
　And neither my wife nor my son   740
　Knows or suspects the first thing about it.
　It's high time to be good to myself
　For a change. Life's too short now
　For anything but wine and song . . .
　And love, *toujours l'amour.*
　Actually, it's completely appropriate
　For somebody my age to have a final fling.
　When a man is young and energetic,

It's the right time to settle down
And try to make his fortune.   750
Old age, that's the time to take it easy
And indulge in love's fun and games.
Each new day is an unearned dividend.
From now on I plan to put my money
Where my mouth is. Meanwhile,
However, I better check in at home
Where my wife has been waiting for me.
Lord, that woman will drive me
To an early death with all her kvetching.
Nevertheless I firmly intend . . .   760
On second thought I better see my neighbor
I need him to rent a place for me,
Some place my girl can live in.
Here he comes now . . .

Scene 3

LYSIMACHUS: As soon as I find him, I'll bring him to you.

DEMIPHO: (*Aside*) He's talking about little old me.

LYSIMACHUS: Demipho, what's happening, man?

DEMIPHO: Is that girl safe in your house?

LYSIMACHUS: What do you think?

DEMIPHO: Maybe I could just sneak a peek.   770

LYSIMACHUS: Take it easy. Wait a minute.

DEMIPHO: What shall I do?

LYSIMACHUS: You better think it over first.

DEMIPHO: What's to think about?
  I think I should go straight inside.

LYSIMACHUS: You do, huh? You old ram?
  Straight inside . . .

DEMIPHO: What else can you think of?

LYSIMACHUS: Listen up. Pay attention now.   780
  If you go in there now,
  Next thing you'll be hugging and kissing
  And messing around . . .

DEMIPHO: You are a mind reader.
  You know exactly what I plan to do.

LYSIMACHUS: And I know you'll do the wrong thing.

DEMIPHO: Look, when a man is passionately in love—
  Can't he even, you know?

LYSIMACHUS: You dirty old man!
  You foul-mouthed old goat,
  Do you want to kiss that sweet thing   790
  On an empty stomach
  And turn her stomach against you?

DEMIPHO: Hey, I'll take care of it.
  If you think it's a good idea,
  Let's get a cook to make dinner
  For us here at your house this evening.

LYSIMACHUS: Now you are cooking with butane.
  Now you sound about half-smart.

DEMIPHO: What are we doing standing here?
  Let's go to the market   800
  And make a nice day of it.

LYSIMACHUS: I'm with you, neighbor.
And, take my advice, you better
Find a place for her to stay.
She can't stay here tomorrow
When my wife gets back from the country.

Scene 4

CHARINUS: Stink pot! Dumb bunny! Spinach!
I am completely miserable everywhere.
If I'm at home, all my thoughts
Are elsewhere. When I am elsewhere,   810
Every thought is headed for home.
I am burning alive in the flames of love.
If it weren't for my copious tears,
My head would quickly go up in smoke.
All that I have is hope. My real life
Is long gone and may not even come back.
If my father does what he said he would,
It's bye-bye life, have a good day.
If my buddy comes through as he promised,
Then it's hello happiness and *la dolce vita*.   820
But even if Eutychus was crippled
With gout he'd be back from the harbor by now.
But wait a minute. Here comes somebody,
a man running this way. I'll go meet him.
Uh-oh, he's stopped. Now he's moving
In slow motion. It looks like bad news
For the good guys. Hey, Eutychus . . .

EUTYCHUS: Oh, there you are, Charinus.

CHARINUS: Don't wait to catch your breath.
Give me the news. Am I here   830
Or already counted among the dead?

EUTYCHUS: Neither one, actually.

CHARINUS: Then I am home free.
  He bought the broad and fooled my old man.
  There's nobody alive can do a deal like him.
  So tell me please, sir,
  If I'm neither here nor there
  Where I am?

EUTYCHUS: Actually, nowhere.

CHARINUS: Keep talking like that and you'll bore me to
    death.   840
  Just the news, please, good and bad.

EUTYCHUS: First, our clever plan is *kaput*.

CHARINUS: Tell me something I don't already know.

EUTYCHUS: They have taken the chick away from you.

CHARINUS: Stop before you commit a crime.

EUTYCHUS: What do you mean?

CHARINUS: I'm your buddy and your pal
  And nevertheless your news is killing me.

EUTYCHUS: Lord have mercy!

CHARINUS: It's like a knife at my throat.   850
  Any minute you'll cut me ear to ear.

EUTYCHUS: Try to indulge in more positive thinking.

CHARINUS: Tell me the rest.
  Who bought my beautiful slave girl?

EUTYCHUS: Beats me.
   They auctioned her off before I even got there.

CHARINUS: First you dump misery all over my head.
   And now you are fixing to torture me, too.

EUTYCHUS: What on earth have I done?

CHARINUS: You've wrecked my life   860
   And lowered my self-esteem to zero.

EUTYCHUS: God knows it isn't my fault.

CHARINUS: That's just like you.
   Calling on God as a witness,
   And he's not even here.
   Why should I believe anything you say?

EUTYCHUS: Believe whatever you want to.
   I can only tell you the truth.

CHARINUS: Oh, you're quick enough in conversation,
   But when you go out to do a deal,   870
   You're crippled, deaf and dumb, blind,
   Disabled, handicapped, challenged.
   You said you would fix things with Father
   And I actually believed you.

EUTYCHUS: What else could I do? I ask you.

CHARINUS: What kind of a dumb question is that?
   You could at least have found out something—
   Who the guy is, where he comes from.

EUTYCHUS: They said he's an Athenian.

CHARINUS: Even if you couldn't get his name,   880
   You could at least have found out his address.

EUTYCHUS: Nobody knew.

CHARINUS: Well, you could at least have asked
  Them what he looks like.

EUTYCHUS: Well . . . picture this.
  He's an old guy, gray-headed,
  Knock-kneed, dipper-mouthed, built like a keg,
  And with a lantern jaw and black eyes and big flat feet.

CHARINUS: That's no way to describe somebody.
  What else can you tell me?   890

EUTYCHUS: That's all I know.

CHARINUS: This is too much for the heart.
  I'm going into exile.
  The big question is, where is the best place
  To go. Megara? Eretria? Corinth?
  Crete? Cyprus? Lesbos? Maybe California . . .

EUTYCHUS: So, okay, you run away from love.
  What happens when love catches up with you?
  Will you just keep on moving from place to place?
  Your exile will go on forever   900
  And you'll never have a place to call home.
  I think your slickest move would be
  To go out in the country somewhere
  And just stay there in the deep boonies
  Until you have managed to forget this broad.

CHARINUS: Are you all through?

EUTYCHUS: Yep.

CHARINUS: You have wasted our time and argued in vain.
  I have made up my mind for good and all.
  I will go home now and see my father   910

And mother, and then, without telling anybody,
I'll split for far places.

EUTYCHUS: Wasn't that something else?
Enter running, exit pursued by a bear.
The worst thing is if he really does it,
If he flees the country, everybody will blame
Me. I better do something quick.
I'll hire the town criers, I'll go
To the cops. Anything to find that woman.

ACT IV

Scene 1

DORIPPA: I heard from my husband out at the farm   920
That he didn't want me to go there in the first place.
And now, acting on feminine intuition,
I'm hot on the trail of the old scamp.
But where is my Syra?
Here she comes now, Miss Slowmotion, 35 B.C.
Can't you move any faster than that?

SYRA: Lordy, Miz Dorippa, I surely can't
Carry this heavy load on my back.

DORIPPA: What load? I don't see any load.

SYRA: I'm talking about the weight of eighty-four years,   930
Plus the wear and tear of being all hot and sweaty,
Not to mention the whole slavery thing.
It's heavy ma'am.

DORIPPA: Let me have something to make
　　An offering here at our neighbor's altar.
　　Just let me have that laurel branch
　　And you can go ahead inside.

SYRA: Yassum.

DORIPPA: O Lord Apollo, I pray thee to vouchsafe
　　Thy favor and blessing, health and safety,   940
　　To our whole family. And may you please
　　Look on my son with special favor.

SYRA: Help! Murder! Police!
　　Lord have mercy!

DORIPPA: Syra, have you lost your mind?
　　What are you carrying on about?

SYRA: Lordy, Miz Dorippa, you poor thing!

DORIPPA: What on earth are you screeching about?

SYRA: There's a strange woman in our house.

DORIPPA: What? A woman?   950

SYRA: A jezebel in the flesh
　　If I ever saw one.

DORIPPA: If you are joking . . . !

SYRA: You were right as can be to come home from the farm.
　　I mean, it's perfectly clear that that woman is
　　Your husband's new girlfriend.

DORIPPA: I'm afraid you're right.

SYRA: Come with me and I'll show you
  The lay of the land.

DORIPPA: I'm coming as fast as I can.   960

Scene 2

LYSIMACHUS: Trouble enough that Demipho is in love,
  But does he have to carry on
  Like the last of the bigtime spenders?
  If we had a dinner party for a dozen
  We could never eat up everything he bought.
  And he's yelling at the cooks like a football coach.
  I hired a cook, too,
  But he still hasn't showed.
  Wait! Who's that coming out
  Of our house?

Scene 3

DORIPPA: I am the saddest, most miserable
  Woman in the world, married to such a slob!
  This is the man I gave a dowry
  Of two thousand pounds.
  What did I get? Insults and embarrassment.

LYSIMACHUS: Holy Smoke! Is my ass in the sling
  Or what? Here she is, full throttle,
  Back from the farm. I reckon
  She's already seen my sweety.
  But I can't quite make out   980
  What she's saying. I better move closer.

DORIPPA: Lord, help me!

LYSIMACHUS: No, Lord, better help *me!*
   She has seen that girl, that's for sure.

DORIPPA: This is exactly why I didn't want to go out to the farm
   In the first place.

LYSIMACHUS: My best move is to try to brazen it out.
   Hi there, honey, how are things
   Down on the farm?
   Did you get tired of hanging out with hicks?   990

DORIPPA: Some of my best friends are hicks.
   City folk could learn some manners from them.

LYSIMACHUS: That's an interesting idea.
   Tell me all about it.

DORIPPA: Quit trying to fool me.
   Whose woman is that slut in our house?

LYSIMACHUS: Woman? Oh, you saw her, then?

DORIPPA: That I did.

LYSIMACHUS: And now you are wondering
   Whom she belongs to.   1000

DORIPPA: Oh, I'll find out, all right.

LYSIMACHUS: You just want me to tell you . . .
   I don't know what to say.

DORIPPA: Cat got your tongue?

LYSIMACHUS: You could put it that way.

DORIPPA: Well, speak up. Speak up.

LYSIMACHUS: Give me half a chance.

DORIPPA: You have just about run out of chances.

LYSIMACHUS: You keep after me
Like I was guilty.   1010

DORIPPA: Not you. You wouldn't be
Guilty of anything at all.
Would you?

LYSIMACHUS: You have such confidence
In your good judgment.

DORIPPA: Go ahead. Tell me.

LYSIMACHUS: Okay. I will.

DORIPPA: Say it as it should be said.

LYSIMACHUS: Certainly . . . Do you want to know
Her right name, too?   1020

DORIPPA: Quit stalling. I've got the goods
On you this time.

LYSIMACHUS: Now wait. The whole thing is
That girl.

DORIPPA: What girl?

LYSIMACHUS: You know, the girl . . .

DORIPPA: Whose girl?

LYSIMACHUS: It's all pretty complicated.

DORIPPA: So you don't know who she is?

LYSIMACHUS: Sure I know. It's business   1030
   I've been appointed advocate in her case.

DORIPPA: Oh, I see.
   And now you're having a conference with her.

LYSIMACHUS: I didn't say that.
   I'm just acting as a temporary trustee,
   A guardian, so to speak.

DORIPPA: Some trusty trustee!
   Oh, I've got the message all right.

LYSIMACHUS: You've got it all wrong, believe me.

DORIPPA: Don't defend yourself before you know   1040
   What the charges are.

LYSIMACHUS: Enough already.
   I know when I'm whipped.

Scene 4

COOK: Keep moving, you guys.
   We have to hurry and fix dinner
   For the horny old fart.
   He won't eat much, anyway.
   He'll be too busy with the food of love
   To eat my cooking. And we'll take home
   A whole kennel of doggie bags.   1050
   This way, boys.
   Uh-oh, there's the old guy now.

LYSIMACHUS: Oh shit! Here comes the cook.

COOK: Here we are, sir, right on time.

LYSIMACHUS: Beat it, will you?

COOK: What? Get out?

LYSIMACHUS: Yeah.

COOK: Get out?

LYSIMACHUS: Get outta here!

COOK: You're not going to have dinner? 1060

LYSIMACHUS: We're not hungry right now.

COOK: But, sir . . .

DORIPPA: Was all this stuff ordered by
Your clients?

COOK: This must be your lady friend,
The one you told me you are mad for.

LYSIMACHUS: Watch your language.

COOK: Not bad . . .
Got a nice build on her.
A little long in the tooth, but . . . 1070

LYSIMACHUS: Will you please just get the hell out of here.

COOK: I bet she's good company
Between the sheets.

LYSIMACHUS: Hey, look. I am not
The same man who hired you.

COOK: Don't try that one.
You're the same guy, all right.

LYSIMACHUS: Lord, help me.

COOK: You're the one whose wife is in the boonies.
I remember you said she's mean as a snake.   1080

LYSIMACHUS: Who me?
I said something like that?

COOK: That's what you said.
My wife is mean as a snake.

LYSIMACHUS: Dorippa, my dear.
I swear by all that's holy,
I never said anything like that.

DORIPPA: Why deny it?
It's perfectly clear you hate me.

LYSIMACHUS: I absolutely and categorically deny   1090
Any such thing!

COOK: He's right, ma'am.
He never said he hated you.
He said he hated his old wife
That he sent out to the country.

LYSIMACHUS: This lovely lady is my wife.

COOK: Oh, I get it now.
You are afraid of her, right?

LYSIMACHUS: Why not?
She's the one love of my life.   1100

COOK: You want to pay me now or later?

LYSIMACHUS: Come tomorrow. Just go.

DORIPPA: I think I'm going to cry.

LYSIMACHUS: I am the living, breathing proof
  Of the old proverb:
  "Bad neighbors bring bad luck."

COOK: Come on, guys, let's go.
  Sorry, sir, if anything bad has happened,
  It's not my fault.

LYSIMACHUS: Oh no, you've been a wonderful help.   1110

COOK: Oh, I get it now.
  I see what you want.
  You want me to get out of here.

LYSIMACHUS: You could say that. Yes.

COOK: Cross my palm with a little silver
  And I'll be ancient history.

LYSIMACHUS: You've got a done deal.

COOK: Fine, sir.
  Now if you'll just wait a minute   1120
  While my men set down their baskets . . .

LYSIMACHUS: Won't you please just disappear?

COOK: Set everything down here, boys.
  We'll come back for things tomorrow.
  Thanks a lot, sir.
  Have a nice day.

LYSIMACHUS: Maybe you are a little surprised
  To run into the cook like this.
  I can explain everything . . .

DORIPPA: Nothing about you surprises me anymore.   1130
   And I have no intention of living like this.
   Mud sluts living in luxury in my own house!
   Syra? Go get my father
   To come here at once.

SYRA: Yassum.

LYSIMACHUS: Now, wait a minute, dear.
   You don't understand all this.
   I'm ready to take a solemn oath.
   Oh Lord. This is a disaster.
   Now look. She's gone, too.   1140
   Well now, Demipho my neighbor,
   I hope you and your chickie babe
   Catch the clap and go rotten to the core.
   Look how he has stirred up suspicions against me.
   How he has created enemies in my own household.
   And my wife is the most dangerous enemy
   Anyone could imagine.
   I'm going to find Demipho and tell him
   I'll kick the girl's sweet ass out into the street
   If he doesn't come and get her   1150
   Out of my house immediately.
   Darling? My dear?
   Better have all these elegant provisions
   Brought into the house.
   We can use the stuff at dinner.

Scene 5

SYRA: The latest news.
   Naturally her father was not at home.
   He's gone to the country. And I
   Have come back to tell her.

EUTYCHUS: I'm worn out from wandering all over the city   1160
    Looking for that girl. Not a sign
    Or a trace of her anywhere.
    But I guess Mother is home from the farm;
    For there's old Syra in front of our house.
    Syra!

SYRA: Somebody calling me?

EUTYCHUS: Just me . . .

SYRA: Greetings, young Master.

EUTYCHUS: Is Mother back from the country so soon?
    Go ahead. Tell me.   1170

SYRA: It's a good thing for her
    And the whole family that she is.

EUTYCHUS: What's the problem?

SYRA: Your randy old daddy
    Has brought his girlfriend into the house.

EUTYCHUS: Get serious.

SYRA: When we got home from the country,
    Your mother found her in the house.

EUTYCHUS: That's hard to believe.
    Is the woman still there?   1180

SYRA: You better believe it.

EUTYCHUS: Come on. Hurry . . .

Scene 6

SYRA: It's tough, hard cheese to be a woman.
The whole patriarchal system is grossly unfair.
Like he brings a whore home
And his wife finds out.
Then what? Nothing. No sweat for him
But just let a wife go cruising one time
And he's got grounds for divorce.
We need the same rules for both of them.   1190
Every good wife is happy with only her husband.
How come a man wants more than his wife?
Lord save us, if husbands had to pay the price
For fooling around, you can bet your ass
The city would be full of single men.

ACT V

Scene 1

CHARINUS: *Arrivederci*, Athens. So long
Doric and Ionic and Corinthian.
Farewell to my father's house.
Now and forever. I ask the gods
To look after this house and my parents   1200
In this treacherous, abominable city.
I hate the place. Athens
Is a garden of vices where
Truth and falsehood, friends and enemies
Are all the same. Where they took
My honey away from me.
I wouldn't hang around here
If they offered me the throne.

Scene 2

EUTYCHUS: Lord, you have answered all my prayers
    And filled my heart with gladness.   1210
    Could a god be any happier than I am?
    What I was hunting turned out to be at home.
    I have found the six blessed things:
    Life, joy, country, friendship, liberty, and levity.
    And I have banished all the baddies:
    Rage, grief, tears, ruin, exile, and poverty.
    Now, Lord, let me find him soon.

CHARINUS: Well, here I am, all alone and ready.
    I am my own assistant.
    I am horse and rider, officer   1220
    And enlisted man. I'm the redcap
    And the bellhop. I owe it all
    To Cupid who deals out hope
    Then trumps it with the ace—despair.

EUTYCHUS: Wonder where he's at?
    I don't know where to begin.

CHARINUS: I will follow her to the ends of the earth.
    Rivers and mountains and raging oceans
    Will not deter me. Neither heat nor cold,
    Rain, hail, or snow will stay   1230
    This lover from his appointed rounds.
    Bring on hard labor and the toughest times.
    I'll find my true love or I'll die trying!

EUTYCHUS: I hear a voice from somewhere near.

CHARINUS: Gods of the highway, keep me in your care . . .

EUTYCHUS: That sounds like Charinus. Can it be?

CHARINUS: Fellow citizens of Athens,
I bid you my affectionate farewell.

EUTYCHUS: Hold it! Stop, Charinus!

CHARINUS: Who calls me back? 1240

EUTYCHUS: Hope, salvation, the thrill of victory.

CHARINUS: What do you want from me?

EUTYCHUS: Let me come with you.

CHARINUS: Find somebody else. I already have
A full crew of companions.

EUTYCHUS: Who are they?

CHARINUS: Tears and lamentations, grief, misery and woe!

EUTYCHUS: Expel them, kick them off the squad.
Come back here with me.

CHARINUS: Follow me if you want to negotiate. 1250

EUTYCHUS: Stop right now.

CHARINUS: Hey, the sun is going down.
Don't try to stop me now.

EUTYCHUS: Ahoy, the wind has turned around
And blows fair. Come about.
Come home to safe harbor, Charinus.
There are dark clouds on the horizon,
Thunder and lightning. Change course.

CHARINUS: I guess I'll go back. Why not?

EUTYCHUS: Good move.   1260
   Come here, Charinus. Take my hand.

CHARINUS: Take it.

EUTYCHUS: I do . . .
   Where did you think you were going?

CHARINUS: Into exile.

EUTYCHUS: To do what?

CHARINUS: Whatever miserable exiles do with themselves.

EUTYCHUS: Chill out and forget it.
   Put on a happy face. You are
   About to hear what you want to hear,   1270
   Which will make you happy.
   Your sweetheart . . .

CHARINUS: What about her?

EUTYCHUS: I know where she is.

CHARINUS: You do? Are you sure?

EUTYCHUS: She's safe and sound.

CHARINUS: Where is she?

EUTYCHUS: I know.

CHARINUS: I'd like to know, too.

EUTYCHUS: Stay cool.   1280

CHARINUS: How can I? My mind
   Is in total turmoil.

EUTYCHUS: Nevertheless I'll give you a sense of serenity.

CHARINUS: Fuck serenity!
  Where's my honey? You saw her?
  Don't just stand there. Tell me.

EUTYCHUS: She's not far from us right now.

CHARINUS: Show me. Can you see her?

EUTYCHUS: Not now. I did see her, though.

CHARINUS: Let me see her, too!   1290

EUTYCHUS: Well, I will. I will.

CHARINUS: Like when?

EUTYCHUS: Let me explain things, okay?
  My best friend in the whole world
  Is the one who has her for his own.

CHARINUS: Fuck him! Tell me about her.

EUTYCHUS: That's exactly what I'm doing.

CHARINUS: Cut to the chase.
  Where is she right this minute?

EUTYCHUS: In a word . . . in our house.   1300

CHARINUS: O blessed domicile! If you're not kidding.
  But how can I believe you?
  Have you actually seen her,
  Or is your information secondhand?

EUTYCHUS: I myself saw her in person.

CHARINUS: Who brought her to your place?

EUTYCHUS: Not a good question.
  I mean, what difference does it make?

CHARINUS: You are absolutely, positively sure
  That you aren't jiving me?   1310

EUTYCHUS: Man, you are a shameless mess.
  I said she's there and she is.

CHARINUS: Then, good buddy, I owe you one.
  Ask me anything you like—anything!
  Just let me see her again
  And everything will be peachy-keen.
  Let me get out of these traveling clothes . . .

EUTYCHUS: That's a definite improvement,
  If you ask me.

(CHARINUS *stops a passing slave*)

CHARINUS: Hey you, take my stuff   1320
  And give me yours, okay?
  And you, old buddy, stay right here
  Until I check this all out.

EUTYCHUS: You still don't believe me?

CHARINUS: Sure I believe you,
  But I can't help wondering
  Why you don't take me in to see her.

EUTYCHUS: Patience. Don't rush things.

CHARINUS: Why wait around?

EUTYCHUS: Timing is everything. 1330
    Look, it's not the best time.

CHARINUS: Why not? Answer me that.

EUTYCHUS: Let's say it's not convenient for her.

CHARINUS: Convenient?
    Not convenient for the love of my life?
    You've got to be putting me on.
    (*To* AUDIENCE)
    This guy is too much to be believed.
    (*To* SLAVE)
    Give me my stuff back.
    And a little traveling music, please.

EUTYCHUS: Wait just a big-ass minute! 1340

CHARINUS: (*To* SLAVE) Here's your coat, kid.

EUTYCHUS: Listen!
    My mother is in her tantrum mode
    Because Daddy brought your chicky-babe
    Home while Mom was out at the farm.
    Mom thinks the chick is Dad's latest erection.

CHARINUS: Don't forget my belt, boy.

EUTYCHUS: Mother is in there having a fit
    Right now.

CHARINUS: And now I've got my sword . . . 1350

EUTYCHUS: If I take you in there . . .

CHARINUS: Ladies and gents, I'm outta here.
    A pair of footprints and a cloud of dust.

EUTYCHUS: Wait, Charinus. Don't go.

CHARINUS: You can fool most folks
   But not this pig.

EUTYCHUS: I'm not trying to deceive you.

CHARINUS: Me either. I'm long gone.

EUTYCHUS: I won't let you go.

CHARINUS: (*To* SLAVE) Don't just stand there, kid.   1360
   Beat it. Get lost.
   Meanwhile, as the sun sinks slowly in the west . . .

EUTYCHUS: You have lost your marbles?

CHARINUS: Feet, commence moving
   Me toward Cyprus.

EUTYCHUS: Quit talking that way.

CHARINUS: I will never cease hunting for her
   High and low, wherever she may be.

EUTYCHUS: But she's right there in the house.

CHARINUS: Your story is touching   1370
   But it sounds just like a lie.
   And here we are safe and sound
   In jolly Cyprus . . .

EUTYCHUS: Okay, okay. Come with me,
   Old friend, and we'll see the girl.

CHARINUS: I have asked and asked
   But I can't seem to find her anywhere.

EUTYCHUS: I'd rather face my mother's rage
  Than listen to this bull.

CHARINUS: My search will never end   1380
  Now we are landing in Chalcis.
  I run into an old friend from Zacynthus
  At the airport and ask him what he knows.

EUTYCHUS: Drop the subject and come inside.

CHARINUS: He tells me he knows
  That good figs grow in Zacynthus.

EUTYCHUS: He's right about that.

CHARINUS: And he tells me the word on the grapevine
  Is that my honey is still in Athens.
  And so I have returned   1390
  From search and exile.
  Well, hello, Eutychus, old pal,
  How are they hanging? Know anything
  About my parents? Are they well?
  How kind of you to invite me to your lovely home.
  I come to yours, you come to mine.
  That's the socially correct thing to do.

EUTYCHUS: My poor friend is mad as an otter.

CHARINUS: Hatter! The expression is mad as a hatter.

EUTYCHUS: Just come along with me.   1400

CHARINUS: Here I come, laughing and scratching.

EUTYCHUS: Take it easy. You're walking
  On my feet. Listen . . .

CHARINUS: I've listened too long already.

EUTYCHUS: I want my parents to make a truce.
  She's still enraged . . .

CHARINUS: Move it or get out of my way.

EUTYCHUS: . . . because of that girl.

CHARINUS: Come on, man. Let's go in.

EUTYCHUS: Then you take care of it.   1410

CHARINUS: Fret not, buddy.
  I'll arbitrate and they will be
  As happy together as Juno and Jove
  Are . . . some of the time.

Scene 3

DEMIPHO: Don't tell me
  You've never been in a fix like this.

LYSIMACHUS: Never in all my born days.
  I'm half-dead already and my wife
  Is totally out of control,
  Ballistic!   1420

DEMIPHO: Don't worry.
  I'll get you off the hook
  And she'll calm down again
  Sooner or later.

LYSIMACHUS: Let's go.
  Wait, I see my son.

Scene 4

EUTYCHUS: I'll find my old man and tell him
Mother has calmed down.
Be right back.

LYSIMACHUS: That's not bad for a beginning.   1430
What say, Eutychus? What's happened?

EUTYCHUS: Sir, your wife is ready
For an armistice. All quiet
On the home front.

LYSIMACHUS: Praise the Lord!

EUTYCHUS: And to you, Demipho,
I'm happy to report you have no mistress.

DEMIPHO: The hell you say!

EUTYCHUS: Gentlemen, give me your attention.
I will speak up loud and clear.   1440

DEMIPHO: We're at your service.

EUTYCHUS: Proposition: when good men and true,
Of excellent background, go bad,
Then they've got nobody to blame but themselves.

DEMIPHO: I'll buy that.

LYSIMACHUS: You're the one he's talking to.

EUTYCHUS: It was definitely inappropriate
For you, a man of your age, sir,
To bird-dog the sweety of your son,
Somebody he loves and paid cash for.   1450

DEMIPHO: What? She's Charinus's girl?
He told me he bought her for his mother.

EUTYCHUS: And that's why you bought her, lover boy?

LYSIMACHUS: Way to go, my lad!
Let's give him the old high-low
Two on one . . .

DEMIPHO: I've lost it all now.

LYSIMACHUS: Such an injury inflicted
On his very own son.

EUTYCHUS: The selfsame son that I brought home   1460
When he was bound and determined
To go into exile.

DEMIPHO: Has he gone?

LYSIMACHUS: Shut up, you old scarecrow.
A man of your age ought to know better.

DEMIPHO: Okay. Okay. I did the wrong thing.
I was . . . insensitive.

LYSIMACHUS: Shut up and listen here.
Our lives are like the seasons of the year.
It's not right for autumnal men   1470
To pretend they're in the springtime
Of young love.

EUTYCHUS: Someone with wisdom and experience
Has to navigate the old ship of state.

LYSIMACHUS: Let the young bucks have their season.

DEMIPHO: The hell with it! Take her,
    Lock, stock, and barrel, for yourselves.

EUTYCHUS: Give her back to him.

DEMIPHO: Done! He can have her
    All to himself. See if I care.   1480

EUTYCHUS: A good choice, sir.
    Seeing it's the only choice left.

DEMIPHO: Please help me make peace and amends
    To him. If I had known the truth,
    I swear to you I would never have messed around
    With his true love.
    You've got to help me, Eutychus.
    Help a poor old man do the right thing.

LYSIMACHUS: Blame it all on your hot young blood.

DEMIPHO: Hey, give me a break.   1490
    One of these days I may get a chance
    To pay you back (pardon the expression)
    Tit for tat.

LYSIMACHUS: Not bloody likely. I've given up
    On the game of love long ago.

DEMIPHO: Me, too . . . at least from now on.

EUTYCHUS: Quit kidding yourselves.
    You'll never change. You'll die
    With a hard-on.

DEMIPHO: None of us will escape whipping.   1500

LYSIMACHUS: Your wife will be glad to hear that.

DEMIPHO: She doesn't need to know
　　Everything that pops into my head.

LYSIMACHUS: Don't worry. Mum's the word.
　　But listen, let's go inside the house.
　　No need to wash dirty laundry in public.

DEMIPHO: Good idea! And if we go in now,
　　It will shorten this play that we're stuck in.

EUTYCHUS: Your son is inside already.

DEMIPHO: Fine and dandy.   1510
　　Let's go home and wrap things up.

LYSIMACHUS: Wait, Eutychus, I need one thing settled
　　And for sure before I go inside.

EUTYCHUS: What's that?

LYSIMACHUS: Everybody's got his own agenda.
　　Know what I mean?

EUTYCHUS: Go on.

LYSIMACHUS: Your mother, are you absolutely certain
　　She isn't still angry at me?

EUTYCHUS: You have my word.   1520

LYSIMACHUS: Are you really sure?

EUTYCHUS: I'm telling you, Dad
　　Pas de problème . . .

LYSIMACHUS: I hope you're right.

EUTYCHUS: Don't you believe me?

LYSIMACHUS: Sure . . . It's just, well . . .
   That old woman scares the shit out of me.

DEMIPHO: Let's go inside, okay?

EUTYCHUS: Wait. Let me propose this to the audience.
   We need a law applying to old men.   1530
   Social insecurity, so to speak.
   Whenever a man is sixty or over,
   Married or celibate, no matter,
   And he takes up wenching again,
   He will be subject to public ridicule
   And expensive private shame.
   Nobody will be allowed to prevent
   Youthful sons from having some fun
   And games with willing girls.
   The fine will be higher than the cost.   1540
   Got it? And all old goats
   Will be subject to the law
   From this day forward.
   As to you all, fare well
   And have a good day.
   And if there are any young people
   Out there, make yourselves known
   By giving me and the others a great big hand.

THE SAVAGE SLAVE

(*TRUCULENTUS*)

Translated by James Tatum

INTRODUCTION

In Cicero's dialogue *De Senectute* (*On Old Age*), Cato the Elder explains why one should not fear old age but look forward to it as a welcome fulfillment to life. For artists there can be special rewards. Sophocles produced *Oedipus at Colonus* when he was in his eighties. As for the Romans, exclaims Cato, "What delight did Naevius take in his *Punic War!* How Plautus delighted in *Truculentus* and *Pseudolus!* (*De Senectute* 14). Because of this passage, the *Truculentus* is customarily assigned to Plautus's old age, around the time of the *Pseudolus* (definitely known to be 191 B.C.). But the precise date of the original production remains a matter of speculation; so does the Greek comedy on which the *Truculentus* is based. For readers and audiences today, the basic question raised by this often-quoted passage in Cicero is why Plautus would rejoice in the *Pseudolus* and the *Truculentus* together. No two plays could have less in common. The *Pseudolus* is like Plautus's more popular *Menaechmi, Mostellaria*, and *Miles Gloriosus*. Its tone is generally sunny, and its ending cheerful. Not so the *Truculentus*. Even in a theater that delights in the comic inversion of traditional values and conventional behavior, it stands out as by far the most sardonic of all Plautus's comedies.

Phronesium of Athens is in the business of making as much money as she can from her lovers. With the able assistance of her maid Astaphium and an old flame, Diniarchus, she succeeds in convincing the braggart warrior Stratophanes that she has given birth to a baby and that he is the father of the boy. An even easier conquest is the dim-witted country boy Strabax, son of her next-door neighbor. The boy's slave Truculentus tries to save him from ruin but fails, and in the end even succumbs himself to the charms of Phronesium's house. The play ends with Strabax and Stratophanes

319

arguing over who has given more gold to Phronesium. As she turns to go inside to her waiting lovers, Phronesium pauses to invite members of the audience to join her if they are so inclined.

The *Truculentus* has a remarkable plot. Scene after scene illustrates Diniarchus's opening lines:

> A lover can spend his whole life learning
> yet never really learn
> how many ways there are to die for love.

The most original feature of the play is its static exposition of character. There is no development of a plot, only a relentless exposition of the jaded and the gullible.[1] What gives the *Truculentus* its power in the theater is the cumulative effect of its scenes. When Truculentus first appears he scorns Astaphium and her charms (II.2); then a long sequence ensues in which Phronesium, with Diniarchus's aid, snares Stratophanes (II.3–II.8); then Strabax falls victim (III.1); then Truculentus, his guardian slave, succumbs (III.2); and *then*, when the audience thinks nothing more could happen, Diniarchus reenters with yet another speech in praise of Venus:

> No one has ever been born, or will be born,
> or will ever be found, to whom I'd wish better luck
> than Lady Venus! (IV.1)

In performance, the effect of this delirious entrance can be explosive.

Here is the sharpest delineation in Roman comedy of specifically male folly. Plautus depicts every stage of the seduction and victimization of the customers of the clever courtesan Phronesium and her maid Astaphium, for that is what the men in this play are—a mob of gullible customers, even though each of them thinks of himself as Phronesium's only lover. Diniarchus, world-weary and urbane, is the first victim; then the rustic youth Strabax and his slave Truculentus; and finally the richest prize of all, Stratophanes, the *miles gloriosus*. At the end of the play, Diniarchus lives up only too well to the theme of his opening lines. First he leaves his own child on loan to Phronesium so that she can successfully carry off her plot

[1]See Cynthia S. Dessen, "Plautus' Satiric Comedy: The *Truculentus*," *Philological Quarterly* 56 (1977): 145–68.

to convince the soldier Stratophanes that he, Stratophanes, is the
father of the child. Then, incredibly, although he has seen the plotting and treachery of Phronesium from close range, Diniarchus vows
to return to her as soon as he can after a perfunctory marriage to the
child's disgraced mother.

The *Truculentus* makes exceptionally heavy demands on its
actors and director. Long expository and moralizing monologues
(I.1, II.1, IV.1) alternate with *cantica* (I.2, II.5, II.7) and some of the
most vivid scenes in all of Plautus, such as the encounter among
Stratophanes, Phronesium, and Cyamus (II.6–7) and the "mirror
scenes" of Truculentus and Astaphium (II.2 and III.2). The stereo-
typical characters of New Comedy are present and recognizable by
their eloquent or significant names, yet Plautus manipulates these
stock types in unexpected ways. It is not a clever slave like Chalinus
or Chrysalus who carries out the deception, but Phronesium. Furthermore, while Truculentus, Strabax, Cyamus, Stratophanes, and
Callicles each act out their two-dimensional roles in one or at most
two scenes, the three central characters—Diniarchus, Phronesium,
and Astaphium—are given much deeper parts. Each of them is a
character we get to know very well, and, perhaps, better than we
would like to.

Diniarchus's role is by far the longest and the most difficult. He
provides much of the exposition of the plot and sets the tone of the
drama. His endless capacity for self-deception and illogic will put a
severe strain on actor (and thus audience) unless we realize that
Diniarchus is not supposed to make sense:

> I'd far rather help her who wishes well for me
> than help myself. Why, I'm my own worst enemy! (II.4)

Diniarchus is at once a fellow conspirator in the plot to trick Stratophanes and a willing victim of the same women. He is "like a brother" to Phronesium and her maid Astaphium. He is no longer either a
threat (through demands for sex) or a source of worry (through pro-
posals of marriage), but only an ally in the game Phronesium plays
with the two men still playing the game of sex. In effect, Diniarchus
is neutered by his long contact with Phronesium.

If Diniarchus is the most pathological type of lover in the play,
Phronesium is the very antithesis of love or passion. As her name

implies, she is a woman coolly in control of all the action of the play, even more than her willing accomplice Astaphium. Diniarchus carefully translates *phronesis* into Latin (*sapientia*) so that the audience will not miss the significance of her name:

> Phronesium,
> the courtesan who lives here in this house:
> her name is one I should learn from but don't.
> *Phronesis,* you know, is Greek for "good sense." (I.1)

She manages drink, sex, and intrigue with equal ease:

> A courtesan who can't drink and tend to her business
> is a blithering fool, a cheap clay pot;
> the rest of her body can be pickled,
> but her brain had better be dry. (IV.4)

She and Astaphium are far more intelligent than any male character in the play. Her successful charade of motherhood and childbirth reveals a woman who is completely free of every traditional role.

Still, if Phronesium and Astaphium are ruthless in their scheming and exploitation, an audience will feel little sympathy for their victims. Strabax gleefully anticipates throwing his mother and father's wealth to the "wolves" (*lupae*, which is also slang for "whores"). Stratophanes is a vainglorious fool who is denied the opportunity for that moment of self-recognition that Plautus gives to his most famous braggart warrior, Pyrgopolynices, at the end of the *Miles Gloriosus:*

> Well, I see I've been tricked. That wretch Palaestrio!
> He got me into this trap! It's a fair penalty.
> If other adulterers had this kind of experience,
> there would be less adultery going on:
> they'd have more to be afraid of,
> and less appetite for affairs like this.

The one person who might be expected to be more stable is the old man Callicles (IV.3), yet he is more concerned with a reduction of his daughter's dowry to penalize Diniarchus than with the well-being of his child and grandchild. The *Truculentus* reduces paternity and maternity to matters of finance. Interest, the metaphorical offspring of money, becomes more important than the literal offspring children (II.5, V.1).[2] What could be the binding love between a husband and his wife is reduced to the *negotium*, "business," of prostitution.

Only one character makes a genuine effort to resist the charms of Phronesium and Astaphium: the slave Truculentus, who gives this Greek play its very Roman name. But his efforts are half-hearted at best. In spite of a ferocious first scene, he begins to weaken even in his first encounter with Astaphium; she predicts his downfall as soon as he is offstage (II.2). A *servus rusticus*, a country slave endowed with what the Romans liked to think of as superior country virtues, he makes an effort to save his stupid young master Strabax from himself. In the end he fails, but at least he is alive to the immorality of Phronesium's world and tries to challenge it. His is also the only character to change, and his second scene with Astaphium (III.2) marks a comic peripeteia in character. It is not a change for the better, as he himself acknowledges in his parting lines:

> The tavern I'm being led to specializes
> in gobbling up high fees for low service.

Truculentus is the savage slave who knew better, and the *Truculentus* is a disturbing comedy by a playwright who is here at his most savage about the human comedy.

James Tatum

[2]This may reflect a wordplay in the unknown Greek model for the *Truculentus*, since the Greek *tokos* means "interest" (born of money) as well as "offspring" (born of men and women).

THE SAVAGE SLAVE

CHARACTERS

PROLOGUE

DINIARCHUS, a young man of Athens and future son-in-law of
    Callicles
ASTAPHIUM, maid to Phronesium
TRUCULENTUS, a country slave of Strabax
PHRONESIUM, a courtesan
STRATOPHANES, a soldier
CYAMUS, a cook and servant of Diniarchus
STRABAX, a country youth and master of Truculentus
CALLICLES, an old man of Athens and father of Diniarchus's future
    wife
MAID, a slave of Callicles
SYRA, a slave of Phronesium
Attendants to Phronesium, Stratophanes, Callicles, and Cyamus

SCENE: *A street in Athens with the houses of* PHRONESIUM *and*
STRABAX's *father.*

PROLOGUE

It's Plautus's plea that you provide a plot
within your pretty city, please—a spot
where he can rear his Athens proud and high,

325

all by himself: no architects need apply.
So what's your pleasure?
                     Please don't turn me down.
What's that?
              I get the finest spot in town?
Then how about a little tip off the top?
—Oh, very well, then.
                 I know when to stop.
Old-fashioned virtues flourish here, I see—
how fast your Roman tongues say *no* to me!   10
Well, nothing ventured. Enough of playing with you.
I'll do the business I came here to do.
Upon this stage, then, Athens is depicted—
at least until our comedy is acted.
Phronesium lives here. She professes
the morals of our day, and our excesses.
From every lover she asks one favor,
to add another gift to what they gave her.
Prayers and robbery supplement her scheming
once she knows she has her victims dreaming.*   20
Her days are filled with whoring, extortions,
mock marriages, and fake abortions.
Her newest scheme will shock some of you, maybe:
you see, the secret weapon is . . . a baby!
The plot I'll now unfold is good and fertile,
though some details may cause your blood to curdle.
Old Callicles once sired a pretty daughter,
a virgin pure, till Diniarchus caught her:
Diniarchus, Athens' reigning pupil,
expert in all things prostitutional.   30
For maiden's hand he swore to ask her daddy,
but took maiden *head;* no order had he.
In real love life each side must give consent,

---

*Unfortunately, only the first seventeen lines of the prologue survive, with three more
lines after a lacuna that ends with the cryptic words "Quid multa?" ["Why say more?"]. The
problem is that for performance at least, the prologue must say more. Hence the text has been
supplied from this point onward with lines about Diniarchus's seamy past and the three latest
victims of Phronesium and Astaphium.

but Diniarchus came, and then . . . he went.
The girl conceived, making him a father,
and that good news proved really quite a bother.
Most young men will act in bona fides;
for him, that's as rare as joy in hades.
Now he's returned, blind to her he should adore,
to see the only one he loves—his whore.   40
He'll loan the baby boy for good measure
to help her fleece two others of their treasure:
Stratophanes, soldier *gloriosus*,
first victim of this whorish hocus-pocus.
And then comes wealthy Strabax after him,
a youth of simple speech and wits so dim
his father guards him with a trusty
Roman slave, a beast with manners rusty.
Since he's the only man who's *compos mentis*,
we take his name and call this Truculentus.   50
Now enter Diniarchus with a lover's plea.
It's time for you to stay, and me to flee.

(*He exits*)

ACT I

Scene 1

(*Enter* DINIARCHUS, *a dissipated young man with circles under his eyes*)

DINIARCHUS: A lover can spend his whole life learning
   yet never really learn
   how many ways there are to die for love.
   Venus never renders balanced budgets,
   though she's in charge of all accounts

a lover calls his own:
how many ways he's made a fool of,
how many ways he's brought to ruin,   60
how many prayers he needs to pray,
how much pouting,
how much petting,
how much punishment—
if you can believe it, gods—
how many lies he needs,
even when he's paid his fees!
Charge number one: a payroll every day
of the year. For that haul you'll get three nights.
Meanwhile, she adds on charges for money,   70
or wine, or oil, or flour
to find out whether you're generous or thrifty.
(*Warms to the subject*)
Think of a fisherman casting a net
on a fish pond. When the net hits bottom,
he gives it a little line. If a fish gets
inside, he's careful not to scare it off.
He tugs gently; sweeping first this way,
then that way, he snares the fish and finally pulls
it from the water. The same fate awaits a lover.
If he gives whenever asked,   80
and is generous instead of thrifty,
extra nights are tacked on,
and in the meantime he's swallowed the hook.
If he gets one undiluted dose of sex,
love juice runs through his vitals, and before he knows it,
he's lost himself and his money and credit as well.
And just let a lover have his whore
get mad at him, and he'll die two deaths:
first his money goes, then his brains.
And if another man is more her type, he's dead again.   90
Why, even when they get along with one another,
the lover still loses. If he spends only an
occasional night, his brains turn to soup.
If he sees her every night, he survives

well enough, but his money doesn't.
Before you can give her even one present,
she's ready to ask for a hundred others.
She's completely out of money,
her dress is an old rag,
she's bought a new maid,   100
there's a silver vase she must have,
or that bronze one,
or a fine carved couch,
or a trinket box some Greek made,
or anything else she can think of
that a lover should give his whore.

It's a full-time job hiding how we
abuse our money, our credit, and ourselves.
God forbid our parents should learn what's going on!
If they found out and were able   110
to rein in our youthful passions now,
their austerity through us would enrich our posterity;
then, I guarantee, there'd be fewer whores and pimps
than there are now, and fewer bankrupts too.
As it is, pimps and whores swarm almost
as thick as flies in the heat of summer.
If you want to see them, there's no better place to look
than at the bankers' tables. Whores and pimps are there every
    day,
too many to count, really. There are
more whores at the tables than there are   120
weights for the bankers' scales.
What business they have there is a mystery to me,
unless they mean to keep track of the latest
interest rates—rates for credit to their customers,
just in case you thought they had any creditors.
In short, this is how we live today.
(*Slips into Roman officialese*)
In this *great* nation of ours . . .
among this *great* people . . .
the state being at peace and at ease . . .

our enemies having been conquered . . .   130
(*Returns to more normal tone*)
a time when every man deserves a little love,
if he can pay for it.
Now, consider my case. Phronesium,
the courtesan who lives here in this house:
her name is one I should learn from, but don't.
Phronesis, you know, is Greek for "good sense."
I'll admit I have been an ardent suitor,
one always on the *closest* of terms with her,
terms a disaster to my bank account.
Now she's found somebody else who is   140
willing to pay more money than I,
a bigger fool with his money than I am.
The witch tells me he's only "a plague," "a burden,"
"a Babylonian soldier." Now this fellow is
said to be about to arrive from overseas,
and she's hatched a plot that goes like this:
She'll pretend she's just had a baby
so she can kick me out and live it up
with the soldier in regular Greek luxury.
She'll pretend that the soldier is the father of the boy.   150
That's why the slut needs this baby on loan.
Does she think she's tricking me?
Does she think she could keep *me* from finding out
if she really were pregnant?

(*Starts to go off; pauses, adds as afterthought*)

You see, I just got back to Athens the day before yesterday. I was
an ambassador on official business at Lemnos.
(ASTAPHIUM *enters from* PHRONESIUM'*s house*)
But here comes her little maid Astaphium, of all people! I've had
dealings with her too. Strictly business, of course.

(*Draws to one side*)

Scene 2

(Enter ASTAPHIUM *from* PHRONESIUM's *house)*

ASTAPHIUM: *(To servants inside)* Listen at our door and guard
our house's gate. No man should ever leave us heavier than he
found us. No barren hands that come to us should go off big with
gold.   162

(In the manner of a blues singer)

I know my men.
Oh, how I know my men,
the young ones
best of all.
Five or six will come at once,
those beaming broths of . . . bores,
to pay a social call,
on their sweetheart whores.   170

(Brightly)

Or so they say. Their plans *are* nicely laid!

(Resumes)

One pins a girl
with kisses in a corner,
and if they see
someone come to warn her,
they're all playing, joking,
until her guard's off guard.
(Rapidly)
Then it's stuffing,
and huffing,
and puffing,   180
and nothing left to eat in the house.

They're sausage stuffers,
and *they* are the sausage!

(*To audience*)

This is exactly what happens, and there are men here who know
me and know I never lie. To steal loot from looters like us: what a
novel, glorious thing to do! We do return the favor, though. First
the fools bring us their money, then they watch while we count it
up in piles.

DINIARCHUS: (*Aside, eyeing* ASTAPHIUM)
She's got a tongue like a whip, and my scars show it. I've deposited
funds there before.   190

ASTAPHIUM: (*Answering someone inside the house*)
Yes, you're right, I just remembered! I'll bring him back with me
to our house, if he's at home.

(*Starts toward* STRABAX's *house*)

DINIARCHUS: Wait a minute, Astaphium! Don't go yet.

ASTAPHIUM: (*Stops, not turning*) Who says, "Don't go"?

DINIARCHUS: Turn around and you'll find out.

ASTAPHIUM: (*Not turning*) And who's there?

DINIARCHUS: (*Advances to her*) Someone who wants nothing but
riches for you.

ASTAPHIUM: Give them then, if you want us to have them.

(*Not turning, she holds out her hand*)

DINIARCHUS: (*Does not respond*) I'll see to it. Just look this way.

ASTAPHIUM: (*Still looks away*) You're wasting my time, whoever you
   are.   202

(*Starts to go off*)

DINIARCHUS: (*Stops her*) You bitch! Wait!

ASTAPHIUM: Ah, a gentleman. And a bore.
   (*Feels his empty hand; her curiosity is aroused*)
   Now, could that be Diniarchus?
   (*Gropes him*)
   Indeed it is.

(*Turns around at last*)

DINIARCHUS: Greetings to you.

ASTAPHIUM: Likewise.

DINIARCHUS: Give me your hand and step this way.

ASTAPHIUM: Your slightest wish is like law to me.   210

DINIARCHUS: And how are you?

ASTAPHIUM: I am as well as the one whose hand I hold.
   (*Without enthusiasm*)
   Since you've been away, we'll have to have a dinner party.

DINIARCHUS: How nice, how *kind* an invitation, Astaphium.

(*Begins to fondle her*)

ASTAPHIUM: (*Withdrawing*) *Please.* I'm on an errand for my mistress.

DINIARCHUS: By all means. But tell me . . .

ASTAPHIUM: What is it you want?

DINIARCHUS: Where are you going? Who is it? Who are you bringing here?

ASTAPHIUM: Archilis the midwife.   220

DINIARCHUS: Naughty, naughty! The smell of your trade follows you
wherever you go. Now I've caught you in an open lie.

ASTAPHIUM: How so, if you please?

DINIARCHUS: Just then you said you were going out to bring a *him*
here, not a *her* here. What was a man has now become a woman.
An enchanting bit of bitchery! Tell me then, who is this man,
Astaphium? Some new lover?

ASTAPHIUM: (*Removes his hands*) I think you have a lot of free time
on your hands.

DINIARCHUS: Why do you think that?

ASTAPHIUM: You're free to spend your time minding other people's
business, and at your own expense.   231

DINIARCHUS: And *you* gave me the free time to do it.

ASTAPHIUM: How so, if you please?

DINIARCHUS: I'll tell you how. I lost all my money at your house.
You're the ones who ran off with my business. If I had saved my
money, I'd still be in *business*.

(*Embraces her with a suggestive bump*)

ASTAPHIUM: (*Escapes easily*) Ha! Do you think you can farm the
public lands of Venus or of Love and not go out of business?

DINIARCHUS: You've got it all wrong. Phronesium is the one who's farming public lands, not me. She let me pay the tax, then took my whole herd. *That's* against the law.   241

ASTAPHIUM: Most men who are bad at business do what you do: when they can't pay the pasture tax, they blame the tax collector.

DINIARCHUS: Since the grazing at your place didn't work out for me, I'd like a change, a little piece of land to plow, as much as you can give me.

(Feels her behind)

ASTAPHIUM: *(Slips away)* We don't have any plow land here, only grassy pastures. If you want to plow, you'd better go to the boys. They're used to being plowed. Our taxes are for *this* pasture land; their taxes are for another service.   250

DINIARCHUS: I know both fields well enough.

ASTAPHIUM: And that's why you have so much free time on your hands. First you failed with the boys, then with us. Tell me, whose business would you like this time?

DINIARCHUS: *(Reckons on his fingers)*
Let's see. You're harder to control. They tell more lies. Whatever they get they lose, with nothing left to show for it; at least when *you* get something, you eat and drink it up. In short, they're shameless, and you're of no account and proud of it.   260

ASTAPHIUM: You're insulting nobody but yourself, Diniarchus, certainly not us or the boys.

DINIARCHUS: And how do you arrive at that conclusion?

ASTAPHIUM: This is how: anyone who finds fault in someone else had better be sparkling clean himself. As clever as you are, you haven't a thing of ours, and we "no-accounts" have everything of yours.

DINIARCHUS: (*Melts, whining*) O Astaphium, you never used to talk to me like this before. You were so polite when I had what's now in *your* house in *my* house.

ASTAPHIUM: (*Surveys* DINIARCHUS *up and down*)
When a man's *alive*, you know him; when he dies, let him rest in peace. I knew you as long as you were *alive*.   270

DINIARCHUS: (*Covers his crotch*) You don't think I'm *dead*, do you?

ASTAPHIUM: *Please*. What could be more obvious? You were once known as the greatest lover in the world, and now you bring Phronesium nothing but complaints.

DINIARCHUS: It's all your fault. You rushed things too quickly. You should have taken your time robbing me; then I would have lasted a lot longer.

ASTAPHIUM: A lover is like an enemy town . . .

DINIARCHUS: . . . and your proof is . . .

ASTAPHIUM: . . . the sooner he can be sacked, the better it is for his mistress.   281

DINIARCHUS: I'll grant that. But friends and lovers aren't the same. The best friend you'll ever have is the one you've known the longest. That's a fact.

ASTAPHIUM: If he's still *alive*.

(*Goes off*)

DINIARCHUS: (*Desperate*) *I'm not dead yet! I still own land and houses!*

ASTAPHIUM: (*Returns*) Then *why on earth* are you standing in front
of our house as if you were a stranger and a foreigner? Do go
inside. You're no foreigner here. No man in the world is dearer to
Phronesium's heart and soul than you, if you *really* do have land
and houses.   292

DINIARCHUS: (*Declaiming*)
Though your tongue and speech be dipped in honey,
your hearts and deeds are sicklied o'er with gall and bitter
  vinegar;
you utter sweet words with your tongue,
your hearts are filled with deeds of bitterness.

(*Moved by his own eloquence, he stares into the middle distance*)

ASTAPHIUM: You dear, sweet boy. That's no way for you to talk.
People who talk that way war against themselves. They have chas-
tity belts for purses.

DINIARCHUS: You're as bad as ever, and as alluring too.   300

ASTAPHIUM: How we've waited for you to return from abroad! How
much the mistress has wanted to see you!

DINIARCHUS: Why?

ASTAPHIUM: Of all her lovers, you're the only one she loves.

DINIARCHUS: (*Aside*) Bravo, land and houses! Your help came just in
time. Now, Astaphium . . .

ASTAPHIUM: Yes, dear.

DINIARCHUS: Is Phronesium at home now?

ASTAPHIUM: No matter what she is for others, she'll be at home for
you.

DINIARCHUS: Is she well?   310

ASTAPHIUM: Oh, yes, and I hope she'll be even better once she sees you.

DINIARCHUS: (*Strikes a pose; to audience*) Here's our greatest fault. The moment we start to make love, we're ruined. If we're told what we want to hear, we're fools enough to believe it, even if it's a lie—and we aren't outraged, even though we should be.

ASTAPHIUM: Oh, tut-tut, that isn't how things are at all.

DINIARCHUS: (*Turns back to his conversation with* ASTAPHIUM) You say she really loves me?

ASTAPHIUM: You and you alone.

DINIARCHUS: I've heard she's had a baby.

ASTAPHIUM: O Diniarchus, please hush!   320

DINIARCHUS: What's the matter?

ASTAPHIUM: (*Pathetically*) The very mention of her labor sets poor little me all atremble. You came very near to having no . . . Phronesium.
(*Brisk again*)
Go inside, please, and see her. But you'll have to wait. She'll be out soon; she was taking a bath.

DINIARCHUS: What are you saying? How could a woman who was never pregnant have had a baby? I know her belly *very* well, and I've seen no signs of swelling.

ASTAPHIUM: She kept it a secret. She was afraid she might not be able to persuade you to let her keep the boy. She thought she'd have to have an abortion and lose him.   331

DINIARCHUS: Then that Babylonian soldier must be the father, and
she's waiting for him now!

ASTAPHIUM: Yes, we've had a message from him that said he'd be
here soon.
(*Looks up and down the street*)
I'm surprised he hasn't arrived already.

DINIARCHUS: Shall I go in now?

ASTAPHIUM: Why not? Go as boldly as you would into your own
home. You're just one of the family now, Diniarchus.

DINIARCHUS: How soon will you return?   340

ASTAPHIUM: I'll be back soon. The place I'm going to isn't far away.

DINIARCHUS: Hurry back! In the meantime, I'll wait for you inside.

(*Goes into* PHRONESIUM's *house*)

ACT II

Scene 1

ASTAPHIUM: Ha-ha-ha! Peace and quiet!
The bore has gone inside!
At last I'm alone!
Now I'll freely say
what I want to say
just as it pleases *me*.
(*Advances to address audience*)
Inside at home my mistress sang a dirge,
lamenting this lover and his property.   350

He mortgaged his house and land as security
to pay for Love's real estate. It's true, he shares
in all my mistress's most important plots;
he's more a friend for his advice than for his *active* duty.

While he could give, he gave. Now he has nothing:
what he had, we have; what he has, we had.
The exchange is *only* human.
Fortunes have a way of changing in a flash.
Life is uncertain.

We recall when he was rich;   360
he knew us when we were poor.
What each of us remembers is what has *changed*.
Anyone would be a fool to be surprised at this.
If he's broke, we'll have to endure that.
He got his love from us, fair and square.
Why, it would be a *sin* for us to pity
any man who can't control his money!

A proper whore must have good teeth,
to laugh at men and flatter them;
she needs evil plans in her heart   370
and friendly words on her tongue.
A courtesan should be like a cactus:
any man she touches should suffer a sting, or a loss.

She should never heed a lover's pleas.
When he pays nothing, she should send him home for
desertion in the ranks. No man can be an honest lover
unless he's his own money's worst enemy.
The man who's best loved in our house is
the one who forgets that he has given.
As long as he has it, he can have *it*;   380
once he doesn't have it, let him get *it*
somewhere else. When he doesn't have it,
he ought to be sensible and make way for one who does.
He gives you only trifles unless he wants to give again.

The best kind of lover at our house is the one
who first drops his affairs, and then his fortune.

Yet men are always saying to each other
that *we* do all the wrong, *we're* the greedy ones.
Why so? I ask you, what wrong do we really do?
No, the truth is that no lover ever gives   390
enough to his mistress; none of us
ever gets enough, none of us ever asks enough.

Now, when a lover comes with hands barren of gifts,
if he swears he has no gifts to give,
we believe him; we take no deposit from him
when he has no deposits left to give.
We always look out for new depositors,
ones who have untouched treasures.
Take the country boy who lives here.
(*Indicates the house of* STRABAX)
Goodness, what a charmer, and only too ready to pay!   400
But his slave is a raging monster.
When he sees one of us here, he chases us
as if he were driving geese from a granary.
He's so . . . so *rural*.
But I'll give a knock, no matter what happens.
Yoo-hoo! Is anyone in charge of this door? Is anyone here?

(*Knocks vigorously*)

Scene 2

TRUCULENTUS: (*Enters raging, with a hoe*)
  Who's battering at our door? Are you a ram, or what?

(*Charges past* ASTAPHIUM; *looks around the stage*)

ASTAPHIUM: (*Behind him*) Just me. Do turn around.

TRUCULENTUS: (*Over shoulder*) Who's "me"?

ASTAPHIUM: Don't I look like me to you?   410

TRUCULENTUS: (*Turns*) You! Why did you come here? Why did you try to beat our door down?

ASTAPHIUM: Good health to you.

TRUCULENTUS: Enough of your "good health." Don't need it. Not healthy anyway. Rather be sick than healthy with your "good health." What I do want to know is, *what's your business with this house?*

ASTAPHIUM: For the sake of your mistress, calm down!

TRUCULENTUS: Make her *come*, did you say? That's your style, eh. You want to make me make our *mistress* come? You have no shame, trying to trick an honest country man into taking a tumble.

ASTAPHIUM: But I only said "calm down" for your mistress's sake. You took *l* out of the word when you heard it.   423
(*Aside*)
And then took *l* out on me. This creature is too truculent for words.

TRUCULENTUS: (*Raising his hoe as if to strike her*)
What! More of your insults, is it . . . you . . . you . . . *woman*, you?

ASTAPHIUM: Insults? What insults?

TRUCULENTUS: Saying I'm succulent, that's what.
(*She begins to protest, but he silences her*)
Now, look here, woman, if you don't clear out of here at once or tell me what I want to know, then *damned* if I don't stomp you under my foot like a sow stomps a litter.   432

ASTAPHIUM: (*To audience*) That one came straight off the farm.

TRUCULENTUS: (*Bellows with rage*) You chattering tribe of monkeys!
You're a disgrace, that's what you are!
(*She walks seductively toward him; for a moment he watches her,
mesmerized*)
You came here to show yourself off, didn't you? Every limb cov-
ered with trinkets. I'll bet you dyed that rag of a dress by holding it
over some campfire.
(*She approaches closer*)
You think you're pretty because you've got these bronze bracelets!

ASTAPHIUM: (*Against him, twirling her fingers in his hair*)
You're cute when you curse like that.   440

TRUCULENTUS: (*Tries to remain oblivious to her actions*)
Then try this one on for size. You think that if you wear that cheap
paste you'll be a high-class lady? I'll bet those jewels hanging from
your ears are fake.

(*Snatches at an earring*)

ASTAPHIUM: (*Yanks his hand away and places it around her waist*)
Don't you lay a finger on me!

TRUCULENTUS: *Me* finger *you?* Ha! By this trusty little hoe, I swear
I'd rather be off in the country embracing some broad-beamed
cow. I'd rather spend every night of my life in the straw with her
than eat at your place for a hundred.
(ASTAPHIUM *is very busy with his hair, ears, etc.; her success is
shown by the trembling of the hoe*)
So it's a disgrace to come from the country? Well, you've met one
man who thinks it's a disgrace to do what you do. What's your
business with this house, you . . . you . . . *woman*, you? Why do
you come here every time we come to town?   451

ASTAPHIUM: (*Rearranging herself*) I want to meet the women of the
house.

TRUCULENTUS: You talk to me of women when there's not so much as a female fly inside these doors?

ASTAPHIUM: What? No women at all live here with you?

(*Moves in closer*)

TRUCULENTUS: *They've gone off to the country, I tell you! Get out!*

ASTAPHIUM: Why are you shouting so, you silly boy?

(*Locks her arms around him and presses close*)

TRUCULENTUS: (*Realizing what she is doing, he frees himself and holds her off with his hoe*)
If you don't hustle yourself out of here in double time, I'll yank those false, dainty, frizzled, frilled, perfumed locks out by the roots, brains and all!   461

(*Pushes her away*)

ASTAPHIUM: (*Plays the helpless female*)
Whatever for?

TRUCULENTUS: Because you dared to come near this house, because you drip with perfume, because you were shameless enough to color your cheeks with . . . with . . .
(*Weakens slightly*)
with such a pretty little ruby tint.

ASTAPHIUM: (*The innocent virgin*) Oh dear, I swear I blushed red because of your terrible shouting . . . poor thing that I am.

TRUCULENTUS: (*Examines her cheeks closely*)
You blushed yourself red, did you? As if there were a single part of your body that could show any more color.   470
(*She snuggles up to him; he jumps back*)

You witch! You've painted your cheeks with red paint and your body with white powder. You're the worst woman alive!

ASTAPHIUM: And what harm have the most wicked women in the world done you?

TRUCULENTUS: (*Draws himself together*) I know more than you think I know.

ASTAPHIUM: And what might it be that you know?

TRUCULENTUS: (*Raging again*) I know our master's son Strabax is being ruined in your house. You're ruining him, snaring him in your wicked schemes and scandals.   480

ASTAPHIUM: If I believed you were in your right mind, I'd say you were slandering me. As it is, no men are ever ruined in our house the way you say. Why, there's no need for us to assist them at all! Each one is able to ruin himself quite nicely—and, I might add, quite unaided. After they've spent everything they have, they're welcome to depart whenever they wish.
(*With renewed interest*)
I don't believe I've had the pleasure of meeting this young man of yours.

TRUCULENTUS: Is that so? What about that wall that separates your garden patch from ours? It gets lower and lower every night as he walks through on the road to his ruination.   491

ASTAPHIUM: (*Fiddling with her jewelry, coyly*)
That's not strange at all. The mortar is old.
(*Suggestively*)
All old garden walls fall down eventually.

TRUCULENTUS: (*Follows her eyes and immediately covers his crotch*)
So! That's your line, eh? "Old garden walls fall down"! I'm going to denounce your scheme to the boy's father! If I don't, may no mortal soul ever trust my oaths or prayers again!

ASTAPHIUM: Is he as foul-tempered as you?

TRUCULENTUS: (*Without realizing it,* ASTAPHIUM *takes his hoe and leans on it, listening intently to his tirade*)
You can be sure of one thing: he doesn't spend his money to keep cheap whores in luxury. He uses it in thrifty, hard-headed ways. And it's his money that's being exported in secret to your house! Damn you! You gobble it down, spray it on, drink it up! You think I'll keep my mouth shut about all this? No. I'm going to the forum right now to tell the boy's father everything I know. This back is one field that will never know a whip's furrows.   504

(*Stalks off down the street. Immediately on exiting, he realizes that he has left his hoe. He comes back, snatches it from* ASTAPHIUM, *and leaves again.*)

ASTAPHIUM: (*To audience*) If that fellow had been fed on nothing but a diet of mustard seed he couldn't be more sour. Too tart even for me! My goodness, he does live only for his master, doesn't he? All the same, I hope to change his ways with flattering words, abject prayers, and all the other tricks we courtesans use. I've seen wild horses tamed who never thought to yield; the same thing can happen to other *beasts* as well.   511
(*Fusses with her hair and jewels*)
I'll look in a bit on my mistress now.
(DINIARCHUS *enters*)
Oh dear, here comes my burden back again. But how subdued! He must not have met with Phronesium yet.

Scene 3

DINIARCHUS: (*Despondently*) I'm sure that fish who pass their entire lives in water don't bathe as much as that Phronesium. If women spent as much time making love as they spend taking baths, all their lovers would have to serve double time as bath attendants.

ASTAPHIUM: What's so *hard* about having to wait a little while?

DINIARCHUS: I'll tell you what's *hard!* Waiting is what's *hard!* I'm so
tired now I need a bath myself. Please, Astaphium, go inside and
say that I'm here. Get her to hurry on out here! She's bathed
enough.   /   523

ASTAPHIUM: Very well.

(*Starts to go in*)

DINIARCHUS: Oh, listen . . .

ASTAPHIUM: What is it?

DINIARCHUS: May the gods curse me for calling you back! Didn't I
just tell you to go?

ASTAPHIUM: Then *why* did you call me back, you worthless fool!
You've made a mile's worth of delay for yourself.   530

(*She exits*)

DINIARCHUS: (*To audience*) But why did she stand here so long in
front of their house? She's on the lookout for somebody. I'll bet it's
that soldier. Yes, *he's* the one they're after! They're like vultures:
they see three days ahead of time when they're going to have a
good meal. He's the one they're gaping for! He's the one on their
minds! The minute he arrives they'll pay no more attention to me
than if I'd been dead for two hundred years. How nice it must be
to save your money! Too bad for me. I've reformed after the fact.
I've aborted the goods my parents gave birth to. If I could somehow get my hands on one more inheritance, a great big juicy one,
now that I know the sweet and the bitter things that money brings,
I'd save every penny. I'd be so stingy from one day to the next,
why . . . why   543
(*Ruefully*)

inside a few days, I'd have it down to nothing. Yes, that's how I'd
show those carping critics of mine.
(*The door to* PHRONESIUM'*s house opens*)
Ah, that steaming hot door is opening, the one that gobbles up
everything that passes through it!

Scene 4

(PHRONESIUM *appears at her door with two servants; she drapes
herself seductively on the threshold*)

PHRONESIUM: Why, dear, you don't think my *door* will bite, do you?
Is that why you're afraid to come inside, darling?

DINIARCHUS: (*Transported*) Ah, behold, the spring . . .   550
she blooms . . .
perfumes . . .
her eyes . . .
breed sighs.

PHRONESIUM: (*Advances, followed by servants*)
Why are you so rude, Diniarchus? Here you are returned from
Lemnos, and not one kiss for your mistress?

DINIARCHUS: Ahhhhh! I'm in for a terrible beating now!

(*Trying to escape, he turns to go*)

PHRONESIUM: Why did you turn away?

DINIARCHUS: (*Returns*) Greetings to you, Phronesium.

PHRONESIUM: And to you. You'll have dinner with us, won't you,
now that you're back safe and sound?   561

DINIARCHUS: (*Tries to escape*) I'm already spoken for.

PHRONESIUM: Where might that be?

DINIARCHUS: (*Collapses*) Wherever you say.

PHRONESIUM: Then here. Dine with us and make me happy.

DINIARCHUS: And me happier still. You mean you'll spend the whole
day with me, my Phronesium?

PHRONESIUM: I would if it were possible.

DINIARCHUS: (*As if already in the dining room, to an imaginary
slave*)
Here! Put these sandals on! Hurry up! Get the dining table out of
here!   570

PHRONESIUM: (*Alarmed*) Oh dear, are you all right?

DINIARCHUS: (*Reeling*) No, I can't drink now. I feel so faint.

(*Staggers about the stage*)

PHRONESIUM: Wait, don't go off! We'll find some way to work things
out.

DINIARCHUS: (*Comes to momentarily*) Ah, your words have revived
me like a drink of cool water. I feel better already.
(*Again transported to his imaginary dining room*)
My sandals! Take them off! Give me a drink!

PHRONESIUM: (*Smiles*) You're your old self again, I see. But tell me,
how did you enjoy your little trip abroad?

DINIARCHUS: Any trip that brought me back to you would be a
pleasant one. Just *seeing* you is reward enough.   581

PHRONESIUM: (*Perfunctorily*) Embrace me.

DINIARCHUS: Gladly. Oh, this is sweeter than the sweetest honey. Jupiter, now I'm luckier in love than even you!

PHRONESIUM: (*Flatly*) Kiss me.

DINIARCHUS: Not once but ten times!

PHRONESIUM: (*Backing away*) There, see why you're poor? You're always promising more than I ask from you.

DINIARCHUS: I only wish that you had been as sparing of my money as you are now of your kisses. 590

PHRONESIUM: If I could possibly save you anything, I would.

DINIARCHUS: All finished with your bath now?

PHRONESIUM: Why, yes, I am, so far as I can tell. You don't think I'm *dirty*, do you?

DINIARCHUS: Oh, no, of course I don't. There was a time when we didn't mind it if we both got dirty. Now I'm back. What new plot have you hatched while I was gone?

PHRONESIUM: What do you mean?

DINIARCHUS: (*Sarcastically*) Well, first of all, congratulations on your growing family. I'm glad you passed through that ordeal so well. 601

PHRONESIUM: (*To her servants*) Go back inside and shut the door, girls.
(*They go inside*)
Now you and you alone shall hear what I have to say. I'm entrusting all my most secret plans to you. The fact is that I didn't have a baby boy. The fact is I wasn't even pregnant. I did pretend to be pregnant, I can't deny that.

DINIARCHUS: Whom did you do that for, light of my life?

PHRONESIUM: For that Babylonian soldier. He kept me like a wife the year he lived here.

DINIARCHUS: That's what I thought happened. But why did you? What good was all that pretending?   611

PHRONESIUM: To make a little bond, a tie to guarantee he'd come back to me. Not too long ago he sent a letter saying he'd return to find out just how much I cared for him; if I didn't kill the child I'd had, but brought it up, he'd give me everything he owned.

DINIARCHUS: Do continue. I'm all ears. What happened next?

PHRONESIUM: Now that the ninth month has passed, my mother told her maids to go looking here and there, and to find a baby boy or girl that could be passed off as mine. Not to go on too long about it: you know our hairdresser Syra, the girl who lives with us?

DINIARCHUS: Yes. What has she to do with you?   621

PHRONESIUM: Well, her work takes her from one house to the next, so she kept her eyes open for a boy and brought one to me in secret. She *said* someone gave it to her.

DINIARCHUS: What witchery! The baby wasn't born to the mother who first bore him, but to you by a second birth.

PHRONESIUM: You've got it all in the right order. Now, according to the soldier's letter, it won't be too long before he gets here.

DINIARCHUS: And in the meantime you're going to see to it that you look like you've just had a baby?   630

PHRONESIUM: Why not? Especially when it can be managed so easily without the labor. As the saying goes, "Everyone is best at what they do best." I'm best at this.

DINIARCHUS: But what will happen to me once the soldier comes?
You think I can live without you?

PHRONESIUM: When I get from him what I want from him, I'll have
no trouble finding ways to cause discord and divorce at home.
After that, my love, I promise to abide by you forever.

DINIARCHUS: I'd rather have you in a *bed* by me forever!

PHRONESIUM: (*Ignores his meaning*) Now a sacrifice is due the gods.
It's required five days after a baby's birth.   641

DINIARCHUS: Of course.

PHRONESIUM: So, will you give me some little present?

DINIARCHUS: Oh, my love, I think I grow richer every time you ask
me for anything!

PHRONESIUM: I feel the same way, too, once I get it.

DINIARCHUS: I'll see to it right away. I'll have my little slave Cyamus
come at once.

PHRONESIUM: Yes, do just that.

DINIARCHUS: I hope you'll like whatever he brings.   650

PHRONESIUM: I'm sure you'll have no cause to regret anything you
send me.

DINIARCHUS: There's something more you want?

PHRONESIUM: Only that you come back when you have a free
moment—and that you fare well.

(PHRONESIUM *sails into house*)

DINIARCHUS: Farewell.

(*Solo*)

By the immortal gods, for her to do what she's just done was not the act of a faithful, loving woman! She's a trusting comrade whose heart's the same as mine! To confide in *me* that she had borrowed that baby boy! That's something not even one *sister* would do for another! Now that she's revealed to me her inner thoughts, I know she'll never be unfaithful as long as she lives. How could I not love her? How could I not wish her well? I'd sooner stop loving myself than leave off loving her. How could I not send her a present? I'll order Cyamus to see that she receives five minas of gold at once, and one more mina for food, at least that much!   666

(*Goes; pauses*)

I'd rather help her who wishes well for me than help myself. Why, I'm my own worst enemy!

(*Brightly, exits*)

Scene 5

(*Enter* PHRONESIUM *in dressing gown; her servants carry a crib and baby*)

PHRONESIUM: (*Matter-of-factly, handing the baby over to an attendant*)
Nurse this baby.

(*Begins a lyric lament*)

Oh, how wretched are we mothers,   670
Oh what cares upon our hearts do weigh,
Oh the tortures that we suffer . . .

(*Breaks to confide to audience, rapidly*)

Why, what an awful fabrication!
When I stop to think of it,
all we girls are known too well
for our clever, wicked ways—
or should I say too slightly?
Everything I talk about
I first learned at home.

(*Reclines; resumes lament*)

Oh what worry for the spirit,   680
Oh what heartache to support . . .

(*Breaks again, rapidly addressing audience*)

To avoid a nasty headache, that is:
the baby's death would spoil my sport.
And since I'm called his mother,
I'm all the more eager that he live.
Now that I've dared this first part of the plot,
I'll now take up the other.
Because of money I am greedy and live
in scandal. I'll even adopt another
woman's labor as my own! Still,   690
it never pays to undertake an
underhanded matter unless you do it
with pride in your profession.

(*Rises from couch and addresses audience*)

See for yourselves
how properly I'm dressed: I mean to look
as though I've just given birth.
No matter what evil a woman undertakes,
if she doesn't finish it,
it makes her sick,
it makes her sad,   700

it makes her miserable
in her misery.
If she starts to do anything good,
very soon she comes to hate it.
Far too few of us grow tired of evildoing
once we start it; even fewer of us
can finish a good deed once it's begun.
Evildoing is a burden we bear
far better than doing good. I owe
my badness to my mother's training,   710
and no little to myself. That's why
I can pretend to be pregnant by a
Babylonian soldier. Now I want
that soldier to discover just how
carefully contrived my badness can be.
He should be arriving any moment.
I'm already set for him and made up
so I'll look sick and confined to my bed.

(*To servants*)

Put some myrrh and offerings on the altar
to honor Lucina, dear goddess   720
who presided at my child's birth.
(*Sharply to servants*)
Now put that down and get out of my sight!

(*Returns to the weakened tone of her lament*)

O Pithecium, help me lie down.
Come help me. Ah, that's the way to treat
a new mother. Take off
my sandals. A cloak for me, Archilis.
Where are you, Astaphium? Bring
rosemary and fruit for my confinement.
Some water for my hands . . .

(*In a determined tone*)

Now, by God, I'm ready for that soldier to appear!   730

Scene 6

(*A grand pause. Then* STRATOPHANES *enters in triumphal procession. He is preceded by dancing girls, drummers, and slaves bearing spoils and trophies. At a signal from him, the dancing and chanting cease and his scribe takes up his position at the warrior's elbow. Throughout the scene the scribe tries to take down* STRATOPHANES' *more eloquent lines.*)

STRATOPHANES: (*Addresses the audience; his gestures and
    delivery are those of an orator and statesman*)
    Expect me not, spectators, to declaim my deeds.
    It is my way to make my valor known by these hands.
    I have no need of empty words.
    I know that the very mention of the military
    brings to mind nothing but thoughts of their mendacity.
    I know that those who would boast
    of exploits equal to the deeds of warriors
    immortalized in Homer stand condemned
    for fighting battles that never were.

(*Warming to his subject, he is increasingly oblivious of others*)

    I have no use for a man who is praised   740
    more by those who hear about his deeds
    than by those who have actually seen them.
    One eye-balled witness is worth more
    than ten whose ears bring them report.
    Those who hear things can tell
    only what they have heard;
    those who see know the truth firsthand.

(*Cheers from the retinue. The scribe has fallen asleep.* STRATO-
PHANES *wakes him with a sharp kick, whereupon he begins to
write feverishly. Only after the scribe signals that he has caught
up does* STRATOPHANES *continue his discourse.*)

I have no use for any man whom fops in town greet
with praise while veterans keep silent in his presence;
nor for him who utters words   750
in the safety of his home that outdazzle real swords
in the line of battle. Men of action are worth
far more to their people than your clever,
scheming types. Valor easily finds
a moving eloquence all its own.

(*The scribe has dozed again, but before the kick lands, he jumps
back, writing all the while.* STRATOPHANES *regains his balance
and continues as if nothing has happened.*)

I regard your citizen who is clever
but lacking in courage as a hired female mourner:
she knows how to praise others well enough,
but in truth cannot praise herself.

(*The entire procession is asleep, some leaning on their instru-
ments, some on each other; a few are prone and audibly snoring.
He awakens them by a loud clearing of his throat. They applaud
vigorously and exit with ad libs about his bravery, eloquence, etc.
The last to exit hurries back to snatch the scribe away just as
another kick is aimed at him. He is dragged off writing furiously.*
STRATOPHANES *turns the incomplete kick into a grand gesture
and continues.*)

Now after nine months, I've come back to   760
Attic Athens to see what my dear girl—
she whom I left filled with the potency
of my manly embrace—is up to.

(*He strides up and down posturing, rehearsing speech, etc.*)

PHRONESIUM: See who is talking about us so nearby.

ASTAPHIUM: (*Looking toward center stage, where* STRATOPHANES *is pantomiming the speech he will deliver*)
Your Stratophanes is here, Phronesium. It's time for you to start looking sick.

PHRONESIUM: Hush! Do you think you can teach me anything about plotting? I taught you everything you know.

(*Pinches baby: sound of a baby crying*)

STRATOPHANES: (*Brightly, to audience*) The woman seems to have had a baby!   770

ASTAPHIUM: Do you want me to approach him?

PHRONESIUM: Yes.

(*During the following exchange,* ASTAPHIUM *blocks* STRATOPHANES' *view of* PHRONESIUM, *who is busy arranging her garments and the couch for her sickbed scene*)

STRATOPHANES: Ah, excellent! Astaphium comes to meet me.

ASTAPHIUM: (*With a formal salute*) Hail to thee, Stratophanes! You're looking well.

STRATOPHANES: (*Returns salute*) Yes, I know. But tell me, has Phronesium given birth?

ASTAPHIUM: She has, and to a boy that's too sweet for words.

STRATOPHANES: Ahhhh! And is he anything like me?

ASTAPHIUM: You have to ask? Why, the instant he was born he was asking for a sword and shield.   781

STRATOPHANES: That's proof enough for me. He's my boy.

ASTAPHIUM: He's only too much like you.

STRATOPHANES: Ah, marvelous! Is he big now? Has he served in a
legion yet? What sort of spoils did he get?

ASTAPHIUM: He was born only *five* days ago!

STRATOPHANES: (*Anxious*) Well, what *happened* then? With all that
time on his hands he should have done *something!* What disaster
could have befallen him so soon after he left his mother's womb?

ASTAPHIUM: (*Silently appeals to audience to witness this stupidity;
shrugs*)
Follow me and greet your wife. Give her your thanks.   790

STRATOPHANES: I come.

(*Strikes a noble attitude and follows her to* PHRONESIUM's *couch*)

PHRONESIUM: (*Weakly, in the style of the mother's lament*)
Where is the maid
who left me just now, I pray?
Where is she?
Where has she gone?

ASTAPHIUM: Here I am. I bring you the Stratophanes you've so
longed to see.

PHRONESIUM: (*Half rising; her weakened eyes cannot focus*)
Where . . . is . . . he?

STRATOPHANES: (*Grandiloquently*) Mars, returning from abroad,
sends greetings to his wife, the fair nymph Neriene.   800

(PHRONESIUM *and* ASTAPHIUM *look at one another, then at the
audience, in disbelief*)

Since you have managed all affairs in proper fashion,
since you have increased our estate with child,
since you have given birth to a thing of great credit
to me . . . oh, yes, *and* to you . . . congratulations!

(Salutes)

PHRONESIUM: *(Salutes weakly, then falls back)*
Oh hail to thee! Thrice welcome, you who nearly
deprived me of life and limb. You had your fun,
then left me with something that has ruined
my health and left me with a sickness unto death.

(Rises, then falls back again)

STRATOPHANES: Tut-tut, my beloved, this labor has not befallen you
unrewarded. You've given birth to a son who will fill your home
with spoils.   811

PHRONESIUM: We stand in much greater need of having our store-
houses filled with grain! We'll be long dead from hunger before *he*
wins any spoils.

STRATOPHANES: Be of good cheer.

PHRONESIUM: *(Tries to rise; falls back)*
Give me a kiss. Ah! I cannot lift my head . . . the pain is too great.
I cannot walk without your help.

STRATOPHANES: *(Lifting her awkwardly from the couch)*
If you ordered me to come to your embrace in the middle of the
sea, I swear I would plunge straight in, my honeybuns.
(Everyone winces)
You know that well enough.   820
(He places her next to the pile of gifts his servants have left)
Now, my dear Phronesium, you will see the proofs of my love for
you. Behold my gifts to you! I've brought you two serving maids
from Syria.

(He claps his hands and motions to attendants)
You there, bring them here. Both came from a royal house. I
should know. I laid waste the entire country.
(Scribe brings two young women forward and delivers them to
ASTAPHIUM; PHRONESIUM *does not even look at them)*
This is my gift to you.

PHRONESIUM: Aren't you ashamed, when I already have too many
    servants to feed? Now you bring me still more to gobble up my
    groceries?

STRATOPHANES: *(In disbelief, aside)* The gift is not a welcome one!
    You, boy, hand me that little sack there. My best beloved, behold:
    I bring this cloak to you from Phrygia!   832

PHRONESIUM:
(Glances at a magnificent robe disdainfully and hands it to AS-
TAPHIUM)
This teeny-tiny thing? Is this all I get for my labors?

STRATOPHANES: *(Aside)* Ah, wretch that I am, I am undone! My son
    is costing me his weight in gold! And it didn't matter that the cloak
    was made of royal purple.
(To PHRONESIUM)
From Arabia I bring frankincense; from the Black Sea, balsam.
They're all yours, my delight.

PHRONESIUM: I'll take them.
(Hands them to ASTAPHIUM *without so much as a look)*
Astaphium, get these *trinkets* and *Syrians* out of my sight.   840

*(*ASTAPHIUM *and scribe with young women exit)*

STRATOPHANES: Now do you love me?

PHRONESIUM: Not a bit. You haven't earned anything at all.

STRATOPHANES: Will nothing satisfy you?

(*Aside, to audience*)
She hasn't said one friendly word to me. I'll bet she could get
twenty minas for the gifts I've given her. She seems angry now.
(*Looks at her;* PHRONESIUM *quickly puts on her best scowl*)
Remarkable! Yes, she's plainly angry. Then I'll be off.
(*He starts off, but noticing that she has not noticed, comes back*)
Now, what would you say if I were to invite myself to dinner, my
delight? I'll come back then for the night.
(PHRONESIUM *ignores him*)
Why are you so quiet?
(*Aside*)
I'm done for!   850
(PHRONESIUM *returns to her couch and weakly turns her face
away from him; she is a study in tragedy and suffering. Suddenly
there are distant sounds of* CYAMUS's *parade.*)
But what's this strange sight? Who is that fellow leading this pa-
rade? I'll take up a sentry post here and watch what they do.
They're bringing something in to her. Whatever it is, I'll know
soon enough.

(*Stands off to one side, with insufferable dignity*)

Scene 7

(*Enter* CYAMUS *with a train of servants carrying food, wine, etc.
They dance merrily to the rhythm of his opening lines.*)

CYAMUS: This way, this way, step over here,
    you ambulating asses with a fool for a master!
    You housecleaning harpies breeding doom and disaster!
    The only thing you're good for is carrying out the loot!

(*They ignore him and continue dancing. He turns to the audience.*)

Can a man in love be anything but a zero?
A man who turns his purse inside-out   860
to pursue the not-so-fine art of whore-mongering?
Does anybody here need to ask
why I know the answer to these questions?
Well, we've got a lover at home who lunges
from one scandal to the next. He treats
his property like so much dung:
"Take it out! Take it out!"
that's his command.
Maybe he's afraid of fleas?
The place is spotless!   870

(*Chuckles*)

He wants a clean house, and we see to *that* well enough. Everything inside gets carried outside! Since Diniarchus's passion is to ruin himself with passion, I see no harm in helping him— discreetly, of course. He would race to his doom soon enough without help from anyone, but just to speed him on his way, I drag one drachma off every ten he gives me for the groceries. Accounts deceivable, so to speak.

(*Raises his arms to heaven*)

O great Hercules!

(*Sings*)

Your tithe
is my tithe.   880

(*Signals to his followers*)

If you want to understand what is going on, picture a raging flood. If a man should redirect some of that great torrent of water onto his own fields, what's the harm in that? If the water weren't chan- neled off, it would all run out to sea anyway. That's a fact. This stuff

(Points to the provisions)
is running out to sea, to a miserable, rotten end! When I see such things going on
(Rhythmic chant is cheerleaderlike)
I embezzle!

ATTENDANTS: Yeah!

CYAMUS: I bamboozle!

ATTENDANTS: Yeah!   890

CYAMUS: I deboot them
  of their booty,

ATTENDANTS: Yeah!

CYAMUS: because . . .

(He and his attendants sing and form a chorus line)

A whore and the ocean are much the same.
Way we see it, just a difference in name.
Give what you got, 'cause they won't overflow.
Just stick it all in, no limit they know.

(Addresses audience again)

I'll say this much, though:
whatever you do sink in   900
stays well hidden.

(Sings again)

Give all you want, you won't see it again.
It stays in the lady on the other end.

(Rapidly)

That's what happened to my poor master when a whore brought
him straight to the door of disaster. She stripped him of property,
life, reputation, friends . . .
(*At last he comes to his senses; notices* PHRONESIUM)
Say! Speaking of strippers, there she is now! I'll bet she's heard
everything I said.
(*Puzzled*)
Why, she's pale, as if she had just given birth to a baby boy.
(*Brightly, aside*)
I'll address her as if I knew nothing.   910
(*To* PHRONESIUM *and* ASTAPHIUM)
I earnestly desire your good health, ladies.

PHRONESIUM: Ah, Cyamus, my dear, what are you up to? How are
things? You're well, I hope?

CYAMUS: I am well. I come to one who's not so well, but I bear
something that will make her more . . . well.
(*Grand gesture*)
My master, that little apple of your eye,
(*Indicates his own eye*)
has ordered me to bring you the gifts borne by these slaves.
(PHRONESIUM *reacts, but he stops her with upraised hand and
purse*)
Here also are five minas of silver.

PHRONESIUM: (*showing the purse to* ASTAPHIUM *and cooing*)
Oh, by the gods, is it any wonder that I love Diniarchus so!

(STRATOPHANES *groans audibly and while following the conversation appeals to the audience to witness such treachery*)

CYAMUS: He also commands me to beg that these gifts will please
you.   921

PHRONESIUM: They *do* please me; they are so welcome! Now, Cyamus, please be a dear and have these fellows take everything
inside.

CYAMUS: (*To his servants, clapping his hands*)
Didn't you hear the lady's orders? Get to it! I don't want these
wine jugs carted off, so tell the slaves inside to pour the wine into
empty jugs and return these to me.

PHRONESIUM: Why, Cyamus! How presumptuous of you!

CYAMUS: Me?

PHRONESIUM: You.   930

CYAMUS: Oh, really! You call *me* presumptuous when you yourself
are a stable of vices?

PHRONESIUM: (*Begins to respond but decides not to lower herself;
smiles*)
Tell me, where is my darling Diniarchus?

CYAMUS: At home.

PHRONESIUM: Inform him that because of the gifts he has sent me, I
now love him more than any other man in the world. Tell him that
I hold him in the very *highest* esteem and that I yearn for him to
come to me.

(STRATOPHANES *roars in agony and rage; gnaws at his knuckles*)

CYAMUS: (*Perfunctorily*) As you say.
(*Notices* STRATOPHANES *for the first time*)
Who is that fellow over there chomping on himself?   940
(PHRONESIUM *shrugs as if she does not know*)
That miserable-looking one with the evil eye. He's in a foul mood,
whoever he is.

PHRONESIUM: (*As if seeing* STRATOPHANES *for the first time*)
Yes, and he deserves every bit of it. He's worthless.
(CYAMUS *moves toward* STRATOPHANES)
Look carefully. Don't you recognize him?

(CYAMUS *looks more closely.* STRATOPHANES *is frozen in rage, his fist stuffed in his mouth.*)
He's the soldier who used to live in my house. He's the father of this little boy here. I've driven him off,
(CYAMUS *pushes* STRATOPHANES)
and still he stays around, listening and observing everything I do.

CYAMUS: I know the worthless fellow. Is that him?

(*He stands eyeball to eyeball with* STRATOPHANES)

PHRONESIUM: Yes, that's him.

CYAMUS: (*As* STRATOPHANES *groans*) He moans at me! He glares at me!   951
(*Another growl from* STRATOPHANES)
That sigh was wrenched from the very bottom of his belly!
(STRATOPHANES *begins to pound on his thighs in impotent rage*)
And look at this! He's gnashing his teeth like a charging horse!
He's slapping his thigh.
(*A thundering roar;* CYAMUS *runs over to* PHRONESIUM)
Is he a soothsayer beating himself into a frenzy?

STRATOPHANES: (*Explodes at last*) Now shall I unleash the raging spirits
and the smoldering wrath that bubbles and boils
in my bosom! How dare you address such rude words to me?
Me!

CYAMUS: (*Mildly*) Passing fancy.

STRATOPHANES: Don't you dare talk to me that way!   960

CYAMUS: Then try this way: I don't give a damn who you are.

STRATOPHANES: (*To* PHRONESIUM) And what about you? How dare you say you love another man?

PHRONESIUM: Passing fancy.

(She walks away and with ASTAPHIUM *begins an inventory of the gifts)*

STRATOPHANES: Oh, is that so?
  (Aside)
  I'll test that little remark first.
  (To PHRONESIUM*)*
  Do you mean to tell me that for the sake
  of such trivial gifts as these vegetables,
  these scraps of food,
  this vinegar water we drink on campaigns,   970
  that for all this you've fallen in love with a
  Dimple-assed gigolo?
  A pile of curly hair?
  A milky-white from indoor sports?
  A mere tambourine thumper?
  Less than a man?
  Not even a mouse?

*(*PHRONESIUM *neither looks up nor acknowledges his anger, only nods yes)*

CYAMUS: Now, just a minute there! You shameless wretch, you fountain of iniquity and lies, do you dare speak ill of *my* master?

STRATOPHANES: Add one more word to that list, and damned if I don't take this sword and hack you into hamburger!   981

CYAMUS: You lay one hand on me and I'll split you down the middle like a lamb ready for the roasting pit!
  (Draws kitchen knife)
  You may be a great warrior in the legions, but around here the king of the kitchen is me!

PHRONESIUM: *(Looking up calmly from her examination of the gifts, to* STRATOPHANES*)*
  If you had any sense of fair play, you wouldn't attack my guest so

viciously. After all, everything I got from him was fine and welcome; everything I got from you was worthless.

STRATOPHANES: Then, by the gods, am I stripped now of life and
    property alike!   990

PHRONESIUM: Well, of course you are.

CYAMUS: Why do you keep hanging around her when all your efforts
    lead to nothing? What a bore.

(*Begins to trim nails with his knife*)

STRATOPHANES: (*Exasperatedly*) Now, by the gods, may I perish
    this very day if I don't drive this beggar away from you!

CYAMUS: Ha! Come on! Just step this way!

STRATOPHANES: *You* would threaten *me*, you villain? Now I'll whit-
    tle you down to toothpicks! What do you mean coming here?
    (CYAMUS *defiantly blows* PHRONESIUM *a kiss, which she returns*)
    What's your traffic with my woman?
    (CYAMUS *throws a bump*)
    What were you doing near my girlfriend?   1000
    (*More bumps and grinds; he draws his sword*)
    You'll die this very minute unless by force of arms you prevail!

CYAMUS: (*Stops his lascivious dance*)
    "Prevail by force of arms," you say?

(STRATOPHANES' *sword is at his throat. He gingerly removes it, takes
a piece of string from his pocket, measures the sword, and then
measures his kitchen knife. With the same string, he pantomimes the
sword going through his body.*)

STRATOPHANES: (*Snatches his sword away from* CYAMUS)
    Do as I tell you! Stand up like a man! Now I think I will hack you up
    into hamburger after all. A fitting end for a cook!

(*Advances menacingly, but* CYAMUS *stops him with a gesture*)

CYAMUS: Ah, but there's a slight catch: that battle sword you have is
far longer than this kitchen knife.
(*They stop and remeasure the weapons.* STRATOPHANES *counts on his fingers.*)
First, let me fetch my spit from the hearth. If I have to wage war
with a warrior like you, I want to do it in proper style.
(*Aside*)
A perfect opportunity to get out of here while my guts are still in
place!   1010

(*He signals slaves and makes a fluttery but silent exit.* STRATO-
PHANES *is left still counting inches.*)

Scene 8

PHRONESIUM: (*To* ASTAPHIUM *and her maids*)
Bring me my sandals. Take me inside at once. I have a headache
from all this windy talk!

STRATOPHANES: *You* have a headache? And what about me? I have
nothing *but* headaches to show for my generous gift of those two
maids from Syria.
(PHRONESIUM *exits; he stalks to her door*)
Gone already, are you? So that's your style, eh? How could I have
been locked out more firmly than I am now? A fine trick you've
played on me! But let that go. It would take very little persuasion
for me to smash the anklebones of everyone in this house.
(*Turns to audience*)
What could be more fickle than a woman? As soon as she has
produced my son, her pride soars out of sight. It's as if she'd said to
me, "I neither ask you nor forbid you to come inside." Well, I don't
want to go in, and I won't. I'll see to it that in a few days she'll
begin to think of me as a rough, iron-willed brute.   1024
(*To his company*)

Follow me! This way!
(*Turns; to audience*)
Enough of mere words!

(*He exits*)

ACT III

Scene 1

(*Enter* STRABAX, *a simple country youth whose face shows not the remotest gleam of intelligence*)

STRABAX: (*Bouncing a purse that hangs from his waist*)
Early this morning Father ordered me off to the country to give our cows some acorns for an early breakfast. After I got there, the gods be praised, this fellow comes up to our farmhouse and says he owes Father some money. Father had just sold him some of our Tarentine sheep. So he asks for Father. I say, "Father is in the city." I ask him, "Why do you want to see Father?" The man unties a moneybelt he has around his neck and gives me twenty minas.
(*Giggles*)
I take them gladly and put them in *my* moneybelt. The man goes away. I come straight back into town. Minus no minas, of course!
(*Doubled over with amusement at his own cleverness, he holds up the purse that dangles from his waist*)
Mars must really be angry at Father dear. His sheep are not too far from the wolves now!   1037
(*Starts toward* PHRONESIUM'*s door*)
I'll knock those city slickers out of action with one blow, and then I'll kick them all out of doors.
(*Leans forward, suppressing his giggles*)

First I'll snip off Father right down to the roots; then I'll do the same to Mother. I've brought this money to a woman I love more than my own mother.   1042
(Approaches the door and knocks)
Knock knock! Is anybody home? Will somebody open the door?

(ASTAPHIUM peers out; STRABAX swings the purse)

ASTAPHIUM: What have you got there?
(Hefts his purse suggestively)
Why, Strabax darling! You're no stranger here. Why didn't you come right inside?

STRABAX: *(Shyly)* Was *I* supposed to do that?

ASTAPHIUM: *You* especially are supposed to.
(Leaning on him, still clutching his purse)
You're one of the family.

STRABAX: Here goes. I don't want you to think I'm slow.   1050

ASTAPHIUM: Ooh, what a charmer you are!

(They exit, ASTAPHIUM leading him by the purse; another grand pause, then . . .)

Scene 2

(Enter TRUCULENTUS, quite tame and solicitous)

TRUCULENTUS: How strange! Young master Strabax is not home yet from the farm. I hope he hasn't somehow slipped in secret to this place. If he did, he's lost for sure.

(ASTAPHIUM enters and sees him first)

ASTAPHIUM: (*To audience*) Oh gods! If he catches sight of me, he'll start bellowing again!

TRUCULENTUS: (*Sees her*) I'm much less savage than I was, Astaphium. I'm not the same Truculentus. You'll see. Don't be afraid. What do you say?

ASTAPHIUM: What do you want?   1060

TRUCULENTUS: Just a little kiss from you.
(ASTAPHIUM *recoils in horror*)
Talk to me, order me to do anything you want. I've got a new character now. I've lost my old one. I can make love or do anything else a whore likes to do.

ASTAPHIUM: (*Overcoming her astonishment*)
What marvelous news! But tell me, do you by any chance have just a little . . .

TRUCULENTUS: . . . "money ready," you were going to say?

ASTAPHIUM: You're marvelous! You understood exactly what I was going to say.

TRUCULENTUS: Be careful! Now that I come to town so often, I'm becoming quite a suffocated wit!   1071

ASTAPHIUM: You're becoming a *what?* I suppose that bit of nonsense means that you're quite so*phis*ticated?

TRUCULENTUS: Suffocated? Sophisticated? What's the difference?

ASTAPHIUM: (*Giving up*) Follow me inside now, my delight.

TRUCULENTUS: (*Hands her a purse*)
Here, take this as a downment for bedding down with you.

ASTAPHIUM: I can't stand it! A "downment"! What kind of beast do I have here? Do you mean to say "down *payment*"?

TRUCULENTUS: Sure, I just saved the *pay* for myself. Why, I even know folks in the country who can find their peckers in a wood-pecker, or a dork in a stork, or . . .   1081

ASTAPHIUM: (*At wit's end*) *Please* come inside.

TRUCULENTUS: I should wait here until Strabax gets back from the country.

ASTAPHIUM: But Strabax has just returned from the country! He's inside right now!

TRUCULENTUS: (*Flares up*) Before he even saw his own mother? What a worthless fool!

ASTAPHIUM: Now, now! Up to your usual ways?

TRUCULENTUS: (*Thinking better of it*)
Now, now! I didn't say a word.   1090

ASTAPHIUM: Come, dear, let's go inside. Give me your hand.

TRUCULENTUS: Here.
(*She takes his hand and leads him in; he pauses and turns to the audience*)
The tavern I'm being led to specializes in gobbling up high fees for low service.

(*They exit*)

ACT IV

Scene 1

(*Enter* DINIARCHUS, *transported by ecstasy*)

DINIARCHUS: No one has ever been born, or will be born,
or will ever be found, to whom I'd wish better luck
than Lady Venus! Gods above, how happy I am!
I'm swept away by happiness!
Cyamus brought me a message of pure joy:
every gift he took inside was a delight
and was accepted straightaway by Phronesium.   1100
Even sweeter was the news of how
unwelcome the soldier's gifts were.
Pure joy, that's me! I've got the ball now!
With the soldier jilted, the woman's mine forever.
I'm saved at last, because I'm lost;
if I weren't lost this way, I'd be ruined another way.
Now to watch what goes on inside,
who comes outside and who goes inside.
I'll keep watch from here on my future fortunes.
I have nothing! She has everything! I'm at her mercy!   1110

(*Perches outside* PHRONESIUM's *door*)

Scene 2

(*Enter* ASTAPHIUM *from house*)

ASTAPHIUM: (*To servants inside*) I'll take care of my business out
here as cleverly as I can: you be sure to do what *you*'ve got to do
inside. Love what you ought to love—your own interest. Drain
his pool dry. Now's the time to get his cash, while he has it, while

he likes to spend it. Turn on your charms for your lover. He'll come clean if you pick him clean. I'll be on sentry duty outside as long as this fellow keeps that stream of cash flowing to your door. No bore will get inside to bother you. I won't allow it. Play your game the way you want to.   1120

DINIARCHUS: (*Advances*) Who's being cleaned out now? Tell me, Astaphium.

ASTAPHIUM: Oh dear, it's *you!*

DINIARCHUS: Am I such a bother?

ASTAPHIUM: More than ever! Anybody who isn't of use to us is a bother to us. Now, please listen; I want to say something.

DINIARCHUS: Well, what is it? Does it have anything to do with me?

ASTAPHIUM: I won't hide it from you. Oh what hauls she's making inside!

DINIARCHUS: What? You mean there's some new lover there?

ASTAPHIUM: She's opened up a full, untouched treasure.   1131

DINIARCHUS: (*Hysterically*) WHO?

ASTAPHIUM: I'll tell you, but keep it a secret. Do you know this fellow Strabax?

DINIARCHUS: Of course.

ASTAPHIUM: Well, he's tops with us now. He's the new crop we're harvesting. The fellow manages his affairs with a light heart and an empty head.

DINIARCHUS: He's come to a bad end, and so have I. I've got a poor return on my investment, being shut out like this.   1140

ASTAPHIUM: You fool, you're trying to make mere words unmake what is already made.
(*Archly*)
Even Thetis stopped crying for Achilles in the end.

DINIARCHUS: Then I'll not be admitted to your house?

ASTAPHIUM: Why you more than the soldier?

DINIARCHUS: Because I gave more than he did.

ASTAPHIUM: Ah, but the reason you were admitted more often was that you were paying. Now be a good sport and let those who pay get the services *they* pay for. You've learned your lesson well. Now that you know it, let someone else learn too.   1150

DINIARCHUS: (*Embracing her*) By all means, as long as I can have a brushup lesson. I don't want to forget how.

ASTAPHIUM: (*Escapes*) What about your teacher, while you're repeating your lessons? She likes repetition just as much as you do.

DINIARCHUS: How so?

ASTAPHIUM: She needs her tuition again and again.

DINIARCHUS: But I've already given today! I've even ordered five minas of silver to be brought to her, plus one mina's worth of groceries.

ASTAPHIUM: That's *exactly* what got here. Everyone's doing well, thanks to your thoughtfulness.   1161

DINIARCHUS: Oh gods, no! Are my enemies gobbling it all up? I'd rather be dead than put up with this!

ASTAPHIUM: You're a fool.

DINIARCHUS: Why so?

ASTAPHIUM: I'll explain.

DINIARCHUS: Well, why?

ASTAPHIUM: I'd rather have my enemies
  envy me than have me envy my enemies.
  To envy somebody else's good fortune   1170
  when your own is down is sheer misery.
  Those who envy are those who're poor.
  Those who are envied are those who're rich.

DINIARCHUS: You mean I don't get a share of my own groceries?

ASTAPHIUM: If you wanted a share, you should have taken it home.
  We keep our books the way they keep books in hades: once your
  account is entered on the ledger, it's on the ledger. Good day.

(*Turns to go*)

DINIARCHUS: (*Holds her*) Wait a minute!

ASTAPHIUM: (*Struggles free*) Let me go!

DINIARCHUS: Let me inside!   1180

ASTAPHIUM: Inside your own house, yes.

DINIARCHUS: No, I want to go inside your house!

ASTAPHIUM: It's impossible. You ask too much.

DINIARCHUS: Let me try!

ASTAPHIUM: No, try waiting. What you want to try is housebreak-
  ing.

DINIARCHUS: Tell her I'm here, then.

ASTAPHIUM: Go away. She's busy. That's the truth.

DINIARCHUS: Will you come back or not?

ASTAPHIUM: (*As if hearing* PHRONESIUM's *call*)
Only if someone calls me who has more power over me than you
do.   1191

(*She goes*)

DINIARCHUS: One word . . .

ASTAPHIUM: Say it.

DINIARCHUS: *Will you let me inside?*

ASTAPHIUM: You liar, get away from here! You said "one word" and
then said *five* of them. Lies, all lies!

(*Goes inside house*)

DINIARCHUS: She's gone inside. She's shut the door. Should I put up
with this? You hooker, you! Now, it's my turn to play games! I'll
shout it out in every street! *It's against the law for you to take
money from so many men!* I'll turn your name over to every magistrate in town! Then I'll make you pay damages four times over. You
witch! You baby snatcher! I'll expose all your crimes! Nothing will
stop me now. I've lost everything I had; now I'll lose all shame.
And I don't care if I look like a stupid hayseed either!   1204
(*Starts to go off*)
But why all this shouting? What if she should order them to let me
back inside? I swear I wouldn't go! Absolutely not! Not even if she
wanted me to.
(*Collapses*)
Oh, what's the use? You can pound on clubs with your fists if you
want to, but your hands will know which hurts more. Nothing

comes of getting angry at nothing, not when she thinks you're
worth nothing.   1211
(*Hears commotion; looks down the street*)
But what's this? Ye immortal gods! I see the old man Callicles, the
one who was nearly my father-in-law! He's bringing two maids all
tied up: one of them's Phronesium's hairdresser; the other is one
of his own slaves. I'm terrified! As if *this* disaster here weren't
enough! Now I'm afraid all my old sins have been found out.

(*He freezes in position against the wall of* PHRONESIUM's *house*)

Scene 3

(*Enter* CALLICLES, *his slaves driving two maids forward ahead of
him with goad and whips. He brandishes his cane.*)

CALLICLES: (*To his maid*) Why, would *I* curse you?
(*To* SYRA, *a maid of* PHRONESIUM)
Would *I* harm you? You both already know from experience just
how gentle and easygoing I can be. I questioned you both when
you were strung up by your thumbs on the whipping post. My
memory's sharp. I know exactly what you confessed. Now that
we're here, I want to know if you'll make the same confession
without punishment. You both have the cunning of a serpent, but
I'm warning you, you'd better not have double tongues, or I'll cut
them off for you! Or would you prefer to be led off to the clink-
clank-clunk of an executioner's chains?   1226

MAID: These thongs cut our arms so. Pain makes us tell the truth.

CALLICLES: If you tell the truth, I'll have you untied.

DINIARCHUS: (*In panic, to audience*)
I don't know what's going on, but I do know I'm scared. I know
what wrongs *I've* done well enough.   1230

CALLICLES: First of all, you two stand apart. There, that's right. I'll
   be a wall so you won't exchange signals.
   (*Stands between them with arms outspread; to his maid*)
   Now talk.

MAID: Talk about what?

CALLICLES: What happened to the boy, the baby my daughter had,
   my grandson? Outline the main points!

MAID: I gave him to her.

(*Points to other maid*)

CALLICLES: Now keep quiet.
   (*To* SYRA)
   Did you receive a baby from her?

SYRA: I did.   1240

CALLICLES: Keep quiet. I don't need anything else. You've confessed enough.

SYRA: I won't deny it.

CALLICLES: Talk like that will get your reddened back time to heal
   over to a darker hue.
   (*Aside*)
   H'm . . . their stories seem to agree up to this point.

(*Reflects a moment*)

DINIARCHUS: (*To audience*) Oh no! Now all my deeds are exposed to
   public view! Everything I hoped would stay a secret!

DINIARCHUS: (*To his maid*) Now you talk. Who ordered you to give
   the baby to her?   1250

MAID: My mistress, your wife.

CALLICLES: (*To* SYRA) Now *you* talk. What did you do with the baby?

SYRA: I took it to my mistress.

CALLICLES: And what did your mistress do with the baby?

SYRA: She gave him at once to my mistress.

CALLICLES: *Which* mistress, damn you?

MAID: (*Volunteering*) She has *two* mistresses.

CALLICLES: (*Turns on her*) Keep out of this unless I ask you something!
(*To* SYRA)
I'm asking *you*.

SYRA: The mother gave the baby to her daughter Phronesium, as a
gift.   1261

CALLICLES: You're talking more now than a little while ago.

SYRA: You're asking more.

CALLICLES: (*To* SYRA) Answer me quickly now: what did the woman
do who was given the baby?

SYRA: She loaned it out.

CALLICLES: To whom?

SYRA: To herself.

CALLICLES: As her own son?

SYRA: As her own son.   1270

CALLICLES: Oh gods, I call you to witness! See how much easier it is for one woman than another to give birth to one and the same baby!
(*Gestures toward* PHRONESIUM's *house*)
Thanks to another woman's labor, *this* woman gave birth to a baby boy without any pain at all. Lucky child! He has two mothers and two grandmothers. What worries me now is how many *fathers* he had!
(*To audience*)
What evils women do!

MAID: (*Sees* DINIARCHUS *hiding*) Goodness, sir, this kind of mischief is more the fault of men than women. A man got her pregnant, not a woman.   1281

CALLICLES: I know that perfectly well enough! And *you* were such a fine guard for her, weren't you?

MAID: (*Assuming didactic pose*) "That man does more who more can do." He was a man, and he did more. He overpowered her and got what he came for.

CALLICLES: And he also got you plenty of punishment in the bargain!

MAID: (*Looks back at her shoulders*)
Even if you hadn't said it, I'd know that well enough.

CALLICLES: But you haven't yet told me who he was.   1290

MAID: I've kept quiet up to now, but I won't any longer. He's here but he doesn't show himself.

DINIARCHUS: (*Still standing rigidly to one side*)
I'm turned to stone, I don't dare move. It's all in the open. My neck's on the line. I did it! It's my stupidity! I'm afraid she'll soon reveal my name!

CALLICLES: Tell me, who has dishonored my virgin daughter?

MAID: (*To* DINIARCHUS) I see you! There you are, trying to prop up the wall because of your sins.

DINIARCHUS: (*With eyes frozen open*)
I'm not alive. I'm not dead. I don't know what I'm doing. I don't know whether to go up to him or to get out of here. I'm scared stiff!

CALLICLES: Will you name him or not?   1301

MAID: Diniarchus, the man you once betrothed your daughter to.

CALLICLES: And where is the man you've named?

(*Looks about him*)

DINIARCHUS:
(*Rushes out; throws himself at* CALLICLES' *feet like a tragic supplicant*)
Here I am, Callicles! By these your knees do I implore, judge wisely this deed I've done so unwisely and pardon me. I did wrong only because I was out of my head with that wicked wine.

CALLICLES: (*Not losing the opportunity to preach*)
It won't do to put the blame on something dumb that can't speak. If wine were able to tell a tale, it would defend itself. It's not up to wine to be sparing with men; rather, men must be sparing with wine—at least men who are worth anything. But if a man is worthless by nature, it doesn't matter if he's drunk or a teetotaler: he's going to *be* worthless.   1312

DINIARCHUS: (*Still on his knees, dryly*)
Because of my offenses, I know only too well that I must listen to a great many things I don't want to hear.
(*Returns to the role of suppliant*)
I confess I've offended you, and I grant I'm guilty!

SYRA: Callicles, don't make the mistake of running an unfair trial. The defendant is pleading his case unbound, but you still have your witnesses tied up.

CALLICLES: (*To attendants*) Let them go.
(*To his maid*)
You, go home.   1320
(*To* SYRA)
And you, too. Give this message to your mistress Phronesium: she's to return the baby when it's sent for.
(*They exit; to* DINIARCHUS)
Come on, you, we're off to court.

DINIARCHUS: Why do you want me to go to court? *You* yourself are my judge. Indeed I beg you, Callicles! Give me your daughter's hand in marriage.

CALLICLES: Let her marry you? It seems you've already decided that point. You didn't wait for me to give her to you; you took her yourself. Now that you've got her, you can keep her. But I'll punish you with a heavy fine: a full six talents deducted from her dowry for your stupidity.   1331

DINIARCHUS: (*Groveling*) You treat me well, sir.

CALLICLES: You'd better get back to that son of yours. What's more, get your wife out of my house as fast as you can. I'm leaving. I'll send message to that relative of mine. He'll have to find some other match for his son now.

(*Hobbles off with attendants;* SYRA *dashes into* PHRONESIUM's *house*)

DINIARCHUS: (*Going to* PHRONESIUM's *house*)
I'll ask her to return the baby; otherwise she'll deny everything later. Nothing to worry about, though, since she's already explained how everything happened.
(*Door opens*)

But what a stroke of luck! Here she comes!   1340
(*As romantic as ever*)
Ah, she has a long sting, that woman; even from that distance she's
piercing my heart!

Scene 4

(*Enter* PHRONESIUM, *sounds of a drunken orgy from inside; composes herself*)

PHRONESIUM: A courtesan who can't drink and tend to her business
   is a blithering fool, a cheap clay pot; the rest of her body can be
   pickled, but her brain had better be dry.
   (*Turns to matter at hand*)
   I'm really sorry my hairdresser got caught so badly. She said it's
   been discovered that the baby is Diniarchus's son. As soon as I
   heard that, I came running out as fast as I could.

DINIARCHUS: (*Aside*) What a pleasure to deal with a woman who has
   everything I own in the world, including my children.   1350

(*Advances*)

PHRONESIUM: Ah, there's the sweetheart who put me in charge of all
   his goods.

DINIARCHUS: (*Sternly*) Woman, I've come to see you.

PHRONESIUM: (*Sweetly*) How are things, my darling?

DINIARCHUS: Don't "darling" me! Enough of that talk! I'm not here
   for that now.

PHRONESIUM: Goodness! I know what you *like*, what you *want*, and
   what you're *waiting* for: you'd like to *see* me, you want to *leave* me,
   and you're *waiting* to get your boy back.

DINIARCHUS: (*To audience, admiringly*) Ye immortal gods! How
plainly spoken! She's covered all the main points in just a few
words. 1362

PHRONESIUM: I know very well that you have a fiancée now, a *baby*
by that fiancée, and that you have to marry her
(*With acid tone*)
and that your heart is really elsewhere, and that I'm nothing but a
cast-off piece of baggage. I know you're leaving. But still, do consider: a mouse may be small, but still it's a wise little beast. It
never entrusts its life to one little mousehole. If one entrance is
blocked, it has another all ready and waiting.

DINIARCHUS: When I have a little more free time, I'll talk this over
with you. Now give me back the baby. 1371

PHRONESIUM: Oh, no, please, let it stay with me just a few more
days!

DINIARCHUS: Absolutely not.

PHRONESIUM: Please.

DINIARCHUS: Why do you need it?

PHRONESIUM: For my personal business. Just let me have him for
three days, while the soldier's being swindled. If I gain the baby,
you'll gain a lot too. But if you take him away, all our hopes for the
soldier will come to nothing. 1380

DINIARCHUS: (*After only a slight hesitation*)
Well, here's hoping it works. There's no way out left for me, even if
I had hoped it wouldn't work. Use the baby, then, and take care of
him, since you're getting paid for your pains.

PHRONESIUM: Dear me, how I love you for doing this! Now, any time
you think there's trouble brewing at your house, just run over
here to my house.

(*Squeals in delight*)
A friend for the greedy is a friend indeedy!

DINIARCHUS: (*Resigned, turns to go*)
  Good day, Phronesium.

PHRONESIUM: Won't you call me the little apple of your eye?

DINIARCHUS: That will come up again in due course, don't worry.
  Anything else?   1391

PHRONESIUM: Only that you take care.

DINIARCHUS: When I have a free moment, I'll come back to you.

(*He exits, drained in every sense of the word*)

PHRONESIUM: He's gone at last! He's left us! Say whatever you want,
  the proverb puts it best: you'll find your wealth where you find
  your friends. Thanks to this fellow, I still have a chance to get to
  that soldier, the one I love more than I love myself—as long as I
  get what I want out of him, that is. Even when we get a lot from a
  man, it never seems enough when we get it. That's the courtesan's
  glory.

(*Enter* ASTAPHIUM)

ASTAPHIUM: Shh! Be quiet!   1400

PHRONESIUM: What is it? What's the matter?

ASTAPHIUM: The baby's father is coming.

PHRONESIUM: Let him come to me—if it really is him—let him
  come.

ASTAPHIUM: It's him all right.

PHRONESIUM: Then let him draw near and do just as he wishes.

ASTAPHIUM: He's right on course.

PHRONESIUM: Before this day is over, I'll have him completely
  snared.

ACT V

Scene 1

(*Enter* STRATOPHANES, *dejected, with purse*)

STRATOPHANES: Here I am again, with a sack of gold for my mistress: a gift as punishment. To make her like what I've lost up to
  now, I've made this addition. But what's this I see!   1412
  (*Notices* PHRONESIUM *and* ASTAPHIUM)
  The maid and mistress at the front door. I must go to them. What
  are you doing here?

PHRONESIUM: (*Peevishly*) Don't talk to me.

STRATOPHANES: Don't be so mean.

PHRONESIUM: Oh, yes, I will. Won't you leave me alone?

STRATOPHANES: Does she have reason to quarrel, Astaphium?

ASTAPHIUM: She's absolutely right to be angry with you.

PHRONESIUM: (*Turns away*) Indeed I am. The truth is, I don't dislike
  you enough.   1420

STRATOPHANES: But, my delight, even if I did sin before, I've
brought you a sack of gold as my penance. If you don't believe me,
just look back here.

(*Holds out purse*)

PHRONESIUM: (*Turns away*) My hand refuses to believe anything
until it has it in it.

(*With increasing fervor*)

The baby needs food!
The mother needs it too! He needs a maid to bathe him,
and he needs a nurse! His nurse needs to drink
vintage wine day and night to have enough milk!
We need wood, we need coal, we need kindling, oil,
     flour,   1430
diapers, pillows, a cradle, bed clothes for the cradle!
We need indeed the whole day long! Our needs
are never met in one day! There's always need!

(*More calmly*)

Soldiers' babies can't be reared like birds, you know.

STRATOPHANES: Turn around and look then! Take it! This will meet
your needs.

PHRONESIUM: (*Takes the purse but does not look at it; gives it to*
ASTAPHIUM *after hefting it*)
All right, but it's not enough.

STRATOPHANES: I'll add another mina to this one later.

PHRONESIUM: It still isn't enough.

STRATOPHANES: At your wish, whenever you command. Now give
me a kiss.   1441

PHRONESIUM: (*Pushes him away*)
    Let me go! I hate you!

STRATOPHANES: I can't do anything right! No love yet, and the day's
    nearly over. I've been tricked into trickling out more than ten
    talents' worth of gold!

PHRONESIUM: (*Gives bag to* ASTAPHIUM)
    Take this and put it inside.

(*Suddenly* STRABAX *enters, drunk, from the house*)

STRABAX: Where on earth is my girlfriend? I can't do anything right
    at the farm or here. I'm going to rot with sitting around. Poor me,
    I've gotten all hard lying around in bed waiting.
    (*At last focuses on* PHRONESIUM)
    But look, there she is. Hey! Girlfriend! What's going on?   1450

(ASTAPHIUM *goes inside with gold*)

STRATOPHANES: (*Incredulously*) What man is this?

PHRONESIUM: (*Coolly*) A man I love far more than you.

STRATOPHANES: Than *me*? How can this be?

PHRONESIUM: This is how.
    (*Turns away to* STRABAX)
    You won't bother me now.

STRATOPHANES: Are you going away, after taking my gold?

PHRONESIUM: I've already stored away what you gave me.

(ASTAPHIUM *reenters*)

STRABAX: Come here, girlfriend, *I'm* talking to you now.

PHRONESIUM: (*Sweetly*) Ah, I'm coming to you, my deliciousness!

(*They embrace*)

STRABAX: By gosh, I mean it! I may seem dumb to you, but I want to
  have some fun.   1461
  (*Winks knowingly*)
  No matter how pretty you are, it'll be too bad for you if I don't get
  to *have some fun.*

(*Winks again*)

PHRONESIUM: You want a nice hug, a little kiss?

STRABAX: I don't care what you do as long as I *have some fun.*

(*Winks again; winces of dismay on all sides;* STRABAX *is oblivious*)

STRATOPHANES: (*Aside*) Shall I endure her being embraced before
  my very eyes? By the gods, no! Far better I were dead at once!
  (*In his old, thunderous style*)
  Take away your hand from that man, woman, unless you desire
  that both of you perish by this sword in my hand!

PHRONESIUM: Your *hand* would do well to have King Philip's coins in
  it if you're so hot for love. You'll keep me from this lover with gold,
  not steel, Stratophanes.   1472

(STRABAX *laughs*)

STRATOPHANES: Damnation! How can a pretty, witty woman like
  you love a man like *this?*

PHRONESIUM: Don't you recall the proverb the actor delivered in
  the theater? "Every man who's good at his trade can hold his nose
  when he has to."

STRATOPHANES: But how can you bear to be embraced by such . . . such . . . such a slob, such a filthy, sloppy . . .

PHRONESIUM: He may be filthy and sloppy to you, but he's clever and handsome to me.   1481

STRATOPHANES: Didn't I give you gold . . .

PHRONESIUM: Me? You gave your *son* groceries. If you want *this*
(*Gestures toward herself*)
to be with *you*, you'd better have another mina of gold ready.

STRABAX: (*Laughing*) You're going to hell, and how: you'd better have a coin for the ferryman at the Styx.

STRATOPHANES: (*To* PHRONESIUM) What do you owe this creature?

PHRONESIUM: Three things.

STRATOPHANES: What three things?

PHRONESIUM: Perfume, a night with me, and most of all . . . a kiss.

(*They embrace again*)

STRATOPHANES: (*Aside*) Tit for tat, obviously.   1491
(*To* PHRONESIUM)
Now, really, even if you do love him, won't you give me just a little, itsy-bitsy share too?

PHRONESIUM: What, pray tell, is it that I should give you?

STRABAX: (*Breaks in*) Don't give that, even if there is any left over!

STRATOPHANES: You try to snare her with words, but I'll take her by force, my good fellow.

STRABAX: Take care you don't hurt yourself with those iron teeth of yours.

STRATOPHANES: (*Disgustedly*) Everyone gets in here: doesn't matter who they are.   1501
(STRABAX *and* PHRONESIUM *embrace yet again*)
Take your hands off her!

STRABAX: You're going to get in lots of trouble yourself, soldier boy.

STRATOPHANES: I gave her gold.

STRABAX: And I gave her silver.

STRATOPHANES: And I gave her a dress of royal purple.

STRABAX: And I gave her sheep and wool, and I'll give her lots of other things when she asks for them. You'd better use minas, not menaces, if you want to fight with me.

PHRONESIUM: What a charming creature you are, Strabax! Do keep it up!   1511

ASTRAPHIUM: (*Aside, to audience*) A fool and a madman are vying for their own ruin! We're saved!

STRATOPHANES: Come on, then! You go first to your ruin!

STRABAX: No! You be the first *and* go to hell!

STRATOPHANES: (*To* PHRONESIUM) I promise a talent of silver for you! Here are your King Philip coins. Take them.

(*Hands over another purse*)

PHRONESIUM: That's much better! Now join us—but see that you buy your own groceries.

STRATOPHANES: (*To* STRABAX) And where is *your* gift? Untie your
   moneybelt, you coarse creature. What are you afraid of?   1521

STRABAX: You're a stranger. I live here. I don't go walking around
   with a moneybelt. I've brought her my flocks all tied up in this
   purse around my waist.
   (*Giggles; to* PHRONESIUM)
   What a gift! I really beat him to the punch.

STRATOPHANES: Absolutely not! My gift was best!

PHRONESIUM: (*To* STRABAX) Go inside now, dear, you'll be with me
   soon.
   (*To* STRATOPHANES)
   After he's done, then you can be with me too.

STRATOPHANES: What do you mean? What did you say? *Me* go
   second, after all I gave?   1531

PHRONESIUM: You've given already, and he's going to. I have *this*
   (*Holds up* STRATOPHANES' *purse*)
   and I'm after *that*.
   (*Tugs on* STRABAX's *purse*)
   This way both of you will be treated just the way you wanted to be.

STRATOPHANES: (*Gives in*) So be it. As I see it, the whole business is
   already finished. I'll have to take what's offered me.

(*Looks hopefully at* STRABAX)

STRABAX: (*Indignantly*) One thing you won't be offered for sure is a
   chance to lie in my bed!

(*They both enter the house, after much struggling to see who goes
first*)

PHRONESIUM:
   (*To the audience, with* ASTAPHIUM, *beaming, looking on*) How

cleverly I've netted them, and just the way I meant to! I've man-
aged this *so* nicely! Perhaps I could take care of some of you as
well?   1542
(*Points to members of the audience*)
If anyone wants anything to do with love, let me know.
For Venus's sake, your applause!
This play was made at her command.

(*She bows; everyone exits*)